CASH TRANSFERS FOR INCLUSIVE SOCIETIES

Behaviourally Informed
Organizations

BEHAVIOURALLY INFORMED ORGANIZATIONS

To date, there has been a lack of practical advice for organizations based on behavioral research. The Behaviourally Informed Organizations series fills this knowledge gap with a strategic perspective on how governments, businesses, and other organizations have embedded behavioral insights into their operations. The series is rooted in work by academics and practitioners cocreating knowledge via the Behaviourally Informed Organizations Partnership (www.biorgpartnership.com) and is written in a highly accessible style to highlight key ideas, pragmatic frameworks, and prescriptive outcomes based on illustrative case studies.

Also in the series:

Behavioral Science in the Wild, edited by Nina Mažar and Dilip Soman
The Behaviorally Informed Organization, edited by Dilip Soman and
    Catherine Yeung

Cash Transfers for Inclusive Societies

A Behavioral Lens

EDITED BY JIAYING ZHAO, SAUGATO DATTA, AND DILIP SOMAN

UNIVERSITY OF TORONTO PRESS
Toronto Buffalo London

Rotman-UTP Publishing
An imprint of University of Toronto Press

© University of Toronto Press 2023
Toronto Buffalo London
utorontopress.com

Library and Archives Canada Cataloguing in Publication

Title: Cash transfers for inclusive societies : a behavioral lens / edited by
    Jiaying Zhao, Saugato Datta, and Dilip Soman.
Names: Zhao, Jiaying (Lecturer in psychology), editor. | Datta, Saugato,
    editor. | Soman, Dilip, editor.
Description: Series statement: Behaviorally informed organizations |
    Includes bibliographical references.
Identifiers: Canadiana (print) 20230446523 | Canadiana (ebook) 20230446558 |
    ISBN 9781487545178 (cloth) | ISBN 9781487549473 (EPUB) |
    ISBN 9781487547851 (PDF)
Subjects: LCSH: Economic assistance, Domestic. | LCSH: Economic assistance,
    Domestic – Psychological aspects. | LCSH: Income maintenance programs –
    Evaluation. | LCSH: Transfer payments.
Classification: LCC HC79.P63 C37 2023 | DDC 362.5/82 – dc23

ISBN 978-1-4875-4517-8 (cloth)   ISBN 978-1-4875-4947-3 (EPUB)
                                  ISBN 978-1-4875-4785-1 (PDF)

Printed in the USA

Cover design and illustration: Thomas Eykemans

We wish to acknowledge the land on which the University of Toronto Press operates. This land is the traditional territory of the Wendat, the Anishnaabeg, the Haudenosaunee, the Métis, and the Mississaugas of the Credit First Nation.

University of Toronto Press acknowledges the financial support of the Government of Canada and the Ontario Arts Council, an agency of the Government of Ontario, for its publishing activities.

 Canada Council   Conseil des Arts
for the Arts   du Canada

 ONTARIO ARTS COUNCIL
CONSEIL DES ARTS DE L'ONTARIO
an Ontario government agency
un organisme du gouvernement de l'Ontario

Funded by the   Financé par le
Government   gouvernement    Canada
of Canada   du Canada

Contents

Acknowledgments

This book project is made possible due to the support to the Behaviourally Informed Organizations (BI-Org) partnership (https://www.biorgpartnership.com) housed at the Behavioural Economics in Action at Rotman (BEAR) research center at the University of Toronto. BI-Org is supported by a partnership grant from the Social Sciences and Humanities Council of Canada. We thank all of the members of the partnership for their comments, suggestions, and discussions on the materials in this book. Special thanks are due to Cindy Luo for managing this book project, Bing Feng for managing the partnership, and Karrie Chou for editorial assistance. This book grew out of an online conference on cash transfer programs hosted by BEAR and BI-Org,[1] and we thank Liz Kang and Cindy Luo for serving as conference coordinators. We also thank the members of the partnership steering committee and our internal review board – Abigail Dalton, Dale Griffin, Melanie Kim, Katy Milkman, Kyle Murray, Sasha Tregebov, Melaina Vinski, and Min Zhao. In addition, Tanvi Mehta provided developmental editing and her contribution is gratefully acknowledged.

The authors of Chapter 3 acknowledge fellow researchers on the Brazil,[2] Ethiopia,[3] Jordan,[4] Kenya, and Palestine[5] Reach Alliance research teams and those who supported the research process, especially their research assistants and key informants in Brazil, Ethiopia, Jordan, Kenya, and Palestine. They thank Professor Joseph

Wong and Bruno Câmara Pinto for their input on this chapter. The case study research was made possible through the Reach Alliance, a partnership between the University of Toronto's Munk School of Global Affairs & Public Policy and the Mastercard Center for Inclusive Growth.[6] In addition to the support of these two organizations, research for these case studies was also funded by the Mastercard Impact Fund, the Canada Research Chairs Program, and the Roz and Ralph Halbert Professorship of Innovation at the Munk School of Global Affairs & Public Policy.

The authors of Chapter 9 acknowledge that the research reported in the chapter was supported by the Eunice Kennedy Shriver National Institute of Child Health and Human Development of the National Institutes of Health under Award No. R01HD087384. The content is solely the responsibility of the authors and does not necessarily represent the official views of the National Institutes of Health. This research was additionally supported by the US Department of Health and Human Services, Administration for Children and Families, Office of Planning, Research and Evaluation; Andrew and Julie Klingenstein Family Fund; Annie E. Casey Foundation; Arnold Ventures; Arrow Impact; BCBS of Louisiana Foundation; Bezos Family Foundation; Bill and Melinda Gates Foundation; Bill Hammack and Janice Parmelee; Brady Education Fund; Chan Zuckerberg Initiative (Silicon Valley Community Foundation); Charles and Lynn Schusterman Family Philanthropies; Child Welfare Fund; Esther A. and Joseph Klingenstein Fund; Ford Foundation; Greater New Orleans Foundation; Heising-Simons Foundation; Jacobs Foundation; JPB Foundation; J-PAL North America; New York City Mayor's Office for Economic Opportunity; Perigee Fund; Robert Wood Johnson Foundation; Sherwood Foundation; Valhalla Foundation; Weitz Family Foundation; W.K. Kellogg Foundation; and three anonymous donors. The authors – Fox, Magnuson, Noble, and Yoshikawa – are listed in alphabetical order. The Baby's First Years study was designed and implemented by (in alphabetical order) Fox, Gennetian, Magnuson (Social Science Lead Principal Investigator), Noble (Neuroscience Lead Principal Investigator), and Yoshikawa.

NOTES

1 For further details, see BI-Org. (2022). *Cash Transfer Programs Symposium 2021.* https://www.biorgpartnership.com/ctp2021.
2 Reach Alliance. (2015–16). *Reaching the hard to reach: A case study of Brazil's Bolsa Família Program.* https://reachalliance.org/news/case-study/reaching-the-hard-to-reach-a-case-study-of-brazils-bolsa-familia-program/.
3 Reach Alliance. (2017–18a). *Ethiopia's Productive Safety Net Programme: Addressing food insecurity with food and cash transfers.* https://reachalliance.org/news/case-study/ethiopias-productive-safety-net-programme-addressing-food-insecurity-with-food-and-cash-transfers/.
4 Reach Alliance. (2016–17). *UNHCR Jordan's Biometric Cash Assistance Program for Syrian refugees.* https://reachalliance.org/news/case-study/unhcr-jordans-biometric-cash-assistance-program-for-syrian-refugees/.
5 Reach Alliance. (2017–18b). *Cash transfers in Palestine: Building blocks of social protection.* https://reachalliance.org/news/case-study/cash-transfers-in-palestine-building-blocks-of-social-protection/.
6 For further details, see https://reachalliance.org/, https://munkschool.utoronto.ca/, and https://www.mastercardcenter.org/.

CASH TRANSFERS FOR INCLUSIVE SOCIETIES

Introduction

Dilip Soman, Saugato Datta, and Jiaying Zhao

Although much progress has been made in reducing poverty worldwide – especially in the prepandemic era – it is fair to say that an unacceptably large proportion of the world's people still live in poverty, with the most recent estimates suggesting that around 9 per cent of the global population is still living on less than $1.90 a day.[1] Although the share of the world's workforce living in extreme poverty fell by half over the decade from 2010 to 2019, the differential impact of the COVID-19 pandemic on economically underprivileged populations has only served as a reminder of the continuing toll of poverty on people's lives.

As the pandemic has dragged on, its economic repercussions have led to increasing interest in trying to figure out ways in which governments and businesses alike can help people in poverty and reduce inequality. There have been increasing calls for governments to use more cash-based poverty alleviation programs such as cash transfer programs to build more inclusive and equitable societies that can be resilient to future shocks such as the COVID-19 pandemic.[2]

Although cash transfer programs have been widely prevalent and much has been written about them, our goal in putting together this volume was to ask two broad questions: First, what is the state of the art in the development of welfare programs such as cash transfers and what works in these programs and what does not? Second, how can behavioral science better inform the design, delivery, and evaluation of welfare programs?

To better address these questions, we (and the contributors to this volume) draw on two streams of literature more broadly. The first has to do with research on the behavioral antecedents and consequences of poverty. It is now widely established that poverty entails more than simply the lack of income or financial resources. It can manifest itself in other ways that might include hunger, malnutrition, violence, limited access to education and financial services, social discrimination, mental health issues, and isolation, as well as exclusion from collective decision making.[3] More recently, it has been shown that poverty implies not only a lack of economic resources but a depletion of cognitive resources that impair decision making.[4] People who are eligible and will benefit from welfare programs might not enroll in these programs, not necessarily because they are unaware of them or because they believe that the dollar amounts provided by them are insufficient, but because they might not have the cognitive bandwidth to process the information or because they might feel embarrassed or socially stigmatized by receiving such payments.[5]

To successfully design good social welfare programs, we therefore need an understanding not only of the economics and people's ability to generate a sustainable livelihood, but also of the cognitive and psychological burdens that come with poverty. In addition, we need to be careful of the "cognitive tax" that social welfare programs may inadvertently impose on low-income individuals they intend to serve (e.g., via long application forms, complicated enrollment procedures).

One way to alleviate the mental burdens of poverty is to simplify welfare programs to increase take-up.[6] Indeed, the behavioral sciences have a rich tradition of research that has shown the effect of small interventions on human decision making and action. Drawing on the notion that the success or failure of any endeavor is a function of not just the individual who has chosen to undertake the action but also of the environment in which that individual operates, researchers have shown that changes in the environment and the context can have significant effects on people's ability to succeed at tasks or to make better decisions. This stream of research was first made popular with the concept of a nudge, as immortalized in the eponymous 2008 book *Nudge* by Richard Thaler and Cass Sunstein.[7] This book revolutionized the way in which organizations all over the world think about using behavioral science in designing products, programs, and policies. Since the publication of the book, the concept of nudging has also found a companion in the notion of sludge – things in the context that slow people down or prevent them from accomplishing goals.

This stream of research has allowed organizations to better understand the so-called last-mile problem: the idea that well-designed products and programs often do not get enough traction because stakeholders (customers or citizens) fail to engage with them. Indeed, in the early days of some welfare programs, governments learned that the simple act of making cash available to citizens is no guarantee that those citizens will accept the cash and use it effectively. Consider the Canada Learning Bond, a Canadian federal government program designed to provide $2,000 to eligible low-income Canadians to educate their children. Its designers believed that a program providing free money would gain close to universal acceptance because the costs (monetary and hassle) of enrolling in the program were considered to be relatively low. However, despite the supposed ease of the process of enrolling, the take-up rate in the early years of the program was only 16 per cent.[8] Why did 84 per cent of people who were eligible to receive cash not claim it? It turned out that the reasons were twofold. Some of the processes that seemed relatively straightforward to the designers of the program were not at all straightforward for people who operated in a different context. In particular, opening a special bank account and enrolling in a specific government program involved visits to government offices. The people who designed the program thought that these visits should be relatively easy, but for recipients – low-income Canadians who were working multiple jobs and taking care of family – the hassle cost was incredibly high. Furthermore, several people who were eligible for the Canada Learning Bond were perhaps embarrassed by receiving government assistance, and this potential embarrassment prevented them from signing up.

We also note that a lot of these welfare programs are all conceptualized by policy makers as a black box – a conduit for governments to funnel money to the poor to help achieve certain social goals. The primary driver for success is simply the dollar value of the payments, with the assumption being that the greater the amount a recipient receives, the more likely they are to accomplish their social goals. This naive simplicity, coupled with a distrust of the poor and a need for accountability, results in a layer of complex paperwork that recipients need to complete. This complexity creates psychological barriers for recipients and administrative burdens for field staff.

A fuller understanding of the effectiveness of poverty alleviation programs must therefore incorporate these behavioral elements that are driven by design features of the program into their research. This approach is still in its infancy. Although the incidence of poverty and calls to use welfare programs to support citizens have only grown over the past few years, there is as yet little nuanced understanding of how these programs should be designed, keeping in mind the behaviors of the recipients, as well as those of the people delivering the programs. As Lindert et al. argue, this nuanced understanding is urgently needed.[9]

The Behaviourally Informed Organizations partnership[10] was set up at the Behavioural Economics in Action at Rotman center at the University of Toronto, with the express goal of trying to understand how behavioral factors might help organizations design better products, programs, and policies. This partnership involves more than 23 academic researchers and 20 organizational partners drawn from governments, for-profit businesses, large international organizations, and not-for-profit organizations. As the partnership began work on one of its stated goals of helping to improve financial well-being, a group of researchers and practitioners emerged that was particularly passionate about designing better social assistance programs during the pandemic period. This group put together an online conference in 2021, and the seeds of this volume were planted at that time. We started asking questions about how behavioral science can be applied to social assistance programs. What are the general success factors for cash transfer programs? When would they succeed, and when would they not? What behavioral frictions might impede the success of social welfare programs? In particular, what is the role of friction, such as emotions (guilt and shame), cognitive limitations (inability to process information), sludge (complexity of processes), and perceptions (failure to be motivated to seek the desired social goal)? What does an unpacked black box (a glass box) for cash transfer programs look like? Instead of treating cash transfer programs as one entity, could we break them down into distinct phases and think about the role that different design features of the program can play in each of these phases? What can the Global North and the Global South learn from each other? Finally, what does a prescriptive framework for the practitioner look like? Questions such as these motivated us to put together this volume. We realized that although there are many excellent articles about the success of cash transfer programs, no one compendium has showcased the latest thinking in this area – hence our desire to put together this book.

The goal of this book is to develop a nuanced framework for how society more generally, and governments and practitioners in particular, should design cash transfer programs to improve inclusivity and equality and reduce poverty. In particular, our focus is not only on showcasing past successes but on building frameworks and developing prescriptive advice for practitioners who are looking to design a behaviorally informed cash transfer program. Although the book primarily focuses on cash transfer programs, we also introduce an overview of basic income programs, which are a specific subset of cash transfer programs designed to provide unconditional cash payments from the government to members of a society to meet their basic needs, regardless of employment status. Cash transfers, however, include a broader class of cash-based programs, including family and child benefits, negative income tax (e.g., the Earned Income Tax Credit), and targeted cash transfers to individuals and households living in poverty. Although much of the policy debate is over the cost of cash transfer programs, in this book we focus on the behavioral design of these programs to increase inclusion, equity, and impact on poverty alleviation.

Our book is organized into three parts. Five chapters in the first part walk the reader through the state of the art on cash transfer programs.

In Chapter 1, Dwyer et al. provide a comparison of cash transfer programs in the Global North with those in the Global South and give insights into the ways in which these parts of the world can learn from each other. In Chapter 2, Datta et al. from ideas42 draw on lessons from six different cash transfer programs worldwide to illustrate the different ways in which behavioral science can inform the design and delivery of these programs to innovate, adapt, and scale them successfully.

Chapter 3, coauthored by a team of academics and practitioners at the Reach Alliance at the University of Toronto, talks about the Reach challenge – the challenge of delivering critical services and resources to the hardest to reach all across the globe. The authors draw on five examples from diverse countries – Brazil, Ethiopia, Jordan, Kenya, and Palestine – to offer practical lessons on how cash transfer programs can be managed to reach as many people as possible and improve targeting. In Chapter 4, a team of researchers from the University of Toronto and the World Bank talk about the ways in which behavioral insights can help cash transfer programs by presenting a basic framework for thinking through multiple effects of cash transfer programs. In Chapter 5, Evelyn L. Forget of the University of Manitoba leads readers through the landscape of basic income programs and highlights how experiments can help in better designing and making decisions about programs.

The five chapters in Part 2 of the book take a deeper dive into understanding how behavioral science can improve the design and delivery of cash transfer programs. In Chapter 6, Turetski et al. from the University of Toronto present a framework for thinking about the effect of design features on multiple dependent measures that can signal the effectiveness of cash transfer programs. They do this through a synthesis of published research as well as a series of in-depth interviews with practitioners, academics, and experts, and they also draw on some lessons from the private sector. In Chapter 7, West and Whillans ask the question of whether cash is the only thing that should be transferred in welfare programs or whether there are benefits to transferring other non-cash resources. This chapter also presents a framework of the different ways in which cash transfer programs can be designed to minimize wasting recipients' time. In Chapter 8, Jaroszewicz provides a behavioral perspective on an individual's decision to seek formal or informal financial help – a building block for their decision to enroll in welfare programs.

Chapters 9 and 10 provide a rich description of two different sets of programs that illustrate some of the ideas on how behavioral science can help design better programs. In Chapter 9, Gennetian et al. describe the Baby's First Years study and provide a framework for how behavioral science helped in designing and optimizing that program. In Chapter 10, Gachigi describes how behavioral science has helped to shape and improve the effectiveness of cash transfer programs in Kenya.

Finally, Part 3 (Chapter 11) brings together the key ideas from the book and identifies an agenda for future research and practice.

For our partnership, this book is an important milestone because it allows us to not only dive deeply into the behavioral science but also to apply it to a large, meaningful societal problem at scale. We are confident that readers will finish this book feeling as though they have enhanced their understanding of how behavioral insights can better help design welfare programs. We also believe that this book will provide a new model to policy makers to study and shift the discourse on poverty alleviation from purely economic factors to behavioral ones as well. Given that the ultimate goal of these programs is well-being, this shift will increase the ecological validity of the programs and their evaluation. We also hope that the content of this book will provide program designers and field staff with a prescriptive framework and a checklist of ideas on how behavioral science can better help them to design social assistance programs.

NOTES

1 World Bank Group. (2020). *Poverty and shared prosperity 2020: Reversals of fortune.* https://openknowledge.worldbank.org/bitstream/handle/10986/34496/9781464816024 .pdf.

2 Johnson, A.F., & Roberto, K.J. (2020). The COVID-19 pandemic: Time for a universal basic income? *Public Administration and Development, 40*(4), 232–5. https://doi.org /10.1002/pad.1891.

3 Ridley, M., Rao, G., Schilbach, F., & Patel, V. (2020). Poverty, depression, and anxiety: Causal evidence and mechanisms. *Science, 370*(6522), Article eaay0214. https://doi .org/10.1126/science.aay0214.

4 See Mani, A., Mullainathan, S., Shafir, E., & Zhao, J. (2013). Poverty impedes cognitive function. *Science, 341*(6149), 976–80. https://doi.org/10.1126/science.1238041; and de Bruijn, E.-J., & Antonides, G. (2022). Poverty and economic decision making: A review of scarcity theory. *Theory and Decision, 92*(1), 5–37. https://doi.org/10.1007/s11238-021-09802-7.

5 Baumberg, B. (2016). The stigma of claiming benefits: A quantitative study. *Journal of Social Policy, 45*(2), 181–99. https://doi.org/10.1017/s0047279415000525.

6 Bettinger, E.P., Long, B.T., Oreopoulos, P., & Sanbonmatsu, L. (2012). The role of application assistance and information in college decisions: Results from the H&R Block FAFSA experiment. *Quarterly Journal of Economics, 127*(3), 1205–42. https://doi.org/10.1093/qje/qjs017.

7 Thaler, R.H., & Sunstein, C.R. (2008). *Nudge: Improving decisions using the architecture of choice.* Yale University Press.

8 Soman, D. (2014). Behaviourally informed innovations. In D. Soman, J.G. Stein, & J. Wong (Eds.), *Innovating for the global south: Towards an inclusive innovation agenda* (pp. 29–46). University of Toronto Press.

9 Lindert, K., Karippacheril, T.G., Caillava, I.R., & Chávez, K.N. (Eds.). (2020). *Sourcebook on the foundations of social protection delivery systems.* World Bank Publications.

10 See the Behaviourally Informed Organizations partnership webpage at https://www.biorgpartnership.com/.

PART ONE

Why Behavioral Science Matters
for Inclusive Societies

CHAPTER ONE

A Comparison of Cash Transfer Programs in the Global North and Global South

Ryan Dwyer, Kaitlyn Stewart, and Jiaying Zhao

INTRODUCTION

Over the past two decades, unconditional cash transfers have become an increasingly widespread tool to address poverty in low- and middle-income countries. In the same period, though, cash transfer programs have remained virtually non-existent in high-income countries, in part because of the benefits cliff (i.e., potentially losing existing social benefits to receive the cash transfer), funding constraints, and wavering political support. In the past few years, however, cash transfer programs have expanded in North America and Europe, enabling comparisons between the emerging literature in the Global North and the existing evidence in the Global South. The goal of this chapter is to review the research on cash transfer programs in the Global North and South to identify similarities and differences in program design, participation, operation, and outcomes. Our aim is to shed light on the research landscape and to identify knowledge gaps that can help inform the development of future programs.

Cash transfers have become an increasingly used poverty alleviation tool because they are simple, flexible, and effective. Unlike in-kind aid, cash transfers can be delivered instantly and easily via electronic payment, and cash can address diverse needs, such as buying food, paying rent, or making an investment. Cash transfers have been particularly popular in the Global South, where objective poverty rates are higher, and the value of each US dollar can go further in the local community. Indeed, as of 2016, more than 130 countries in the Global South had implemented some form of cash transfer program to address poverty.[1] The proliferation of these programs has generated a growing body of evidence demonstrating that cash transfers provide benefits to health,[2] psychological well-being,[3] food security and assets,[4] education and employment,[5] and financial management strategies.[6]

The accumulating evidence from the Global South has recently inspired new programs in the Global North. Indeed, hundreds of countries around the world – including most countries in the Global North – have turned to cash transfers to help address the social and economic crises caused by the COVID-19 pandemic.[7] Even before the pandemic, there was growing interest in using cash transfers in the Global North to simplify social assistance programs (e.g., stimulus checks) and raise the income floor for low-income and marginalized members of society. Of course, the social, political, and economic contexts in the Global North and South differ in many ways, leading to differences in the design of cash transfer programs. This diversity has led to many open questions about the similarities of and differences between programs in the Global North and South: Who are the primary recipients of cash transfers? How much do recipients receive, and how is the money delivered? What outcomes have been measured, and what are the impacts of the cash?

CURRENT STUDY

To address these questions, we conducted a review of the literature on cash transfer programs in the Global North and South since 2000, when cash transfer programs became widely implemented around the world. We focused specifically on cash transfer programs that are non-contributory and unconditional. *Non-contributory* refers to programs that provide cash with no requirement for a monetary contribution from the individual (e.g., employment pensions).

Unconditional refers to programs without behavioral requirements to receive the cash (e.g., attending a training program). Although previous reviews have focused primarily on conditional cash transfer programs in the Global South,[8] the number of unconditional cash transfer programs has greatly increased in recent years, enabling us to focus our review on these programs, which are more easily comparable across diverse contexts. Although many emergency relief programs have provided cash assistance in response to COVID-19, we excluded these programs given the unique circumstances of the pandemic. To ensure our review covers only programs that have been or will be subject to rigorous evaluation, we also included only programs designed as randomized controlled trials (RCTs) or evaluated using a meaningful comparison group. Ongoing programs were only included if they have a project description that includes their research design (e.g., whether they are an RCT or not).

METHODS

As described, we included only past and current cash transfer programs from 2000 to 2021 that are non-contributory and unconditional and in which recipients were compared with a meaningful control group. To compile our database, we built on preexisting systematic reviews and used additional informal searches to capture all completed and ongoing programs that met our inclusion criteria. Specifically, we included all relevant programs from an extensive systematic review of cash transfer program evaluations in the Global South from 2000 to 2015.[9] We also extracted relevant programs from GiveDirectly's Cash Research Explorer, an online database covering cash transfer programs since 2015 from both the Global North and the Global South. To find newer and ongoing programs, we used additional informal search methods, such as a working database of cash transfer programs in the United States compiled by members of the Guaranteed Income Community of Practice, expert referrals, and Google searches to include ongoing cash transfer trials up to 2021.

To limit the influence of multiple hypothesis testing on the same cash transfer program, we identified one primary impact evaluation report for each program. These primary reports were used to extract information about the program treatment conditions and outcomes, and we visited the program websites when available to confirm details.

Programs were classified as Global North or South on the basis of the World Bank's classification of countries by gross national income (GNI). We defined the Global North as high-income countries (i.e., GNI per capita above $12,696) and the Global South as low-, lower-middle-, and upper-middle-income countries (i.e., GNI per capita below $12,696). To our knowledge, this is the most comprehensive database of rigorously designed unconditional cash transfer programs to date.[10]

RESULTS

Program Location, Funding, Launch Date, and Recipient Samples

We included a total of 87 cash transfer programs in the review. These included 44 programs in the Global South, of which 16 are still active, and 43 programs in the Global North, of which 33 are still active. The top panel of Figure 1.1 shows the geographic distribution of the programs by continent, and the bottom panel shows the geographic distribution by country. The majority of cash transfer programs in the Global South were based in Africa ($n = 29$), but a moderate number were also based in Asia ($n = 9$), South America ($n = 5$), and Europe ($n = 1$). The programs in the North were almost exclusively based in North America ($n = 39$), with only three in Europe and one in South America.

Figure 1.2 shows the number of cash transfer programs funded by governments, by non-governmental organizations (NGOs) or private funding, or with a mix of funding sources. Programs in the Global South were primarily funded by either governments ($n = 22$) or NGOs ($n = 20$), but rarely by both ($n = 2$). In contrast, programs in the North were almost exclusively funded by NGOs ($n = 36$), with only a few programs funded by governments alone ($n = 6$) or by both governments and NGOs ($n = 1$).

Figure 1.1. Geographic distribution of cash transfer programs: (a) number of programs per continent and (b) number of programs per country

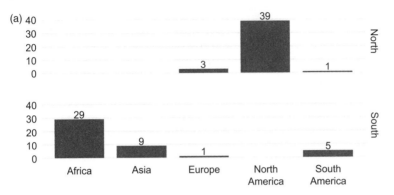

(a)

North

			39	
		3		1

South

29	9	1		5

Africa Asia Europe North America South America

(b)

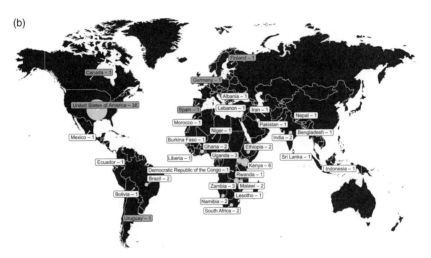

Notes: Countries with darker labels are included in the Global North; countries with lighter labels are included in the Global South. The size of the circle represents the number of programs in that country.

Figure 1.2. Number of cash transfer programs per sponsor, with the program sponsors categorized as government, NGO, or a mixture: (a) Global North and (b) Global South

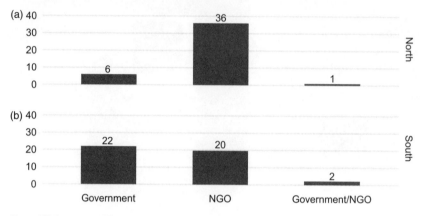

Note: NGO = non-governmental organization.

Figure 1.3 shows that most cash transfer programs in the South launched around 2008 (the median), but most programs in the North launched around 2020 (the median), highlighting that programs in the North began only recently – and roughly a decade later on average than those in the South.

To compare the size of programs in the North and South, we tracked the total number of cash recipients in each program. Figure 1.4 shows the distribution of programs by recipient sample size in increasing orders of magnitude (from zero–99 to more than 10 million recipients). Programs in the South were much larger in size than those in the North. The median number of cash recipients in the South was roughly 22,000, with eight programs exceeding 1 million recipients. Among programs in the North, the median number of recipients was 130, with only three programs exceeding 10,000 cash recipients.

Many cash transfer programs targeted specific low-income groups. To better understand whom the cash transfers were meant to help, we tracked whether the cash transfer was targeted to parents, children, women, vulnerable groups, or ethnic minorities (see

Figure 1.3. Number of cash transfer program launches per year: (a) Global North and (b) Global South

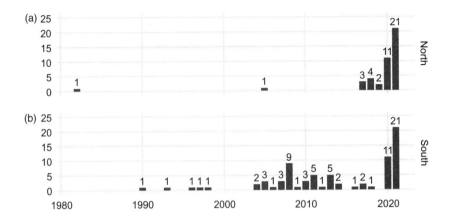

Figure 1.4. Number of cash transfer programs by recipient sample size: (a) Global North and (b) Global South

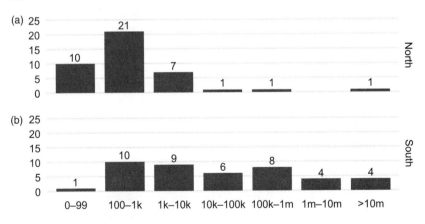

Figure 1.5). Other groups, such as farmers, have also been targeted in the literature but are not shown in the figure because of the small number of such programs. Roughly equal numbers of programs in the North and South targeted children ($n_{North} = 11$, $n_{South} = 10$), parents ($n_{North} = 13$, $n_{South} = 7$), women ($n_{North} = 9$, $n_{South} = 8$), and vulnerable groups, such as youth in foster care or people experiencing homelessness ($n_{North} = 6$, $n_{South} = 5$). Eight programs in the North

Figure 1.5. Number of cash transfer programs targeting specific recipient groups: (a) Global North and (b) Global South

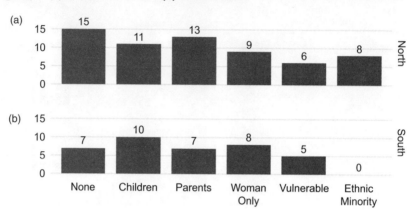

Note: *None* means the program did not target any of these specific groups, but it may have targeted other groups.

targeted ethnic minorities, whereas none did in the South. Only seven programs in the South did not target any of these specific groups, whereas 15 programs in the North did not target any.

Cash Transfer Frequency, Duration, Delivery Mode, and Amount

Although all cash transfer programs provided cash to recipients, the size and frequency of cash payments varied greatly. In fact, 12 programs included multiple treatment groups that received cash transfers of differing amounts or frequency, making a total of 102 treatment arms in our database (n_{North} = 48, n_{South} = 53). Figure 1.6 shows the number of cash transfers by transfer frequency. Across the North and South, a large majority of transfers were provided as monthly payments (n_{North} = 39, n_{South} = 35). A relatively small number provided lump sum payments (n_{North} = 2, n_{South} = 11), and only a few programs distributed cash weekly (n_{North} = 3, n_{South} = 3), quarterly (n_{North} = 3, n_{South} = 4), or annually (n_{North} = 1, n_{South} = 0).

For transfers that were not provided as a lump sum, the length of time recipients continued to receive payments varied (see Figure 1.7). The most common transfers in the South were ongoing, such

Figure 1.6. Number of cash transfer programs by transfer frequency: (a) Global North and (b) Global South

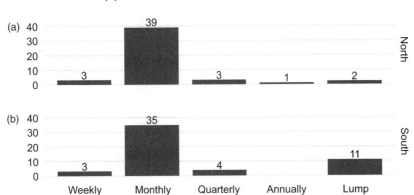

Figure 1.7. Number of cash transfer programs by transfer duration: (a) Global North and (b) Global South

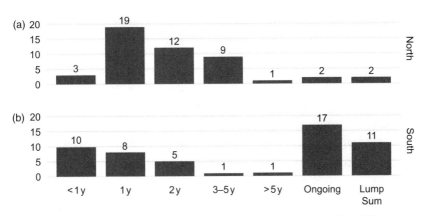

Note: *Ongoing* means that participants in the programs are currently still receiving cash transfers.

that participants continued to receive cash payments as long as they remained eligible (*n* = 17). For example, the Child Grant Program in Zambia provided cash transfers of roughly US$21 (2021 purchasing power parity [PPP]) every two months as long as households had children aged younger than five years. Most other transfers in the South continued for less than three years (*n* = 23), and only a few continued for three years or longer (*n* = 2). Meanwhile, very few transfers

Figure 1.8. Number of cash transfer programs by delivery mode: (a) Global North and (b) Global South

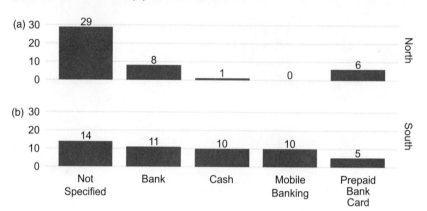

in the North provided ongoing cash payments ($n = 2$). Most transfers in the North continued for one to two years ($n = 31$), with a handful lasting more than three years ($n = 10$) and only a few lasting less than a year ($n = 3$).

Although many programs did not specify how the cash transfers were delivered (see Figure 1.8; $n_{North} = 29$, $n_{South} = 14$), bank transfers ($n_{North} = 8$, $n_{South} = 11$) and prepaid bank cards ($n_{North} = 6$, $n_{South} = 5$) were equally common in the South and North. Programs in the South also used physical cash ($n_{South} = 10$) or mobile banking (e.g., M-pesa; $n_{South} = 10$), but these were almost never used in the North ($n_{North} = 1$ and $n_{North} = 0$, respectively).

To compare cash transfer amounts using a common metric, we calculated how much participants in each program received annually in US dollars, adjusted for inflation and purchasing power. For each program, the amount was first converted from local currency to nominal US dollars using the exchange rate from the mean year of the program. This amount was then adjusted for purchasing power in the same year and then further adjusted for inflation using 2021 as the base year. Thus, all values are reported in 2021 US$ PPP. As shown in Figure 1.9, most programs in the North provided an annualized transfer amount between $6,000 and $13,000 (mean = $7,753, median = $6,403), whereas most programs in the South provided an

Figure 1.9. Number of cash transfer programs by annualized cash transfer amount: (a) Global North and (b) Global South

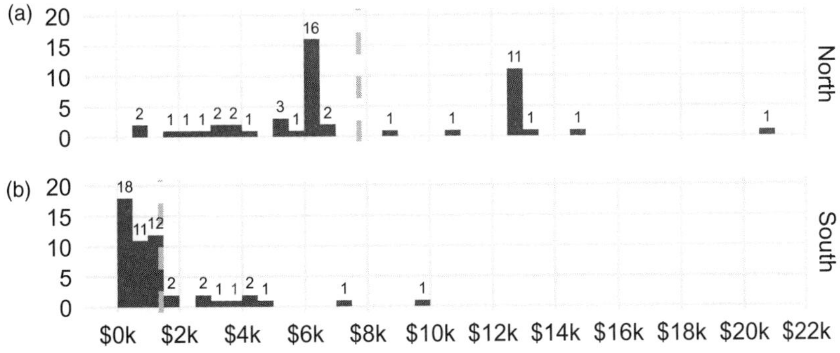

Notes: All values are annual amount converted to 2021 US$ purchasing power parity. Dashed lines represent the mean across programs.

annualized amount around $1,000 (mean = $1,414, median = $799). We excluded one program in the South from this analysis because its cash transfer amount was unspecified.

In addition to the absolute transfer amount, we also calculated the relative increase in wealth provided by the cash transfer by converting the annualized transfer amount to a percentage of the country's median per capita annual income. This was calculated by converting the median per capita gross domestic product (GDP) for the country in each program's mean year to 2021 US$ PPP. Using this metric, 11 programs in the South provided more than 50 per cent of the per capita annual income, of which six programs provided more than 100 per cent of the per capita annual income (see Figure 1.10). However, no program in the North provided more than 50 per cent of the per capita annual income. On average, programs in the South provided cash transfers, which represented a 37 per cent increase in relative wealth (median = 17 per cent), whereas programs in the North provided cash transfers, which represented only a 12 per cent increase in wealth (median = 9 per cent). Taken together, these results highlight the higher cost – and relatively smaller increase in financial power – of cash transfer programs in the North compared with those in the South.

Figure 1.10. Number of cash transfer programs by annualized cash transfer amount relative to country median income: (a) Global North and (b) Global South

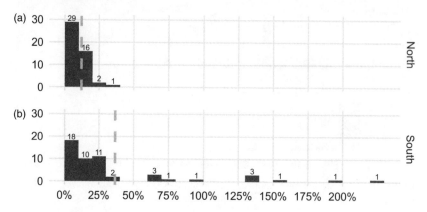

Notes: Percentages show annualized cash transfer amounts relative to country median income. Dashed orange lines represent the mean across programs.

Program Outcomes

Cash can be used in numerous ways, enabling cash transfer programs to affect a range of outcomes from financial stability to education and health. To better understand what outcomes have been influenced by cash transfer programs, we extracted the key outcomes from each program's primary impact evaluation. For each outcome, we tracked how long the follow-up period lasted after the final cash transfer and whether the cash had a significant impact on the recipients compared with the control group. We grouped the outcomes into one of eight domains: health (including measures of physical health, nutrition, health behaviors), assets (including measures of income, savings, and investments), spending (including measures of how the cash transfer was spent), community (including measures of civic engagement and social behaviors), labor (including measures of employment and entrepreneurship), well-being (including measures of emotional well-being, satisfaction with life, and mental health), education (including measures of schooling, training, and skill development), and housing (including measures of housing stability).

Figure 1.11. Number of cash transfer programs by primary outcome domains: (a) Global North and (b) Global South

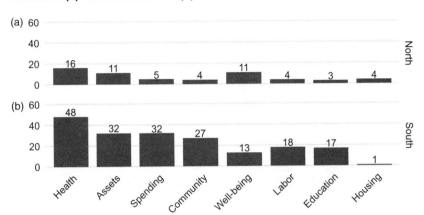

Overall, programs in the North and South have focused on similar types of outcomes, although fewer outcomes are reported in the North (n_{North} = 58, n_{South} = 188) because many ongoing projects have not provided detailed information on outcomes (see Figure 1.11). In the South, the most common outcome was health (n = 48), and a moderate number of programs also tracked assets (n = 32), spending (n = 32), community (n = 27), labor (n = 18), education (n = 17), and well-being (n = 13). Only one study tracked housing. In the North, only 16 programs reported their primary outcomes. The most common outcomes were health (n = 16), assets (n = 11), and well-being (n = 11), and a small number measured labor (n = 4), spending (n = 5), community (n = 4), housing (n = 4), and education (n = 3).

Because the impact of cash transfers may emerge over time (especially for programs that deliver transfers in installments), cash transfer programs have tracked outcomes across a range of time periods (see Figure 1.12). In the South, the most common follow-up period was within one year of receiving the final cash transfer (n = 23), but many programs also tracked outcomes for two years (n = 12) and after three to five years (n = 9). Only a small number of programs studied long-term outcomes beyond five years (n = 6). Programs in

Figure 1.12. Number of cash transfer programs by primary follow-up period: (a) Global North and (b) Global South

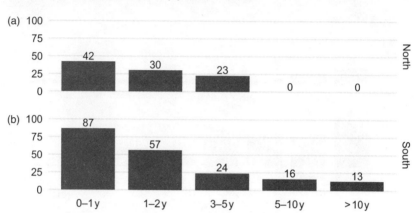

the North followed a similar pattern. The most common follow-up period was within one year (n = 19), but many programs tracked outcomes for two years (n = 15) and for three to five years (n = 8). However, unlike in the South, no program in the North tracked outcomes beyond 5 years.

As a crude snapshot of the effectiveness of cash transfers, we counted the number of effects in each outcome domain that were reported as significant, not significant, or still to be analyzed as part of an ongoing study (see Figure 1.13). The significant effects were further separated into positive impacts (beneficial to cash recipients) or negative impacts (unfavorable to cash recipients). In the South, at least half or more of the completed programs reported positive impacts in most domains: health (n = 27/44; 61 per cent), assets (n = 17/29; 59 per cent), spending (n = 19/26; 73 per cent), community (n = 13/24; 54 per cent), well-being (n = 7/12; 58 per cent), labor (n = 9/17; 53 per cent), and education (n = 8/14; 57 per cent). The only two negative impacts were that in one program the cash transfer led to a significant decrease in trust of individuals but a significant increase in trust of institutions, and in another program it led to a significant increase in moderate and severe anemia for children in the cash group. The only study tracking housing is still ongoing. The initial results in the North show positive impacts of cash transfers and no negative impacts, but most

Figure 1.13. Number of cash transfer programs by impacts

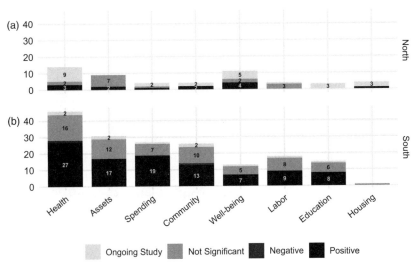

Notes: The number of programs reported here is smaller than that reported in Figure 1.11 because in the evaluation reports, many outcomes were missing statistical details. Counts are shown only for values greater than 1.

programs are still ongoing and do not have outcome data yet. Only seven programs in the North have completed evaluations, so more studies will need to be finished before meaningful conclusions can be drawn.

DISCUSSION

Unconditional cash transfers are an increasingly popular tool used to alleviate poverty around the world, but how do cash transfer programs in the Global South compare with those in the Global North? In this chapter, we conducted the first review of the published and gray literature on rigorously designed unconditional cash transfer programs from 2000 to 2021 in the Global North and South. Our goal was to shed light on the literature landscape and identify knowledge gaps that could help inform the development of future cash transfer programs.

Cash transfer programs have a long and established history in the Global South. The prototypical program is based in Africa, started around 2008, is funded by either government or an NGO, and provides ongoing monthly payments amounting to around $1,000 (2021 US$ PPP) annually to tens of thousands of low-income people. Many programs involved specific populations such as children, parents, and women. A program that fits this prototype well is the government of Malawi's Social Cash Transfer Programme, which has provided more than 200,000 poor households with ongoing payments amounting to roughly $400 (2021 US$ PPP) per year. In contrast, cash transfer programs have a much shorter history in the Global North and were not widely used until 2016. The prototypical program is smaller in scale (involving several hundred cash recipients), based in North America, funded by an NGO, just started in 2020, and provides transfers of around $7,000 (2021 US$ PPP). For example, Growing Resilience in Tacoma is a new privately funded program providing 110 families with monthly payments amounting to $6,400 (2021 US$ PPP) for one year. The relatively new research literature in the North will greatly benefit from additional large-scale RCTs and more support from governments. For example, many of the recently launched programs ($n = 16$) are associated with Mayors for a Guaranteed Income, a coalition of 62 mayors across various US cities advocating for guaranteed income, although funding for these programs is still primarily provided by NGOs.

In both the Global North and the Global South, most cash transfer programs distributed the money as monthly payments, and relatively fewer provided lump sum payments. Previous research in Kenya has found that lump sum cash transfers have resulted in increased spending on durable goods and reduced cortisol levels compared with monthly payments of the same total amount, whereas monthly cash transfers were more likely to improve food security.[11] With these potential differences in mind, future work should continue to explore the advantages of regular and lump sum payments in the Global North and South. For example, GiveDirectly is conducting a long-term study of universal basic income in which they are providing one group with US$23 monthly for 24 months and another group with the same amount as a lump sum. Similarly, the Denver Basic Income Project is giving one group US$1,000 monthly for 12 months and another group US$6,500 as a lump sum and US$500 a month for the next 11 months.

This said, there are challenges with lump sum payments, such as the benefits cliff, that are unique to the Global North and not as problematic in the Global South. That is, if recipients receive a large sum of cash at once, they may be disqualified for a range of social benefits (as in the case of the Finland basic income trial). The benefits cliff still remains a policy barrier for programs that aim to provide large sums of money to low-income people in many countries in the North. One prime example of the benefits cliff is Magnolia Mother's Trust in Jackson, Mississippi, where women received US$1,000 a month as unconditional cash transfers. As a result of clawbacks, the net transfer was only around US$400 a month, and recipients lost housing vouchers and food stamp benefits. One program that successfully avoided benefits cliff is the New Leaf Project that provided $7,500 as a lump sum to individuals experiencing homeless in Vancouver, British Columbia, who still remained eligible for social benefits. This was made possible by an agreement with the BC provincial government that invoked a special exemption that allowed people to keep the cash transfer without affecting eligibility for other benefits.

Although the absolute size of cash transfers was smaller in the South, the relative increase in wealth was much greater. This highlights the higher cost – and relatively smaller increase in financial power – of cash transfer programs in higher-income countries. The smaller relative increase in wealth, combined with the smaller average sample sizes, suggests that existing cash transfer programs in the North will have less statistical power to find significant benefits from cash transfers. Future studies should use larger participant samples with considerably larger transfers, such that the cash injection will meaningfully increase the relative wealth. Of course, additional government support may be necessary to overcome funding and policy challenges (e.g., remove the benefits cliff) hindering large-scale programs in the North.

Programs in the North and South have tracked a range of outcomes over time. The most common outcomes were health, assets, spending, and community engagement in the South and health, assets, and well-being in the North. Most programs tracked outcomes only within one or two years, and very few programs measured outcomes beyond five years. More positive impacts of cash transfers in the domains of health, assets, community, spending, and labor were found in programs in the South, although most programs in the North have not finished rigorous evaluations. This calls for future research to track longer-term outcomes beyond five years to examine the long-run effects of cash transfers.

The goal of this chapter is to provide a comparison of unconditional cash transfer programs in the Global North and South. Although we tried to include only relevant high-quality research projects, this was not a systematic review of exclusively peer-reviewed scientific articles. Instead, our review built on existing reviews and also relied on gray literature of new and ongoing programs. As a result, the programs and reports included in the review are likely to be incomplete and biased by our search methods. Our analysis also overlooked a number of potentially important nuances. For example, we have primarily focused on summarizing programs, giving each program outcome equal weight while giving little attention to sample sizes. As more programs in the North are completed, a systematic review and meta-analysis should be conducted to compare these impacts while taking into account sample size, effect size, and moderating variables. Despite these limitations, this chapter provides an initial broad overview of the known research to date on cash transfers. We are encouraged to see many more cash transfer programs starting in the North as efforts to test guaranteed income ramp up. We have made our database publicly available so others can explore the data and build on this initial analysis.[12] This is a rapidly growing literature, so we expect the research landscape to change quickly, generating more evidence and greater interest in cash transfers as a tool to reduce poverty.

NOTES

1 Bastagli, F., Hagen-Zanker, J., Harman, L., Barca, V., Sturge, G., Schmidt, T., & Pellerano, L. (2016). *Cash transfers: What does the evidence say? A rigorous review of programme impact and the role of design and implementation features*. https://odi.org/en/publications/cash-transfers-what-does-the-evidence-say-a-rigorous-review-of-impacts-and-the-role-of-design-and-implementation-features/.

2 Handa, S., Peterman, A., Huang, C., Halpern, C., Pettifor, A., & Thirumurthy, H. (2015). Impact of the Kenya cash transfer for orphans and vulnerable children on early pregnancy and marriage of adolescent girls. *Social Science & Medicine, 141*, 36–45. https://doi.org/10.1016/j.socscimed.2015.07.024.

3 Haushofer, J., & Shapiro, J. (2016). The short-term impact of unconditional cash transfers to the poor: Experimental evidence from Kenya. *Quarterly Journal of Economics, 131*(4), 1973–2042. https://doi.org/10.1093/qje/qjw025.

4 Ibid.

5 Kilburn, K., Thirumurthy, H., Halpern, C.T., Pettifor, A., & Handa, S. (2016). Effects of a large-scale unconditional cash transfer program on mental health outcomes of young people in Kenya. *Journal of Adolescent Health, 58*(2), 223–9. https://doi.org/10.1016/j.jadohealth.2015.09.023.

6 Hjelm, L., Handa, S., de Hoop, J., & Palermo, T. (2017). Poverty and perceived stress: Evidence from two unconditional cash transfer programs in Zambia. *Social Science & Medicine, 177*, 110–17. https://doi.org/10.1016/j.socscimed.2017.01.023.

7 Gentilini, U., Almenfi, M., & Dale, P. (2020). *Social protection and jobs responses to COVID-19: A real-time review of country measures*. World Bank Group.

8 See, for example Baird, S., Ferreira, F.H.G., Özler, B., & Woolcock, M. (2013). Relative effectiveness of conditional and unconditional cash transfers for schooling outcomes in developing countries: A systematic review. *Campbell Systematic Reviews, 9*(1), 1–124. https://doi.org/10.4073/csr.2013.8; Bastagli et al. (2016); Gaarder, M.M., Glassman, A., & Todd, J.E. (2010). Conditional cash transfers and health: Unpacking the causal chain. *Journal of Development Effectiveness, 2*(1), 6–50. https://doi.org/10.1080/19439341003646188; Glassman, A., Duran, D., Fleisher, L., Singer, D., Sturke, R., Angeles, G., Charles, J., Emrey, B., Gleason, J., Mwebsa, W., Saldana, K., Yarrow, K., & Koblinsky, M. (2013). Impact of conditional cash transfers on maternal and newborn health. *Journal of Health, Population and Nutrition, 31*(4, Suppl. 2), S48–S66; Kabeer, N., & Waddington, H. (2015). Economic impacts of conditional cash transfer programmes: A systematic review and meta-analysis. *Journal of Development Effectiveness, 7*(3), 290–303. https://doi.org/10.1080/19439342.2015.1068833; Lagarde, M., Haines, A., & Palmer, N. (2009). The impact of conditional cash transfers on health outcomes and use of health services in low and middle income countries. *Cochrane Database of Systematic Reviews*. https://doi.org/10.1002/14651858.CD008137; Manley, J., Gitter, S., & Slavchevska, V. (2012). *How effective are cash transfer programmes at improving nutritional status? A rapid evidence assessment of programmes' effects on anthropometric outcomes*. EPPI-Centre, Social Science. https://assets.publishing.service.gov.uk/media/57a08a7540f0b652dd00073a/Q33-Cash-transfers-2012Manley-rae.pdf; and Saavedra, J.E., & Garcia, S. (2012). Impacts of conditional cash transfer programs on educational outcomes in developing countries: A meta-analysis (Laper and Population Working Paper WR-921-1). RAND. https://www.rand.org/content/dam/rand/pubs/working_papers/2012/RAND_WR921-1.pdf.

9 Bastagli et al. (2016).
10 A live version of our database is publicly available at Center for Open Science. (2023). *A comparison of cash transfer programs in the global north and south.* Retrieved February 3, 2022, from https://osf.io/z5gn9/.
11 Haushofer & Shapiro (2016).
12 Center for Open Science (2023).

CHAPTER TWO

Innovate, Adapt, and Scale: The Future of Behavioral Science in Cash Transfer Programs

Saugato Datta, Faraz Haqqi, Mukta Joshi, and Catherine MacLeod

SUCCESSES OF BEHAVIORAL INTERVENTIONS IN CASH TRANSFER PROGRAMS

With evidence mounting that they are effective tools for reducing poverty and improving well-being, the number of cash transfer programs in developing countries has increased rapidly in recent years.[1] The proliferation of programs was further accelerated during the COVID-19 pandemic, with many governments incorporating cash transfers into their emergency response strategies.[2] The universe of social protection programs now includes a diverse array of cash-only and cash-plus programs (the latter being ones that supplement cash transfers with additional support mechanisms, such as health or education services).[3] These programs seek to have an impact on a wide range of human development and productive inclusion outcomes, from improving nutrition, parenting, and early childhood development to increasing financial literacy, economic participation, and entrepreneurship.

The success of cash transfer programs in reaching their desired outcomes hinges largely on the behavior of program participants, that is, their ability to make and act on a series of choices. Yet, many of these choices can be complex: participants must first decide (1) what their financial priorities are and (2) how best to allocate financial resources among those priorities. Then, having made those decisions, participants must follow through with appropriate actions and sustain them over time to achieve optimal outcomes. As programs add additional components and services, the behaviors they require of participants become more complex. For example, the addition of training sessions might require participants to attend sessions, process and retain information, and decide to adopt new practices.

Behavioral science can inform interventions to help participants successfully complete each of these steps; making cash transfer programs more meaningful (see also Chapters 4 and 6 for the role of behavioral science in the effectiveness of cash transfer programs). In this chapter, we outline some examples of programs that have successfully incorporated behavioral interventions to improve a broad range of outcomes, often at very little cost. Looking to the future, we outline some considerations for scaling the use of behavioral science in cash transfer programs and, finally, identify opportunities for future behavioral science innovation.

Our work supporting cash transfer programs in countries across Sub-Saharan Africa over the past six years shows that participants often encounter impact-limiting behavioral barriers that keep them from making decisions and acting in ways that would help them realize the outcomes programs want. Program participants are often living in environments of extreme and chronic scarcity.[4] The cognitive burden of scarcity can limit the attention participants are able to dedicate to considering their options and making decisions, which can make it even harder for them to navigate already difficult choices.[5] In addition to its cognitive impact, scarcity can manifest in many different ways, shaping participants' perceived choice sets, their priorities, and their ability to act in accordance with their choices. For example, participants may form an identity of poverty, developing a stagnation mindset that can lead participants to believe that their choice sets are more limited than they really are.[6] Participant decision making may also become increasingly biased toward short-term needs, making it harder for them to build long-term goals and make investments in their future. Finally, scarcity-affected participants may struggle to adhere to their financial choices if they face challenges in mental accounting to separate the resources they have accumulated for different purposes and monitoring their progress toward their goals.[7]

Cash transfer programs are uniquely well situated to address the behavioral challenges their participants face. In providing an infusion of cash, the programs temporarily alleviate participants' scarcity constraints, creating a natural window of opportunity in which to engage participants in reflecting on their longer-term goals and planning how they might use their cash to advance toward those goals. Programs that do not engage participants in this way are missing an opportunity to increase their impact. Our work has aimed to take advantage of this context, as we have been working to design behaviorally informed interventions that can easily be delivered when participants are receiving their transfer to support them in making the most of their cash. In Table 2.1, we highlight examples of design concepts that can be used to address the common behavioral barriers mentioned.

Although the barriers and design concepts are often similar across programs, designs must be customized to the context in which they are used to be effective. We have tested customized versions of these design concepts through randomized controlled trials (RCTs) in multiple countries, including Madagascar, Kenya, and Tanzania, where they have proven to have an impact.

In Madagascar, we have been partnering with the government since 2015 on a program that targets mothers in rural areas, with the goal of encouraging and empowering women to take steps toward improving their children's development. We designed and tested goal-setting and self-affirmation activities alongside community mother leader groups with the goal of improving early childhood development outcomes. The activities were delivered at well-being sessions that the mothers participated in while they were waiting to receive their cash transfer. To assess their impact, a large-scale cluster RCT was conducted, with data collected 18 months after the intervention began. We found positive impacts on key outcomes, including significant decreases in food insecurity, more positive parenting behaviors, and even significant positive impacts on children's social skills, as measured by a reputable child development assessment tool.[8] We are planning to conduct an end-line evaluation in the

Table 2.1. Common behavioral bottlenecks and design concepts

Behavioral barrier	Design concept
Cognitive scarcity	Goal-setting and plan-making interventions facilitated just before cash delivery can give recipients a moment to think through and plan toward their goals.
Identity of being poor	Highlighting the norm that all people, including cash transfer recipients, are capable of saving and investing in their future can help recipients expand their perceptions of what they can achieve.
Stagnation mindset	Self-affirmation activities can help participants adopt a growth mindset.
Present bias	Goal-setting and plan-making activities can give recipients a moment to consider their future goals and plan for how they will use their transfer to reach those goals.
Mental accounting	Partitioning guidance – such as a partitioning pouch or tool – can help recipients put their plans into action when they receive their money, allowing them to physically separate their cash when they receive it and reduce the possibility of spending it on impulsive purchases.

future to measure the impact of the designs on long-term outcomes because we expect that impacts on key development measures, including anthropometric measures such as stunting and wasting, would take effect after a significant amount of time.

In Kenya and Tanzania, we ran smaller, one- to one-and-a-half-month RCTs in 2019 to test packages of behavioral interventions integrated into the countries' national safety net programs. In Kenya, we focused on increasing savings toward productive investments among recipients of the National Safety Net Program, which targets households with orphans and vulnerable children, older people, and people with disabilities. The customized package of interventions included goal-setting and plan-making activities as well as a partitioning pouch for recipients to separate the cash they wanted to save from the cash they planned to use for immediate consumption. Short Message Service (SMS) messages (texts) were also sent to remind recipients to follow their plan when they received their cash, because the interventions were delivered at a community meeting about a week before cash was digitally disbursed through an account-based system. Significant positive impacts were found, including a 9 per cent increase in the incidence of having a productive goal and a 41 per cent increase in the amount saved. In Tanzania, the goal was also to increase savings and productive investments among recipients of the country's Productive Social Safety Net. The intervention consisted of a self-affirmation activity, followed by goal setting, plan making, and a partitioning pouch. The activities were delivered at the cash transfer site, just before cash disbursement. The package of behavioral interventions was found to significantly increase the incidence of recipients who had a productive goal by 3 per cent, and it increased the incidence of saving by 13 per cent.[9] A larger cluster RCT is currently in progress in Tanzania to assess the impact of the nudges on making productive investments within a six-month time frame.

ADAPTATION OF BEHAVIORAL INTERVENTIONS TO NEW PROGRAM CONTEXTS

The initial positive impacts we have found are promising, but as noted, behavioral designs are not one size fits all: design concepts must be tailored to the context. In the ever-changing world, there has been increased demand to adapt the use of behavioral science to improve cash transfer outcomes and to increase programs' value for money. Key changes in the cash transfer ecosystem include the continued shift toward digital payments as well as the rapid expansion of cash transfers during COVID-19, often expanded to urban populations and those who were newly out of work as a result of the pandemic. Key themes that have arisen along with this need for adaptation include the need to adapt programs to digital contexts, support recipients in transitions from humanitarian aid to social protection, and ensure that programs are targeting groups that most need support. In the following section, we share examples of our learning regarding these key themes.

Digital Transitions

Moving toward digital delivery of cash transfers has long been a goal of many programs, and it was sped up during the COVID-19 pandemic as mobile or digital delivery more quickly reached people in need and reduced touchpoints where the virus can spread.[10] In response to the COVID-19 pandemic, the World Bank and the government of the Democratic Republic of the Congo (DRC) developed an emergency response cash transfer in Kinshasa known as the Projet pour la Stabilisation de l'Est de la RDC pour la Paix 2–Contingent Emergency Response Component. This transfer was delivered completely remotely: recipients could register through an SMS survey and receive the money via mobile phone. The program targeted individuals who were vulnerable to falling into poverty and may have lost their jobs or livelihoods because of the pandemic. It provided recipients with US$25 per month over six months. In this program, we saw parallels to the behavioral problems and barriers faced in our previous work: recipients often had priorities for spending their cash but had difficulty planning how to spend it and ultimately with following through. Given the all-digital aspect of the program, we could not facilitate designs in person; however, we knew most recipients had access to a phone because that is how they received their cash. With this in mind, we developed SMS nudges based on design concepts from our previous work. We developed two SMS messages, one that was sent just before receipt of the cash that prompted participants to think of their priority and write down a budget and one that was sent just after the cash was received that reminded them to spend according to their plan. The messages also included general affirmations, reminding participants that they had the ability to improve their family's well-being. We also used evidence from behavioral science on communications best practices when developing the messages, ensuring messages were sent at opportune times to keep participants' plans salient and keeping the message concise to keep participants' attention.

When we tested these nudges by means of an RCT, we found significant positive results: participants who received the nudge SMS messages were 3 per cent more likely to have a priority set, 6 per cent more likely to have a future-oriented priority (such as spending on education or investment in a business), and 4 per cent more likely to report that they spent in line with their priority in comparison with a control group. Given the low cost of SMS messaging, the nudges proved to be very cost-effective: if the program did not incorporate the nudges but wanted to achieve the same impact attributed to the nudges, we estimated that it would require providing participants with about eight times the cost of the nudges in additional cash.

Humanitarian and Social Protection Nexus

The nexus between development and humanitarian aid has also been a growing focus: the COVID-19 crisis created numerous humanitarian emergencies, and after humanitarian aid, a transition to social protection is necessary to continue to support those affected.[11] To this end, it is crucial that behavioral designs for social protection cash transfers are relevant for the specific populations that may be exiting a humanitarian crisis. We have been working with the World Bank and UN Office for Project Services in South Sudan to tweak and test interventions in this context, where a social protection cash transfer program is being implemented in a postconflict context in which emergency situations such as floods, locust swarms, and theft and crime are common concerns. Although the problem we aimed to address was similar to the problem we had addressed previously – recipients had goals for their cash but had trouble planning and spending to reach those goals – some of the barriers we identified were unique to the context. For example, although recipients faced resource scarcity as a result of living in poverty, they also faced time scarcity: as a result of fluctuations in currency value and depreciation, they had limited time to use their cash to keep the full value. Depreciation also made it difficult to save in the traditional sense, and to save, participants had to take the extra step of identifying what they could invest in that would keep its value and then make that purchase. When they identified their goal and planned what they had to purchase to reach it, they also had to consider a detailed risk assessment, because they had to prioritize what to spend on while accounting for potential risks of displacement or theft. In this context, design concepts of prioritizing and planning were still relevant, but they had to be adapted so that people could specifically plan out the items they wanted to buy with their cash that would help them work toward their longer-term goal. Instead of providing a partitioning pouch to simply separate savings out, we also designed separate envelopes so that participants could separate their cash into as many envelopes as items they planned to buy. The envelopes had icons to represent the items, so they served as a reminder when the participant went to the market to make their purchases. Testing of these interventions is currently underway.

Focus on Targeting and Enrolling Groups
Who Would Benefit Most

Because cash transfers have been proven effective at reducing poverty,[12] there is a growing focus on areas beyond just getting cash to households. One key example is women's empowerment, in which evidence has already shown that cash transfers have a positive impact,[13] and behavioral science may be able to further increase their impact through a focus on aspects of the program such as registration and enrollment. In 2020 and early 2021, we worked with the World Bank and the government of Sudan to identify ways in which we could use a behavioral lens to increase women's empowerment through the Sudan Family Support Program, a large nationwide cash transfer program. The World Bank and the project team identified stark gender inequality, highlighted by low participation of women in political life, the labor market, and education,[14] which they aimed to address through the program by increasing women's receipt of the benefits. We worked to diagnose why women might not have been receiving the benefits and, through research and discussions, identified key behavioral barriers women may have faced that could have hindered them from receiving the transfer. For example, social norms could have affected whom a household chose as the recipient;[15] it is possible that if potential transfer recipients did not see women in their community handling cash transfers, they may have believed that men should be the ones to handle them and that the man in the household should be the recipient. In this case, highlighting positive descriptive norms around female recipients might help.

Another potential barrier was related to intrahousehold dynamics: it is often the case that within the household, women have responsibility for dealing with money for day-to-day items such as food, whereas men more often have responsibility for larger investment purchases.[16] The framing of the program could have activated or primed the identity of potential participants, which may have led them to make decisions and take actions in line with the specific identity that was activated.[17] For example, if a transfer is framed as being for daily needs and the woman has the identity of being the

Table 2.2. Summary of projects

Program	Country	Goal of behavioral engagement
National Safety Net Program	Kenya	Help transfer recipients spend their cash on productive investments, such as livestock, farming inputs, or business inputs.
Productive Social Safety Net	Tanzania	Help transfer recipients spend their cash on productive investments, such as livestock, farming inputs, or business inputs.
Human Development Cash Transfer	Madagascar	Support transfer recipients in improving early childhood development outcomes, such as cognitive and social development, by taking advantage of the reduction in cognitive scarcity the cash provides to help them plan activities they will undertake to support their children.
Projet pour la Stabilisation de l'Est de la RDC pour la Paix 2-Contingent Emergency Response Component	Democratic Republic of Congo	Support transfer recipients in identifying priorities on which to spend their cash to improve future resilience and spend accordingly.
South Sudan Safety Net Project	South Sudan	Support cash transfer recipients in identifying and spending their cash in line with their priorities.
Sudan Family Support Program	Sudan	Encourage households to select a woman in the household to be the primary recipient of the cash transfer.

caretaker and the person who deals with daily needs, she may feel empowered to be the recipient of the cash, and the household may be more likely to select her to be the representative. Finally, women often faced hassles in registering that men did not; for example, a photo identification is required to register, which women were less likely to have. Even if it was possible to get their photo taken at the location, some women may not have been willing to get their photo taken without permission from a man in their family or felt comfortable doing so given the context in which they live. Reducing hassles, such as waiving this requirement for women or offering an alternative way to prove their identity, may increase the number of women who register to receive benefits. In Table 2.2, we summarize each of the projects discussed thus far in this chapter and the goal of each of the behavioral engagements.

CHALLENGES AND RECOMMENDATIONS IN SCALING BEHAVIORAL DESIGNS IN CASH TRANSFER PROGRAMS

In addition to the evidence built through our engagements, there is broad and expanding evidence that cash-plus programs that complement cash with non-cash components such as training, coaching, and external linkages are more likely to achieve a longer-term and lasting impact.[18] Behavioral interventions, typically considered as part of this cash-plus package, are no an exception to this finding. Although proven effective, these interventions have still not become mainstream in program design. In this section, we discuss possible reasons driven by our experience and suggest a way forward.

Need for Evidence Generation

Although applied behavioral science has become a more mature discipline, with Kahneman and Thaler being acknowledged for their contributions with a Nobel Prize in economics, it still relies heavily on evidence generation, particularly through RCTs, to assess the impact of behavioral interventions. Even with decades of academic and empirical work in this space, guidance on how much and what evidence is enough to replicate successful behavioral interventions is limited. Such evidence generation has certainly helped to establish the relatively new discipline, as well as its importance and impact; however, at the same time the costs associated with running such trials have slowed the pace of scaling successful interventions.

In our own work in Sub-Saharan Africa, we have seen the willingness of many partner governments to scale the behavioral designs for cash transfer programs based on rigorous user testing versus those based on RCT results. Program staff working closely with us in the field observe how recipients interact with behavioral designs and often clearly see that the behavioral designs offer an actionable solution to the identified problems that they have then in many cases seen throughout their years of experience but that have become more concrete and salient when diagnosed through a behavioral lens. Furthermore, once a program is developed, opportunities to make any changes to it are limited, and such opportunities do not necessarily align with the timing of the RCT. Hence, there may be situations in which such opportunities are foreclosed because of the demands of evidence generation. In some contexts, RCT-based evidence generation is strongly driven by funder mandates, although in recent times we have started to see a more open approach to alternative means of evidence generation versus only RCTs.[19]

To address this bottleneck, one could consider rigorous localized user testing for behavioral interventions as an alternative to running an RCT, particularly when similar interventions have proven effective in other contexts. In the cash transfer domain, these would include exercises such as self-affirmation, goal setting, and plan making, among others. Randomized evaluations can continue to add value to evaluating behavioral interventions that address new problems identified in the cash transfer domain that call for novel designs. Even when a choice is made in favor of running an RCT, attempts should be made to minimize its costs. This includes piggybacking on ongoing evaluation efforts instead of running stand-alone impact evaluations, using administrative data as an alternative to expensive primary data collection exercises, and either skipping a baseline survey altogether or significantly shortening its length.[20]

Additions to the Program versus Integral Part of the Program

Driven to a large extent by the need for evidence generation, behavioral interventions are typically developed as stand-alone additions to existing programs. Although this type of design allows researchers to test these interventions more effectively, it could impose additional burden on already overworked program staff and implementers and create hassles for cash recipients who need to attend additional training or sessions on top of routine program activities. The issue of overburdened staff is relatively well documented and studied in the health space.[21] We have encountered similar issues in many cash transfers programs as well. At least four of the 12-plus programs we tried to partner with did not come to fruition, primarily because of staff bandwidth issues.

Right from the beginning, designers should be mindful of resource and bandwidth constraints that exist in many developing countries and look for ways to efficiently embed interventions into existing entry points and design elements, even during the pilot testing phases. For example, instead of inviting cash recipients to attend behavioral intervention sessions separately, consider offering them according to the preplanned program activity schedule, thus minimizing the need for additional travel. Such an approach would also facilitate a more seamless integration of behavioral interventions in the program during the scaling phase. While integrating the proven behavioral interventions in the program design, we suggest a subtractive approach to program design – doing away with any unnecessary or redundant components when adding the new ones.[22] This would ensure lower burden for the program recipients and implementers and save scarce resources from a program sustainability standpoint.

Cost-Effectiveness of Behavioral Interventions Is Not Routinely Measured

With many governments progressing toward incorporating behavioral interventions into their cash transfer programs and policies, it has become imperative to answer the question of whether behavioral interventions are cost-effective. The question is an important one to ask, given that policy makers with limited resources need to weigh the costs of various programs or program components to make a decision on which ones to move forward with. The cost considerations become even more relevant when making a decision about scaling the proven interventions.

The majority of impact evaluations pertain to microeconomics, which tends to focus on individual-, household-, or firm-level decision making. Whereas the benefit or impact of the program gets rigorously measured in these evaluations, related cost considerations have rarely been studied.[23] Furthermore, measuring the cost of the intervention falls outside the realm of such evaluations, which are primarily conducted to test the theory of change in individual decision making versus the program design elements. In addition, incorporating cost components into the behavioral design may not always be straightforward and requires making some assumptions. For example, if the development (and testing) of a behavioral intervention (the fixed cost) is funded by donors, it is prudent to include only the variable costs related to behavioral interventions (such as materials, training costs, and staff time required to implement the intervention) in the cost components. Note that the fixed costs of developing and testing interventions would decline over time if the proven interventions are scaled.

In our conversations with government partners in Sub-Saharan Africa, we are routinely requested to present cost-effectiveness numbers along with the impact evaluation results. To inform scaling of behavioral interventions, we have thus developed a cost-effectiveness multiplier. This multiplier estimates how much additional cash needs to be given to participants to achieve the same impact (improvement in key outcomes of interest) achieved by incorporating nudges in the program design. Figure 2.1 visually illustrates the cost-effectiveness multiplier.

A cost-effectiveness multiplier larger than one implies that the behavioral interventions are a more cost-effective way of achieving a change in the outcome in question than the provision of additional cash. Put differently, the government would get more impact on the outcome of interest by spending additional resources on the behavioral intervention than by using the same resources to augment the transfer. We present the cost-effectiveness multiplier from our recently completed pilot in the DRC, described earlier, in which the behavioral nudges helped cash recipients spend the cash according to their priorities. The outcome of interest is the amount of the transfer the recipient spent on their stated priority. Table 2.3 shows estimates for various components of the cost-effectiveness multiplier.

When given the cash transfer alone of US$25.00, recipients spent on average US$9.42 toward their stated priority, or 38 per cent of the transfer. The cost of the nudges – the two SMS messages, described earlier – was US$0.22. To create the counterfactual, we calculated how much we would expect the recipient to spend on their priority if they received the cash transfer plus the value of the nudges in cash, which is US$25.22. We assume they would still spend 38 per cent

Figure 2.1. Cost-effectiveness multiplier: A graphic representation

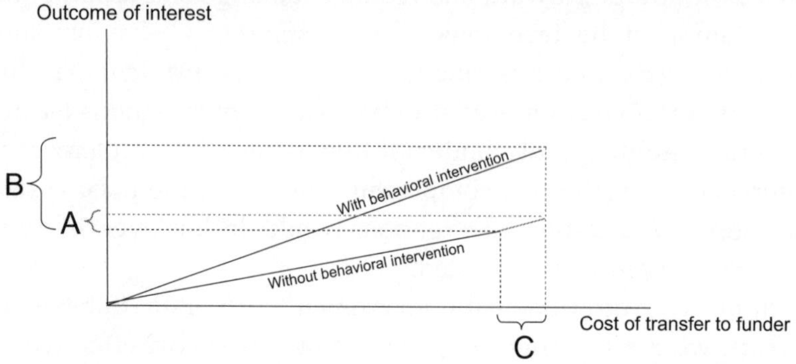

A = Counterfactual (expected change in outcome of interest if monetary value of nudges was given in additional cash)

B = Change in outcome of interest with nudges

C = Value of nudges in cash

B/A = Cost-effectiveness multiplier (additional value of cash that would need to be provided to achieve change in outcome achieved with nudges)

Table 2.3. Estimates for the cost-effectiveness multiplier

Component of cost-effectiveness multiplier	Value from DRC example
Amount spent on priority when given cash	US$9.42
Counterfactual	US$9.50
Amount spent on priority when given cash + nudge	US$10.08
Cost-effectiveness multiplier	8.25

on their priority, meaning that we would expect them to spend on average US$9.50 toward their priority. However, when recipients received the nudges, they spent on average US$10.08 on their priority, or 40 per cent. To calculate the cost-effectiveness multiplier, we divide the expected change if given the value of nudges in cash (US$0.08) by the actual change from the behavioral intervention (US$0.66) and obtain a cost-effectiveness multiplier of 8.25. In other words, to achieve the benefit of the nudges, it would cost 8.25 times the cost of the nudges themselves.

A standardized framework for calculating cost-effectiveness of behavioral interventions in the cash transfers space would be a helpful decision-making tool for governments, especially because there are opportunity costs for every development dollar spent. Although not in the cash transfers context, the work of Benartzi et al. provides an insightful approach to comparing the cost-effectiveness of behavioral interventions relative to traditional interventions (such as education programs and financial incentives).[24] They compare cost–benefit estimates for behavioral and traditional interventions and find that behavioral interventions deliver a higher rate of return on investment than traditional ones in a variety of domains (education, health, energy conservation, and savings). Our own experience in the cash transfers domain suggests that complementing an impact evaluation of behavioral interventions with a cost-effectiveness analysis provides a more complete picture of policy options to governments and equips them to make better decisions in a world with limited resources.

Cash Transfer Programs Are Constantly Evolving

As we previously mentioned, cash transfer programs have evolved at a rapid rate, reaching a diverse set of populations in a variety of contexts, as well as targeting a multitude of outcomes. The COVID-19 pandemic saw an unprecedented rise in the number of these programs as well as in their power to support vulnerable individuals during the crisis. Although these programs had already experienced a push for digitization, the pandemic necessitated digitization in program design to reach more vulnerable people at a faster rate. Digitization has been relied on in all of the key stages of the program cycle – targeting, registration, and disbursement.

Increased digitization of cash transfer programs could facilitate introduction and scaling of behavioral interventions on two levels: first, by leveraging behavioral science to strengthen the impact of digitization by ensuring adoption and usage of digital practices;[25] second, by creating slack for program implementers, whose time (saved as a result of digitization) could then be better invested in running behavioral interventions to improve program outcomes. As new program designs emerge, agile ways to introduce behavioral interventions in the program cycle and developing nimble testing approaches to assessing the impact of such interventions would provide an opportunity to reach greater impact more quickly. As noted earlier, non-RCT-based yet rigorous methods to generate evidence, greater integration of behavioral interventions into programs, and a standardized framework for embedding cost-effectiveness measures to complement the impact evaluation would allow for more nimble testing of newer interventions and thus expedite the scaling process beyond what has been possible in the past.

Implementation Challenges Can Be Limiting

An evaluation showing a positive impact of behavioral interventions on recipients' behaviors and key program outcomes in a cost-effective way still does not ensure their scaling. Scaling is a long, multifaceted process that requires many elements to come together. First, political buy-in is critical for scale, but it could be hard to achieve in countries with low political stability, as is the case in many sub-Saharan African countries. Second, it is important to work closely with all the key stakeholders right from the beginning and make them part of the entire behavioral design and scaling process to ensure their advocacy and operational as well as financial support beyond prototyping and pilot stages. Third, even if there is political stability and support, scaling of interventions would require meticulous planning and their smooth integration into current program designs. Program implementers would need technical support and capacity building during this phase. Last, our experience suggests that in many countries, cash transfers remain uncertain and unreliable, further exacerbating the implementation challenges. It is the responsibility of financial institutions and governments to ensure that mechanisms for timely, effective, and accurate disbursement are put into place and respective authorities are held accountable.

Given that in the near future cash transfers will be here to stay and the fact that billions of development dollars are at stake, it is the joint responsibility of governments, funding agencies, and program designers to make an honest effort to scale effective interventions to help program participants achieve better outcomes and ensure donors get the most bang for their buck.

LOOKING TO THE FUTURE

We have discussed current challenges and recommendations to scaling behavioral interventions, including (1) a need for additional and more nuanced evidence; (2) greater integration into programs; (3) consistency in cost-effectiveness calculations; (4) the moving target presented by the continuous evolution of programs that outpaces behaviorally designed interventions; and (5) implementation challenges resulting from politics, the ongoing COVID-19 pandemic, and funding uncertainties. However, there is also cause for optimism about the potential for innovative behavioral designs to complement cash transfer programs in the future, providing a better fit for program and participant needs. Next, we identify three opportunities for future innovation: (1) the digitization of program platforms, (2) a closer focus on service provider behavior, and (3) novel approaches to evaluation and learning.

Digitization of Program Platforms

As mentioned in the "Challenges and Recommendations" section, digitization provides opportunities to create slack for program implementers and reduce operational costs, and with appropriate application of behavioral science, they can ensure adoption and use of digital practices for those who may traditionally have faced barriers to digital economic inclusion. Applying a behavioral lens to digital transfers may help to spur additional innovation in the design of behavioral interventions. Digital tools offer platforms or channels for the delivery of interventions that can be integrated into the tools themselves for a more streamlined implementation experience. For example, by building goal-setting or goal-planning prompts into the architecture of the digital platform instead of layering additional behavioral tools over it, programs can reduce the number of discrete tools that participants and service providers need to interact with. Similarly, digital platforms may allow for the automation of some steps, allowing the program to set instructive default choices for participants while reducing the amount of time and effort required for service providers to follow up with participants.

Programs could also leverage the shift to digital platforms to become more responsive to individual participants' differing needs. The platforms could be designed to offer participants greater customizability in areas ranging from the schedule on which transfers are made to participants' language preferences. Introducing behavioral tools and features through digital platforms could also improve program learning through rapid testing of alternative tools, features, and designs. The ease of A/B testing with digital tools opens possibilities for greater innovation by providing opportunities for programs to roll out alternative versions of their platforms to participants, quickly and cheaply collecting feedback on designs to identify successful strategies for maximizing impact. In the realm of digital financial services, these principles have previously been used to identify strategies and designs to increase access to and engagement with digital financial tools in Pakistan, Nigeria, and Tanzania.[26]

Focus on Service Provider Behavior

Cash transfer programs have not typically focused on applying behavioral science to provider behavior, because they often require only limited provider–participant interaction. However, the fact that behavioral interventions are often seen as an add-on rather than being integrated, as discussed earlier, in combination with the increasing role of supplementary services and the development of more complex graduation models, opens the door to a larger assortment of behavioral barriers that can hamper program impact. This shift also introduces the behavior of service providers – their ability to act in ways that lead to successful transfers of knowledge and skills – as a significant determinant of program impact, including engaging participants, sharing complete information, and being respectful and inclusive in their interactions with participants. Here, innovative programs may find opportunities to borrow insights from adjacent fields, such as public health and education, where behavioral science has been successfully applied to increase the adoption of best practices,[27] improve the fidelity with which services are delivered,[28] reduce absenteeism,[29] and encourage more respectful interactions between program providers and participants.[30]

Approaches to Evaluation and Learning

The progress made to date in forming an evidence base for behaviorally informed interventions in cash transfer programs creates opportunities for programs to adapt their testing strategies that better accommodate the varying capacities of programs seeking to apply behavioral science insights for the first time. Although some form of rigorous testing is undeniably important to inform scale-up, funders and practitioners must be willing to explore new approaches to testing that are more agile and flexible to make scaling and adaptation easier for these programs. Here, we discuss three ideas for reducing the burden of testing on resource-constrained programs.

One way would be to explore the potential for more light-touch A/B testing within digital tools (as described previously): exploring the impact of adjustments to the design or features of tools that have already been proven effective in other, similar contexts. A systematic cost-effectiveness assessment such as the one outlined earlier could also be a useful tool to help practitioners. Behavioral science practitioners can also put more work into identifying the key contextual factors that determine the success or failure of interventions previously tested in other contexts. Once those contextual features are identified, programs will more easily be able to decide whether to scale interventions without conducting costly new trials if they can (1) confirm the existence of key contextual factors in their local context and (2) customize and adapt the interventions to their local context, conducting rigorous user testing with the interventions' intended end users to ensure that that the final designs will still function as needed to bring about their desired impact.

NOTES

1 See Arnold, C., Conway, T., & Greenslade, M. (2011). *Cash transfers: Evidence paper.* Department for International Development; and Bastagli, F., Hagen-Zanker, J., Harman, L., Barca, V., Sturge, G., Schmidt, T., & Pellerano, L. (2016). *Cash transfers: What does the evidence say?* ODI.
2 Brown, S. (2021). The impact of COVID-19 on development assistance. *International Journal, 76*(1), 42–54.

3 Roelen, K., Devereux, S., Abdulai, A. G., Martorano, B., Palermo, T., & Ragno, L.P. (2017). *How to make "cash plus" work: Linking cash transfers to services and sectors* (Innocenti Working Paper 2017-10). UNICEF Office of Research.

4 Mullainathan, S., & Shafir, E. (2013). *Scarcity: Why having too little means so much.* Macmillan.

5 Shah, A.K., Mullainathan, S., & Shafir, E. (2012). Some consequences of having too little. *Science, 338*(6107), 682–5.

6 Campos, F., Frese, M., Goldstein, M., Iacovone, L., Johnson, H.C., McKenzie, D., & Mensmann, M. (2017). Teaching personal initiative beats traditional training in boosting small business in West Africa. *Science, 357*(6357), 1287–90.

7 Thaler, R.H. (1999). Mental accounting matters. *Journal of Behavioral Decision Making, 12*(3), 183–206.

8 Datta, S., Martin, J., MacLeod, C., Rawlings, L.B., & Vermehren, A. (2021). *Do behavioral interventions enhance the effects of cash on early childhood development and its determinants? Evidence from a cluster-randomized trial in Madagascar* (Policy Research Working Paper 9747). World Bank Group.

9 Ideas 42 & World Bank Group. (2019). *Cash and change: Using behavioral insights to improve financial health in three cash transfer programs.* https://www.ideas42.org /wp-content/uploads/2019/09/I42-1160_CashTransfers_paper_final-4 .pdf.

10 Una, G., Allen, R., Pattanayak, S., & Suc, G. (2020). *Digital solutions for direct cash transfers in emergencies* (Special Series on Fiscal Policies to Respond to COVID-19). International Monetary Fund.

11 See Cherrier, C. (2021). The humanitarian–development nexus. In E. Schüring & M. Lowewe (Eds.), *Handbook on social protection systems* (pp. 295–306). Edward Elgar. https://doi.org/10.4337/9781839109119.00041; and Lyons, A., Kass-Hanna, J., & Molena, E. (2021). *A multidimensional approach to poverty that strengthens the humanitarian-development nexus* (T20 Policy Brief). 2030 Agenda and Development Cooperation. https://www.t20italy.org/wp-content/uploads/2021/09/TF5_PB04 _LM03.pdf.

12 See Bastagli et al. (2016); and Sedlmayr, R., Shah, A., & Sulaiman, M. (2017). *Cash-Plus: Poverty impacts of transfer-based intervention alternatives* (No. 2017-15-2). University of Oxford, Centre for the Study of African Economies.

13 See Lwamba, E., Shisler, S., Ridlehoover, W., Kupfer, M., Tshabalala, N., Nduku, P., Langer, L., Grant, S., Sonnenfeld, A., Anda, D., Eyers, J., & Snilstveit, B. (2021). Strengthening women's empowerment and gender equality in fragile contexts towards peaceful and inclusive societies: A systematic review and meta-analysis. *Campbell Systematic Reviews, 18*(1), e1214. https://doi.org/10.1002/cl2.1214; and Hagen-Zanker, J., Pellerano, L., Bastagli, F., Harman, L., Barca, V., Sturge, G., Schmidt, T., & Laing, C. (2017). *The impact of cash transfers on women and girls.* ODI. https://cdn.odi.org/media/documents/11374.pdf.

14 UN Development Programme. (2021). *Human development report 2020: The next frontier – Human development and the Anthropocene.*

15 See Cialdini, R.B., Reno, R.R., & Kallgren, C.A. (1990). A focus theory of normative conduct: Recycling the concept of norms to reduce littering in public places. *Journal of Personality and Social Psychology, 58*(6), 1015–26. https://doi.org/10.1037/0022 -3514.58.6.1015; and Allcott, H. (2011). Social norms and energy conservation. *Journal of Public Economics, 95*(9–10), 1082–95. https://doi.org/10.1016/j.jpubeco.2011.03 .003.

16 Doss, C. (2013). Intrahousehold bargaining and resource allocation in developing countries. *World Bank Research Observer, 28*(1), 52–78.

17 Akerlof, G.A., & Kranton, R.E. (2000). Economics and identity. *Quarterly Journal of Economics, 115*(3), 715–53.
18 See Andrews, C., de Montesquiou, A., Sánchez, I.A., Dutta, P.V., Paul, B.V., Samaranayake, S., Heisey, J., Clay, T., Chaudhary, S. (2021). *The State of Economic Inclusion Report 2021: The potential to scale*. World Bank Group. https://openknowledge.worldbank.org/server/api/core/bitstreams/33e62d47-7ba8-5d38-ae09-48f1daf3607d/content; and Banerjee, A., Duflo, E., Chattopadhyay, R., & Shapiro, J. (2016). *The long term impacts of a "graduation" program: Evidence from West Bengal* [Unpublished manuscript]. Massachusetts Institute of Technology.
19 Gauri, V. (2018). eMBeDding for impact and scale in developing contexts. *Behavioural Public Policy, 2*(2), 256–62.
20 Muralidharan, K. (2017). Field experiments in education in developing countries. In A.V. Banerjee & E. Duflo (Eds.), *Handbook of economic field experiments* (Vol. 2, pp. 323–85). North-Holland; Holla, A. (2018, July 18). Are we over-investing in baselines? *Development Impact Blog*. https://blogs.worldbank.org/impactevaluations/are-we-over-investing-baselines.
21 See Flanagan, S.V., Razafinamanana, T., Warren, C., & Smith, J. (2021). Barriers inhibiting effective detection and management of postpartum hemorrhage during facility-based births in Madagascar: Findings from a qualitative study using a behavioral science lens. *BMC Pregnancy and Childbirth, 21*(1), Article 320. https://doi.org/10.1186/s12884-021-03801-w; and Wasunna, B., Zurovac, D., Goodman, C.A., & Snow, R.W. (2008). Why don't health workers prescribe ACT? A qualitative study of factors affecting the prescription of artemether-lumefantrine. *Malaria Journal, 7*(1), Article 29. https://doi.org/10.1186/1475-2875-7-29.
22 Adams, G.S., Converse, B.A., Hales, A.H., & Klotz, L.E. (2021). People systematically overlook subtractive changes. *Nature, 592*(7853), 258–61.
23 Evans, D. (2016, May 10). Why don't economists do cost analysis in their impact evaluations? *Development Impact*. https://blogs.worldbank.org/impactevaluations/why-don-t-economists-do-cost-analysis-their-impact-evaluations.
24 Benartzi, S., Beshears, J., Milkman, K.L., Sunstein, C.R., Thaler, R.H., Shankar, M., Tucker-Ray, W., Congdon, W.J., & Galing, S. (2017). Should governments invest more in nudging? *Psychological Science, 28*(8), 1041–55.
25 Davis, K., Kau, M., & Kim, A. (2018). *Behavioral design for digital financial services: How to increase engagement with products and services that build financial health*. ideas42. http://www.ideas42.org/wp-content/uploads/2018/04/ideas42_DFSplaybook.pdf.
26 Ideas42. (2020a). *Bringing digital finance tools to more women: Behaviorally informed text message campaigns in Pakistan*. https://www.ideas42.org/wp-content/uploads/2020/03/JazzCash-Project-Brief_2.pdf; Ideas42. (2020b). *Increasing the use of mobile banking: Behavioral text message campaigns in Nigeria*. https://www.ideas42.org/wp-content/uploads/2020/02/GatesAB_Brief_1-1.pdf; and Ideas42. (2020c). *Bringing mobile banking within reach: Increasing engagement with a mobile banking platform in Tanzania*. https://www.ideas42.org/wp-content/uploads/2020/03/Tanzania-banking-project-brief.pdf.
27 Drexler, A., Fischer, G., & Schoar, A. (2014). Keeping it simple: Financial literacy and rules of thumb. *American Economic Journal: Applied Economics, 6*(2), 1–31.
28 Zurovac, D., Sudoi, R.K., Akhwale, W.S., Ndiritu, M., Hamer, D.H., Rowe, A.K., & Snow, R.W. (2011). The effect of mobile phone text-message reminders on Kenyan health workers' adherence to malaria treatment guidelines: A cluster randomised trial. *Lancet, 378*(9793), 795–803.

29 eMBeD: Mind, Behavior and Development Unit, World Bank. (2018). *How to encourage school principals not to play hooky*. https://documents1.worldbank.org /curated/en/828801524830677726/pdf/125816-eMBeD -Peru-Absenteeism.pdf.

30 Smith, J., Schachter, A., Banay, R., Zimmerman, E., Sellman, A., & Kamanga, A. (2021). Promoting respectful maternity care using a behavioral design approach in Zambia: Results from a mixed-methods evaluation. *Reproductive Health, 19,* Article 141.

CHAPTER THREE

Reaching the Hardest to Reach with Cash Transfer and Disbursement Programs

Kyle Jacques, Marin MacLeod, Sydney Piggott, and Kevin Yin

THE REACH PROBLEM IN CASH TRANSFER PROGRAMS

In recent years, cash transfer and disbursement programs have become a tool of choice for development practitioners, donors, and governments looking to improve the lives of the global poor.[1] On its face, the premise is deceptively simple: people live in poverty, so give them money. A wealth of research and final evaluations have also now consistently demonstrated the positive impact cash transfer programs can have on a variety of outcomes, from household income to education and to health and nutrition.[2] However, how to implement these programs is debated. Program architects can choose from an array of delivery methods, needs-identification procedures, and policies. They must balance reaching the many with reaching the hardest to reach, objectivity with empathy, and standardization with flexibility. Our research into five cash transfer and disbursement programs across Brazil, Ethiopia, Jordan, Palestine, and Kenya revealed complex examples of both challenges and successes. We highlight targeting, conditionalities, data management, technology, and partnerships as five themes that contribute to success in reaching the hardest to reach.

The reach problem, as described by Joseph Wong, is the challenge of delivering critical services to those who are hardest to reach.[3] People can be hard to reach because of where they live, their selected or assigned identities, and their socioeconomic status. The interaction of geographic, social, political, and economic forces makes these people both those most in need of assistance and those hardest to reach with assistance. How best to deliver money, vaccines, legal support, and other important services to these groups constitutes the reach problem.

What is it that makes the cash transfer problem so challenging? For one, resources to deliver cash transfer programs are limited. Effective and affordable targeting is essential to determine which eligible recipients are most in need and then to reach those recipients. Targeting the hardest to reach is usually done by means of several techniques that consider a variety of socioeconomic factors. On the basis of the cash transfer or disbursement program's desired outcomes, implementers will also need to determine whether to implement a conditional or unconditional transfer (see also Chapters 4 and 6). To consistently and accurately identify and deliver services to the hardest to reach, practitioners require dedicated data management systems to store, analyze, and cross-check information on beneficiaries. These data management systems provide implementers with precise information on who to target, where, and how, and they ensure the program's continued relevance by facilitating systematic updates. Coordination, integration, and delivery of cash transfer and disbursement programs often depend on facilitative technologies. For instance, corruption and high implementation costs for cash transfer and disbursement programs can quickly turn a well-intentioned program into an inefficient use of public or donor funds. Appropriate technologies can thus help overcome these challenges and get services to people equitably and efficiently. Last, without meaningful partnerships, delivery of cash transfer and disbursement programs puts program sustainability into question, especially in the context of delivering to hard-to-reach populations. Partnership and stakeholder engagement is critical to reach the hardest to reach with finite programmatic resources.

Table 3.1. Summary of five digital and cash transfer programs reaching the hardest-to-reach

Key information	Brazil	Ethiopia	Jordan	Kenya	Palestine
Program name	Bolsa Família Program	Productive Safety Net Program	Biometric Cash Assistance Program	M-Pesa	National Cash Transfer Program
First year implemented	2003	2005	2012	2007	2010
Primary goal	Reduce poverty and inequality	Alleviate food insecurity and build household and community resilience	Alleviate poverty among the most vulnerable Syrian refugees cost-effectively to ensure more money is available for those who are eligible	Elevate national financial inclusion rates	Reduce the household poverty gap
Target population	Rural families and historically disadvantaged groups, including river-dwelling groups and Afro-Brazilian religious communities	Rural poor who experience the highest degree of food insecurity and vulnerability to climate shocks	Urban-dwelling Syrian refugees, 93% of whom live below the poverty line	Millions of people without access to financial services	People made most vulnerable by the continued deterioration of the economy and as a result of gender, physical impairment, or family composition
Conditionalities	Yes	Hybrid	No	No	No

The Reach Alliance is a student-driven, faculty-mentored research initiative examining how critical interventions and innovations reach those who are hardest to reach. Actionable insights presented in this chapter are based on research that was conducted by Reach researchers in Brazil, Ethiopia, Jordan, Palestine, and Kenya between 2015 and 2021. Each of the five cases demonstrates efficacy in reaching hard-to-reach populations with cash transfer and disbursement programs.

TARGETING RECIPIENTS OF CASH TRANSFER PROGRAMS

Targeting methods identify potential recipients on the basis of their need for poverty alleviation programs within select populations or geographical areas. Because of the many factors that cause poverty and inequality in national and subnational contexts, these recipients are often the hardest to reach and experience multiple barriers to accessing social safety nets. To effectively select recipients, targeting mechanisms must accurately assess the needs of individuals or households in relation to the larger population and use an approach that engages communities in decision making. Mixed mechanisms are often used that include some level of assessment and data collection combined with human intervention to better understand local and individual contexts while improving the accuracy of the selection process.

In Palestine, the Palestinian National Cash Transfer Programme (PNCTP) uses a proxy means-testing formula (PMTF) to identify eligible recipients. It estimates a household's income by collecting information on multiple aspects of its composition and consumption and then running this information through a weighted formula. This process is essential in a context in which many workers are employed informally, if at all, and lack access to formal or verifiable proof of income such as tax or salary slips. However, in recognition of poverty's multidimensional nature, the PMTF goes beyond strictly income-based measures by giving special weight to households considered vulnerable, such as woman-headed households or households with a person with a disability or chronic illness or elderly members. By including 35 quantitative and qualitative factors, households with higher needs that may have been overlooked by an assessment based solely on income are still considered eligible.[4] Recognizing the possibility that recipients in need will be excluded for small demographic differences (such as having one fewer member in the household), the PNCTP complements the proxy means test with a network of social workers who help to identify recipients from hard-to-reach populations.[5]

The Productive Safety Net Programme (PSNP) in Ethiopia identifies recipients through Community Food Security Task Forces – local decision-making bodies that have been recognized as key to the program's successful targeting.[6] Guided by the program implementation manual, communities can select recipients on the basis of demographic factors such as gender, ability, and age while also considering local traditions and cultural norms.[7] Community-based targeting has made the PSNP one of the most successfully targeted social safety nets in Africa: it targets beneficiaries better than the average social safety net program globally.[8]

IMPACT OF CONDITIONALITIES

Cash transfer programs broadly fall into two categories: conditional or unconditional cash transfers (see Chapter 6 for a discussion of the role of conditionality in program effectiveness). Conditional cash transfers (CCTs) require recipients to remain eligible for cash assistance by complying with certain conditions, such as enrolling children in school or working on public works projects. Fulfillment of these conditions is monitored on an ongoing basis to ensure compliance and understand more about different communities' needs, including the underlying causes of poverty among specific populations. Attaching conditions to cash transfer programs is considered to incentivize behavioral change that is attributed to positive social and economic outcomes.[9] Conditional transfers are also considered more politically viable because they appeal to decision makers and constituents across the political spectrum because of their relatively low cost compared with other social protection programs and popularity among lower-income households, allowing programs to continue over a long period under different government administrations.[10]

Unconditional cash transfers (UCTs) are issued to households solely on the basis of their eligibility and do not impose conditions on recipients.[11] Without conditions, households address their needs at their sole discretion, which is why UCTs are associated with rights-based approaches to international development and poverty alleviation.[12] In both cases, however, limited programmatic resources can affect disbursements. Not all households that are found to be eligible through targeting methods receive cash assistance.

Conditional cash transfers have been successful when tackling long-term poverty alleviation goals. For example, the Bolsa Família program (BFP) in Brazil uses CCTs to improve education and health outcomes for recipients by addressing intergenerational poverty in low-income and historically marginalized communities such as Afro-Brazilians and Indigenous peoples.[13] Recipient households must enroll children in school and have them attend regularly and receive vaccinations in local health clinics.[14] Conditions attached to the BFP have been attributed to reducing the infant mortality rate by 9.3 per cent in the first five years of the program and increasing school enrollment rates by approximately 5 per cent for recipient households over a similar period.[15] The BFP has even produced additional health benefits that are not part of the program design. For example, a 2018 study on tuberculosis treatment in Brazil indicated that BFP recipients were more likely to complete treatment and be cured of tuberculosis than non-BFP groups.[16]

In contrast, target populations that require short-term cash assistance in humanitarian contexts have benefited from UCT programs. In Jordan, the Biometric Cash Assistance Program run by the UN High Commissioner for Refugees (UNHCR) supports refugees in accessing monthly income support by leveraging iris-scanning technology to disburse cash transfers.[17] Households are targeted using a vulnerability assessment framework that determines the recipients most in need, but no conditions are imposed, which ensures that people can easily and rapidly access the program.[18] Unconditional transfers are also considered less onerous in terms of administration because they do not require as robust data management systems to monitor compliance over the medium and long terms. Instead, UCTs assess only need and disburse according to available resources.[19]

DATA MANAGEMENT FOR CASH TRANSFER PROGRAMS

Effectively delivering aid to the hardest to reach requires identifying precisely who these eligible individuals are in the first place. This requires multifaceted and context-specific targeting mechanisms but also dedicated systems to store, aggregate, and update data on potential and actual beneficiaries, as well as cross-checking mechanisms to identify data inconsistencies or inaccuracies. Comprehensive data management systems are essential for effective program delivery because they provide implementers with the most reliable information available on whom to target, where, and how. They also ensure the programs' continuous relevance and accuracy by keeping information and eligibility assessments up to date. However, any database that contains family- and individual-level financial information raises the specter of privacy concerns. As we discuss later, these concerns must be actively tackled rather than being used as an excuse to not have good data. The bottom line is this: successful cash transfer programs around the world need to leverage well-developed and well-tested data management systems and analysis to ensure delivery to the last mile.

In Brazil, the BFP relies on the Cadastro Único Para Programas Sociais (Unified Registry for Social Programs, or CadÚnico) as the central database for all information on individuals who qualify or may qualify for Ministry of Social Development (MDS) programs. According to an MDS official in a recent communication, as of 2021, the CadÚnico contained data on more than 31.5 million households, of whom nearly 14.7 million were beneficiaries of the BFP.[20] The CadÚnico stores information on key variables such as family income, employment status, and detailed descriptions of households' locations and conditions. With this, the database functions as a "map" of poverty in Brazil, which the MDS can use to assess potential beneficiaries' eligibility, as well as to locate exactly where they live.[21]

In Palestine, the Portalgate serves a related function as the central database for the Ministry of Social Development's (MoSD's) cash transfer program. In 2018, the Portalgate held data on more than 200,000 poor and vulnerable households in Palestine, of whom 110,000 were recipients of the cash transfer program.[22] Each household in the Portalgate bears a unique user ID that corresponds to multiple data points, including scores from the proxy means test to indicate eligibility, as well as home addresses, family composition, and school enrollment figures.[23]

Such data systems are important not only to correctly assess program eligibility in the first place but also to ensure that this assessment remains accurate over time. In Palestine, MoSD officials emphasize that a significant portion of the administrative work involved in maintaining the Portalgate is reassessing existing entries to ensure that cases still fulfill eligibility requirements. This process of reverification entails social workers revisiting beneficiary households to assess any changes in living situations and update Portalgate data, which can result in adjustments to cash transfer amounts or potential removal from the program so that households on the waiting list can be upgraded and enrolled.[24]

Likewise, in Brazil, MDS officials estimate that only 15 per cent of administrative work on the CadÚnico is directed at enrolling new families, whereas 85 per cent is dedicated to verifying and updating existing data to determine any adjustments in eligibility.[25] Effective data management systems provide benefits beyond those related to the specific programs for which they were developed, including by supporting coordination among related programs or donors. The use of these systems by other interventions helps to keep data updated and is key to integrating policies aimed at the poorest citizens.

In Palestine, Portalgate data are used by other international organizations, such as the World Food Programme and the UN Relief and Works Agency, to cross-check their own beneficiary lists and minimize overlap in the distribution of cash transfer programs.[26] In Brazil, the CadÚnico tracks eligibility data not only for the BFP but also for 30 other government-sponsored social services programs.[27] This means that households that are not eligible for the BFP can easily be referred to other programs for which they qualify, such as MDS electricity subsidies.[28]

Such data-driven processes do not imply overly technocratic or impersonal approaches to program delivery, however. In contrast, these processes rely on dedicated teams of workers who travel to remote locations, conduct regular in-person meetings, and support households through each step of a program's life cycle. For the BFP, municipal-level social workers meet with all program applicants to work through a detailed questionnaire (dubbed the "green book") and then digitally input all data into the CadÚnico.[29] In Palestine, MoSD social workers are responsible for conducting preliminary interviews with potential beneficiaries and completing an extensive screening questionnaire; they then digitally input these data into Portalgate.[30]

This human touch is especially important for the collection of certain data, such as household location, because many potential beneficiaries do not have a fixed or official address and may live in a slum or far away from a city center. Thus, in addition to information on household addresses, local-level social workers in Brazil also note physical descriptions of dwellings, nearby landmarks, and whether such residences are permanent, improvised, or shared.[31] In Palestine, social workers conduct routine follow-up field visits to verify collected data but also to assist households in providing any additional required documentation or information that may be required to confirm eligibility, especially when this information may be technical or hard to understand.[32]

An emphasis on interpersonal connection in data collection also helps maximize these programs' potential reach. Although most applicants to the BFP travel to their nearest social assistance municipal office to initiate the registration process, local social workers are also routinely dispatched to neighborhoods far away from registration centers to survey households that may have been missed. In the town of Dias d'Ávila, for example, the municipality sends a *unidade social móvel* (mobile society unit) to conduct weekly visits to families who live far from the town center. In Palestine, social protection committees consisting of civil society members such as teachers and health care workers can nominate for eligibility households that may have been missed on the basis of what they witness during their own work.[33]

Although detailed and comprehensive data management systems are essential for reaching the hardest to reach, they can also create concerns over data privacy and beneficiary safety. For example, whereas many organizations in Palestine refer to the data contained in the Portalgate as essential for service delivery, they were themselves hesitant to feed their own data into the system out of concerns for data privacy. With respect to UNHCR's Biometric Cash Assistance Program, UNHCR Jordan collaborated with IrisGuard, a leading iris-scanning firm, to encrypt all beneficiary data and develop a server accessible solely to UNHCR.[34] This system allowed partner organizations to confirm beneficiaries' identities when necessary without having access to refugees' biometric information.[35] Human rights groups have nonetheless recently raised concerns around issues of consent in collecting sensitive data from vulnerable populations such as refugees, as well as a lack of clarity on specific privacy policies to protect such data.[36]

TECHNOLOGY AND CASH TRANSFERS

Technology is most useful for cash transfer programs when it improves accessibility and lowers delivery costs. These innovations can help reduce the barriers in receiving transfers, thus improving access for groups that are often left out. Technological innovation also reduces formal and informal costs needed to provide these services, passing on savings to the recipients. By cutting out intermediaries, technology can reduce corruption as well as labor costs. Several case studies show the efficacy of technological augmentation for delivering money.

Eliminating some key barriers to access is the primary channel through which technology can be useful in getting cash to hard-to-reach populations. Many poor households eligible for the BFP, for instance, lack a permanent home or even a formal address. They are also unlikely to have a bank account. Sending checks in the mail or bank account transfers would fail to reach a significant portion of the population because the people who need money the most are the hardest to get it to. To overcome these obstacles, the government opted for electronic cash transfers. Each beneficiary is given a BFP card that can be used at ATMs in bank branches operated by the federally owned commercial bank Caixa Econômica Federal. A person with a card does not need to have a formally recognized home or a bank account with Caixa to receive their funds.[37] In 2015, the program was augmented with the introduction of a mobile app that allows recipients to monitor their account and any related updates, offering a level of flexibility and transparency.[38]

People in Kenya face many of the same challenges to financial inclusion. Having a bank account in Kenya is relatively rare, with about 30 per cent of Kenyans having access to formal accounts. Sending money was also prohibitively expensive.[39] Before the introduction of M-Pesa, a mobile-phone-based money-transfer service, transferring cash was either physical or informal, or both. Someone wanting to send funds to a friend or family member would have to give cash to a driver to deliver it, with a significant portion going to the driver.[40] It was also common to send money informally using prepaid credit, which was costly.[41] M-Pesa filled this need with a technological solution. Without a smartphone or bank account, people could send remittances over long distances. People needed only a SIM card and an M-Pesa agent nearby to withdraw and deposit funds. M-Pesa's convenience and affordability eliminated many barriers to financial inclusion.

Innovations in how critical services are delivered also improve supply-side efficacy by cutting costs and increasing efficient delivery. One issue with cash transfer programs is that beneficiaries may try to register more than once or use another person's identity to collect multiple payments. The precision of iris scanning featured in the UNHCR Jordan program reduces the risk and cost of fraud.[42] Another issue is that refugees are supposed to be physically present in the country to be eligible for cash transfers, which would need to be verified by UNHCR staff. Iris scanning eliminates the need for physical presence checks and frees up staff for other program activities.[43] As a result, the UNHCR program in Jordan has achieved a remarkable level of cost-effectiveness, where approximately $0.95 of every US dollar reaches refugees directly.[44] By closing opportunities for fraud and saving on staff, the biometric scanning feature of

Jordan's cash transfer program is a prime example of how technology can improve delivery of money to those who need it.

Corruption is another cost that can undermine effective cash transfer programs. Bolsa Família mitigates the problem of corruption by directly and electronically transferring the funds to the recipient (see also Chapter 6 for additional benefits of electronic transfer of funds). Because cash transfers are not sent physically, they do not pass through state or municipal governments.[45] In addition to cutting out the administrative costs of passing through multiple state bodies where civil servants would need to document, monitor, and administer the program, BFP's electronic delivery mechanism prevents corruption and fiscal leakage.

This is not to say that technology is without trade-offs, specifically when it comes to access to technology. In Kenya, people who do not have mobile money tend to be less educated, live in more remote regions, lack formal identification, and originate from specific ethnic groups.[46] If receiving cash is dependent on technology, the very obstacles to accessing the technology become obstacles to accessing the cash transfer.

Policy makers must be wary not only of the transfers' delivery mechanism but also of people's perception of that mechanism. Public trust and perception of fairness benefit from a human touch as well. If critical decisions about people's livelihoods and about beneficiary selection are made without transparency and without a sufficient channel for complaint or consultation, support for an effective program may suffer.

These cautions notwithstanding, technology is still a vital pillar of the delivery of cash transfers around the world. Although there are added risks, technology-augmented programs can offer a marked improvement over alternate approaches.

COLLABORATION AND PARTNERSHIPS

Without meaningful partnerships, delivery of cash transfer and disbursement programs is inefficient and puts program sustainability into question, especially in the context of delivering to hard-to-reach populations. Partnership and stakeholder engagement are critical to reach the hardest to reach with finite programmatic resources.

The private sector and its assets – such as technology and infrastructure – can also facilitate necessary programmatic efficiencies. For example, M-Pesa was founded as a partnership between Safaricom (a large telecommunications company based in Kenya) and the Commercial Bank of Africa. M-Pesa leveraged both Safaricom's existing network and brand to help facilitate widespread rapid uptake of the service and the Commercial Bank of Africa's account infrastructure.[47] M-Pesa, also known as a mobile wallet, has helped drive increased financial inclusion in Kenya.[48]

The Common Cash Facility in Jordan is another important example of how leveraging partnership with the private sector has resulted in direct program savings. UNHCR Jordan and the Cairo Amman Bank negotiated a payment structure for cash transfers to Syrian refugees. In Jordan, where several humanitarian organizations work together to meet the ever-growing needs of program recipients, there is a unique opportunity to leverage economies of scale and minimize transfer fees on donor funds flowing through the Cairo Amman Bank to program recipients. Transfer fees can be reduced from a maximum of 2.5 per cent to 5 per cent of total transfer value to a minimum of 1.67 per cent as the amount of money passing through the bank increases.[49] Governments could leverage this payment structure to facilitate more efficient delivery of social service payments.[50]

International stakeholders can play a vital role in supporting consensus building and prioritization. In Ethiopia, PSNP donors formed a donor working group to foster coordination and collaboration among funders. The donor working group builds consensus on program priorities through discussion with government officials, supporting the program's successful implementation. Despite a civil conflict that erupted in the Tigray region of Ethiopia in November 2020,[51] international donors have recommitted their support to the PSNP, including the program's largest donor, the US Agency for International Development (USAID).[52]

The World Bank has been an important stakeholder in Brazil's state-run BFP since its inception. It provided technical support during program set-up and, alongside other external stakeholders, has conducted program evaluations that have generated recommendations to improve program efficiency.[53] The World Bank has recommended Bolsa Família and CadÚnico tools to other countries designing and implementing cash transfer programs and data management systems.

International stakeholders are similarly crucial in Palestine's PNCTP, which was created from cash transfer programs offered by the European Union and the World Bank. This collaborative approach resulted in an enhanced program and supported relationship building and strengthening across government, UN agencies, and non-governmental organizations. The PNCTP's wide-ranging effort resulted in a more comprehensive social service offering, through which recipients could receive health insurance and tuition waivers in addition to cash.[54]

Another ingredient for success is government buy-in, which is important for program sustainability, in the context of both humanitarian response programs delivered by international stakeholders and state-run social assistance programs. In Brazil, a new approach to collaboration and coordination between federal and municipal governments has also resulted in creative solutions to reaching the hardest to reach. For example, the state-owned Caixa Econômica Federal bank operates two ATM boats that facilitate BFP transfers for riverside populations in the Amazon.[55] Another example is in Kenya, where the government and the Central Bank of Kenya have overcome a common barrier to program scale-up and enabled friendly regulatory environments that meant M-Pesa could flourish.

In Ethiopia, the state's organizational capacity has been both a barrier, such as through the misuse of program funds, and a facilitator, such as through building partners across sectors and stakeholders. Overall, the state-led approach has been lauded by internal and external partners for ensuring ownership and sustainability of the program and because it helps advance a demand-driven approach to reach.

CONCLUSION

Cash transfer and disbursement programs have the potential to reduce poverty and foster economic resilience in communities around the world.[56] That said, delivery of cash transfer and disbursement programs to hard-to-reach populations is especially difficult. The hardest to reach are those living in extreme poverty, those who are geographically remote and marginalized. The Reach Alliance asks why these groups are so hard to reach with essential programs, such as cash transfers, and how we can overcome these barriers. In this chapter, we present five themes that underpin success in reaching the hardest to reach. Implementors must first use targeting mechanisms that consider a variety of socioeconomic factors and, second, determine whether conditionalities are appropriate given desired program outcomes for the target population. Third, dedicated data management systems must be used to store, analyze, and cross-check information on beneficiaries, and fourth, appropriate technologies, although useful to overcome challenges such as corruption and fraud, should be used carefully and with special attention to data protection and public trust. Finally, meaningful partnerships and stakeholder engagement are critical to reach the hardest to reach with finite programmatic resources as this collaboration increases programmatic efficiency. We encourage practitioners and policy makers to consider how to overcome barriers to reaching those who are administratively invisible and to design and implement programs that specifically target those on the margins.

NOTES

1 Lindert, K., Linder, A., Hobbs, J., & De la Brière, B. (2007). *The nuts and bolts of Brazil's Bolsa Família Program: Implementing conditional cash transfers in a decentralized context* (Social Protection Discussion Paper No. 709). World Bank. http://web.worldbank.org/archive/website01506/WEB/IMAGES/0709.PDF.

2 Such studies and evaluations are too numerous to accurately list here. For one recent synthesis review, see Bastagli, F., Hagen-Zanker, J., Harman, L., Barca, V., Sturge, G., & Schmidt, T. (2018). The impact of cash transfers: A review of the evidence from low- and middle-income countries. *Journal of Social Policy*, 48(3), 569–94. https://doi.org/10.1017/S0047279418000715.

3 Wong, J. (2015). Achieving universal health coverage. *Bulletin of the World Health Organization*, 93(9), 663–4. https://doi.org/10.2471/BLT.14.149070.

4 Jones, N., & Hamad, B.A. (2021). Case study K: Palestine's national cash transfer programme: An example of cash transfer programming in a humanitarian setting. In E. Schüring & M. Loewe (Eds.), *Handbook on social protection systems* (pp. 313–59). Edward Elgar.

5 Easton, S.D., Safadi, N.S., & Crea, T.M. (2018). The experience of social protection in Palestine: An exploratory study of beneficiary perspectives. *International Social Work, 61*(6), 1007–8.

6 Coll-Black, S., Gilligan, D.O., Hoddinott, J., Kumar, N., Taffesse, A.S., & Wiseman, W. (2011). Targeting food security interventions when "everyone is poor": The case of Ethiopia's Productive Safety Net Programme (ESSP II Working Paper No. 24). International Food Research Policy Institute. https://ebrary.ifpri.org/utils/getfile /collection/p15738coll2/id/124855/filename/124856.pdf.

7 Ministry of Agriculture. (2014). *Productive Safety Net Programme Phase IV programme implementation manual.*

8 Coll-Black et al. (2011, p. 22).

9 Pellerano, L., & Barca, V. (2017). The conditions for conditionality in cash transfers: Does one size fit all? In D. Lawson, D. Hulme, & L.K. Ado-Kofie (Eds.), *What works for Africa's poorest: Programmes and policies for the extreme poor* (pp. 223–42). Practical Action. https://practicalactionpublishing.com/book/2363/what-works-for-africas -poorest.

10 Sugiyama, N.B. (2011). The diffusion of conditional cash transfer programs in the Americas. *Global Social Policy, 11*(2–3), 250–78.

11 Pellerano & Barca (2017).

12 Forget, E.L., Peden, A., & Strobel, S. (2013). Cash transfers, basic income and community building. *Social Inclusion, 1*(2), 84–91.

13 Glewwe, P., & Kassouf, A.L. (2012). The impact of the *Bolsa Escola/Família* conditional cash transfer program on enrollment, grade promotion and drop out rates in Brazil. *Journal of Development Economics, 97*(2), 505–17. https://doi.org/10.1016/j.jdeveco .2011.05.008.

14 De Brauw, A., Gilligan, D.O., Hoddinott, J., & Roy, S. (2015). The impact of Bolsa Família on schooling. *World Development, 70*, 303–16.

15 Shei, A. (2013). Brazil's conditional cash transfer program associated with declines in infant mortality rates. *Health Affairs, 32*(7), 1274–81; Glewwe, P., & Kassouf, A.L. (2012). The impact of the Bolsa Escola/Familia conditional cash transfer program on enrollment, dropout rates and grade promotion in Brazil. *Journal of Development Economics, 97*(2), 505–17.

16 Oliosi, J.G.N., Reis-Santos, B., Locatelli, R.L., Sales, C.M.M., da Silva Filho, W.G., da Silva, K.C., Sanchez, M.N., Freitas de Andrade, K.V., Santos de Araújo, G., Shete, P.B., Pereira, S.M., Riley, L.W., Lienhardt, C., & Maciel, E.L.N. (2019). Effect of the Bolsa Familia Programme on the outcome of tuberculosis treatment: A prospective cohort study. *Lancet Global Health, 7*(2), e219–26.

17 Gilert, H., & Austin, L. (2017). *Review of the common cash facility approach in Jordan.* UN High Commissioner for Refugees.

18 Salemi, C., Bowman, J., & Compton, J. (2018, April). *Services for Syrian refugee children and youth in Jordan: Forced displacement, foreign aid, and vulnerability* (Working Paper Series No. 1188). Economic Research Forum.

19 Caldes, N., & Maluccio, J.A. (2005). The cost of conditional cash transfers. *Journal of International Development, 17*(2), 151–68.

20 CEDAD 2.0. *Cadastro Único.* Retrieved October 21, 2021 from https://cecad .cidadania.gov.br/painel03.php.

21 Ibid.

22 Ban Kim, C., Câmara Pinto, B., Jacques, K., Mano, S., Sarraj, J., & Wong., J. (2019). *Cash transfers in Palestine: Building blocks of social protection.* Reach Alliance, Munk School of Global Affairs & Public Policy, University of Toronto.

23 Ibid.

24 Ban Kim et al. (2019).
25 Garcia, N., Sim, A., Ray, S., Stiller, N., Waud, A., & Wong, J. (2016). *Reaching the hard to reach: A case study of Brazil's Bolsa Família Program.* University of Toronto, Munk School of Global Affairs & Public Policy, Reach Alliance.
26 Ibid.
27 Garcia et al. (2016).
28 Ibid.
29 Ibid.
30 Ban Kim et al. (2019).
31 Garcia et al. (2016).
32 Ban Kim et al. (2019)
33 Ibid.
34 Assefa, E., Boychuk, N., Koswin, K., MacLeod, M., Park, D., Sheikh, A., & Wong, J. (2017). *Case study: UNHCR Jordan's Biometric Cash Assistance Program for Syrian refugees.* University of Toronto, Munk School of Global Affairs & Public Policy, Reach Alliance. https://reachalliance.org/case-study/unhcr-jordans-biometric-cash-assistance -program-for-syrian-refugees/
35 Ibid.
36 Access Now. (2021, April 12). *Iris scanning of refugees is disproportionate and dangerous – What's happening behind IrisGuard's closed doors?* [Press release]. Retrieved November 23, 2021, from https://www.accessnow.org/irisguard-refugees-jordan/.
37 Lindert et al. (2007).
38 Garcia et al. (2016).
39 Central Bank of Kenya, Financial Sector Deepening Kenya, and Kenyan National Bureau of Statistics. (2019). *2019 FinAccess Household Survey Report.* https://www .centralbank.go.ke/wp-content/uploads/2019/04/2019-FinAcces-Report.pdf.
40 Berman, M.S. (2011). *The development, use and cultural context of M-PESA in coastal Kenya* (Independent Study Project Collection No. 1197). https://digitalcollections.sit .edu/isp_collection/1197.
41 Jack, W., & Suri, T. (2011). *Mobile money: The economics of MPesa* (Working Paper 16721). National Bureau of Economic Research. https://www.nber.org/papers /w16721.
42 Hall, S. (2021, May 11). *Multipurpose cash assistance: 2020 post distribution monitoring report.* UNHCR. https://reliefweb.int/report/jordan/multi-purpose-cash-assistance -2020-post-distribution-monitoring-report.
43 Assefa et al. (2017).
44 Ibid.
45 Garcia et al. (2016).
46 Yin, K., Kwang, K., Sharifi, M., & Johnson, Z. (2021). *Left behind: The socioeconomic barriers to last-mile mobile money access in Kenya* [Manuscript submitted for publication]. University of Toronto.
47 Ndung'u, N. (2017, July). M-Pesa, a success story of digital financial inclusion. *Practitioner's Insight.* https://www.bsg.ox.ac.uk/sites/default/files/2018-06/2017 -07-M-Pesa-Practitioners-Insight.pdf
48 International Finance Corporation (2018).
49 Gilert & Austin (2017).
50 Ibid.
51 Pellet, P. (2021). *Understanding the 2020–2021 Tigray conflict in Ethiopia –Background, root causes, and consequences* (KKI Policy Brief KE-2021/39). Institute for Foreign Affairs and Trade. https://kki.hu/wp-content/uploads/2021/09/KE_2021_39 _ET_Tigray_Conflict_in_Ethiopia_Pellet_0810.pdf.

52 USAID. (2021, March 29). *US and Ethiopia launch new $2.2 billion phase of the productive safety net program* [Press release]. https://www.usaid.gov/ethiopia/press-releases /mar-29-2021-us-and-ethiopia-launch-new-22-billion-phase-productive

53 Garcia et al. (2016).

54 Ban Kim et al. (2019).

55 Agência Barco. (n.d.). *O que é*. Retrieved December 14, 2021, from https://www.caixa .gov.br/sustentabilidade/investimentos-socioambientais/agencia-barco/Paginas /default.aspx

56 MacLeod, M., Piggott, S., Sarraj, J., & Dos Santos Stiller, N. (2021, August 9). How to deliver cash transfer programs more effectively to hard-to-reach populations. *Stanford Social Innovation Review*. https://ssir.org/articles/entry/how_to_deliver _cash_transfer_programs_more_effectively_to_hard_to_reach_populations#.

CHAPTER FOUR

Behavioral Insights Can Help Improve Cash Transfer Programs

Daniella Turetski and Renos Vakis

INTRODUCTION

As behavioral science has gained popularity as an important component in the planning, design, and implementation of policies and programs around the world, we (and several other contributors to this book) have asked whether it can help improve the effectiveness and impact of cash transfer and other social assistance programs. One of the most widely used and well-evaluated types of antipoverty interventions in the development world has been cash transfer programs.[1] Our answer to this question is "yes!" The goal of this chapter is to highlight ways in which behavioral science can help fine-tune and complement the design and delivery of cash transfer schemes across the world. Although the widespread evidence for cash transfer programs has shown how crucial they are for supporting families in poverty, a behavioral science perspective can provide complementary, human-centered design elements to further improve their outcomes. Looking at evidence and lessons from the United States, as well as internationally from the Global South, the number of ways in which behavioral science has had a noticeable impact on program outcomes from both the beneficiary and the management perspective is growing. Chapter 6 further develops a framework for understanding the behavioral effects of design features on program outcomes.

Behavioral science has shown time and time again that understanding human behavior amplifies the effectiveness of policies, programs, and other services.[2] For cash transfers, achieving long-lasting program outcomes requires understanding recipients' behaviors before, during, and after the program. This involves understanding their psychological responses to the program and how these reactions may affect program outcomes. Behavioral science can help identify frictions (or "sludge") throughout the program that might hinder its ultimate success.[3] It is important to take a holistic approach and try to understand cash transfer programs from both the recipient and the management perspective, although many of the examples we refer to in this chapter focus on the beneficiary perspective.

One overarching theme in the discussion of how behavioral science may influence welfare programs, and specifically cash transfer programs, is that small, behaviorally informed design changes can have significant and important consequences. In many cases, these changes are often extremely cost-effective, easily implementable, and highly scalable.[4] In the first part of this chapter, we outline evidence for and examples of how these small design changes can yield a large impact. We next emphasize how behavioral science can be particularly effective in addressing well-being and mental health outcomes, which are unfortunately often overlooked in cash transfer program design. We discuss possible ways to directly integrate mental health interventions into the design of cash transfer programs, as well as how cash transfers can specifically target well-being and mental health outcomes. Finally, we provide a road map on where to go from here and what we believe are critical areas to tackle going forward.

IMPROVING CHOICE ARCHITECTURE: SMALL CHANGES CAN YIELD SIGNIFICANT PROGRAM IMPACTS

Thaler and Sunstein's *Nudge* showcases many examples of how organizations can use choice architecture to influence stakeholders.[5] Welfare programs – as we aim to highlight – are no exception.

Behaviorally informed interventions have slowly started to be implemented into policy, and in particular policy design, including the processes underlying cash transfer programs. These interventions may take the form of nudges (choice architecture interventions), as described in *Nudge*, but behavioral science more generally has started to change the perspective with which cash transfer programs are approached. We highlight a few examples of small, cost-effective changes that can make a meaningful difference in the beneficiary's experience during and after the program, which ultimately affects the program's outcomes.

Early models of cash transfer programs had a "cash transfers 101" model, heavily based on participants meeting certain conditions imposed by the designers in order to receive the cash transfer.[6] This predetermined design served as the classic cash transfer program model that made transfers conditional on some sort of required behavior from the recipients. For example, parents might be asked to enroll and take their children to school, so their cash transfer would then be conditioned on the child's attendance. Other similar follow-ups may include baby checkups, training sessions, and so forth. Since then, cash transfer program models have evolved, particularly in terms of their design.

More recently, these classic original models have been augmented by the provision of additional features and are commonly known as *cash-plus models*. These programs are different in their newly found integration of behavioral interventions and use of behavioral insights when designing and rolling out the programs. Behavioral science might suggest that programs that offer additional services, or other non-cash benefits, might succeed relative to those that provide cash only (see also Chapter 7). Numerous randomized controlled trials (RCTs) have taken place in several countries that have specifically looked at the value added of behaviorally informed interventions used on top of the traditional cash transfer.[7] Such RCTs have provided growing evidence that these interventions work, making it highly worthwhile to continue integrating behavioral science into program design.

Many of these interventions are extremely cost-effective, yet with very promising and meaningful outcomes. Much of the evidence for this comes from programs focused on parents and their behaviors.[8] Cash transfers are no longer just about supporting income and smoothing consumption – they can be taken a step further and improve human capital outcomes. This can be done especially well through investment in children. Many of these programs target low-income and vulnerable families. These are exactly the situations in which initially higher human capital deficits are found and in which behaviorally informed program designs can have some of the most impact. It is important that the program design provide this foundation for human capital development (alongside the traditional financial support) to help eventually break intergenerational cycles of poverty. Programs in Latin America, including Ecuador, Honduras, and Nicaragua, have showcased evidence of a very positive impact of interventions in cash-plus models on child development outcomes (e.g., cognition, language). These parenting interventions have effects on cognitive outcomes among children, even above and beyond nutrition interventions. The Progresa program in Mexico, for example, provided evidence that providing mothers with education grants contingent on their children's school attendance significantly and positively affected school enrollment and attendance.[9] In addition to these shorter-term impacts, analyses of the Familias en Acción program in Colombia have shown that such programs also have longer-term impacts on reducing poverty (as well as health outcomes and reduced crime) by improving opportunities and outcomes for youth in a behaviorally informed way.[10] Evidence from the Child Development Grant Programme in Northern Nigeria supports that these interventions can begin as early as in utero.[11] This program paired unconditional cash transfers to pregnant women with information on recommended practices related to pregnancy and infant feeding. These interventions led to marked improvements in child health.

Often, these cost-effective interventions are tangible items that can be provided in tandem with the cash transfer.[12] For example, giving children bed nets, deworming pills, and nutrient supplementation might lead to an increased likelihood that parents themselves will continue to provide their kids with these items in the future once they receive the cash transfer. Through the free distribution of these products, parents were exposed to their benefits, which made them more likely to purchase them in the future.

A key insight illuminated by behavioral science is that recipients of cash transfers are living in the context of their own unique and hectic lives and that an understanding of that context should be central to the design of the programs. Unfortunately, this is often forgotten when programs are designed, which becomes clear when one considers programs focused on parents. Parents do their parenting tasks in the context of many other (often stressful) events going on in their lives. They are employees, they have relationships, they need to find a place to live, and they often act as their children's first teachers. Recognizing this is critical and should inform the design of programs. Evidence from a US-based RCT in which low-income mothers were given monthly, unconditional cash transfers shortly after giving birth shows a clear causal impact of these transfers on their infant's brain activity.[13] Of importance to this chapter, we want to highlight that this program (1) delivers cash to mothers on a predictable monthly schedule and (2) entrusts them with the choice of how to spend that money (see also Chapter 9). Small design features that are created from this behaviorally informed perspective can support parents by factoring in the full extent of their parental responsibilities and life events. Specifically, this would involve alleviating avoidable sludge from the cash transfer process and making it easier for parents to receive and use the cash. Behavioral science has cracked open this problem and can further be used to improve beneficiaries' experiences in cash transfer programs, which would ultimately improve program outcomes.

By blending insights relevant to the specific cash transfer program (i.e., child development insights for cash transfers relevant to parents and child development), behavioral science insights, and economics and psychology research, programs can be designed far more holistically and effectively. As we discuss in the next section, part of this design needs to involve a consideration of the recipient's well-being and mental health in more direct ways, whether through the program's design features or through program outcomes.

INTEGRATING WELL-BEING AND MENTAL HEALTH CONSIDERATIONS INTO CASH TRANSFER PROGRAM DESIGN

An often-neglected area of welfare programs is how to integrate well-being and mental health considerations into the design of cash transfer programs and choice of intended program outcomes. The behavioral interventions that we have highlighted so far have great potential for high impact in these programs. Understanding the nuances and factors that affect recipient well-being and mental health is critical for designing effective cash transfer programs in this area.

A question often debated when designing cash transfer programs is when to pay recipients and what effects different payment schemes have on recipient psychological well-being. Experiments focused on how well-being can be improved by changing the timing of payments have studied the effects of financial strain on worker productivity and how paying workers a few days earlier than their coworkers may affect their well-being and, ultimately, their productivity.[14] The workers chosen were severely financially constrained – they were strapped with lots of debt and had few opportunities to earn money. For these individuals, getting paid a few days earlier was a significant opportunity. Usually, workers are paid at the very end of a pay period, but in these experiments, some workers were surprised by getting paid earlier than their peers. Results showed that this made them significantly more productive in their small-scale manufacturing work. An interesting finding was that there were no announcement effects, that is, simply telling workers that they would be paid earlier had no effect on their behavior. What really mattered was that they received money in their pockets and were able to use this cash to pay bills and tackle other financial stresses. The results of these experiments suggest that psychological factors such as worry and sadness can (1) make people really unhappy and significantly affect their well-being and (2) meaningfully interfere with their work and capacity to be economically productive and resilient (which in turn circles back to their well-being). When workers are critically financially strained, delivering cash at the right moments can therefore be extremely important. Being flexible and understanding when people are truly financially strained (i.e., when they need support the most) is important for supporting their capacity to help themselves. This same logic could easily be applied to the design of cash transfer programs, with examples ranging from making larger payments before the beginning of school years or timing payments so that rural families get larger amounts during preharvest periods when income flows tend to be low.

Although evidence suggests that cash transfers can accomplish many goals, it is unreasonable to expect cash itself to do all the heavy lifting when it comes to addressing severe mental health issues. Evidence suggests that it may be cost-effective to offer some form of psychotherapy as a supplement to cash transfers. Inexpensive versions of psychotherapy (e.g., cognitive–behavioral therapy) have been found to be effective in improving mental health at a very low cost.[15] In addition to being cost effective, many psychotherapy interventions are highly scalable. For example, in-person therapy can be run by non-specialists (i.e., individuals who can be trained in a very short time frame).[16] These interventions simply require laypeople or non-specialists who are willing to help and be quickly trained. Although this surely differs from professional therapies provided by trained psychiatrists and psychologists, this form of therapy is still effective, very inexpensive, and relatively easy to scale. Group therapy is another less expensive alternative to individualized therapy and has been shown to be highly effective.[17] Alongside such in-person examples, online and phone therapies have been shown to be effective and far more scalable than their in-person alternatives.[18] These therapies are starting to take off in the United States with promising results. There are many different opportunities for online psychotherapies, such as cognitive–behavioral therapy via video, chatting with a therapist online, or even chatbots trained in cognitive–behavioral therapy. The potential is undoubtedly enormous; somebody just needs to put the pieces together and figure out the best way to make it work. The ability to reach a large number of individuals could not only drastically improve mental health, but it could also have an impact on labor market productivity and other economic outcomes (i.e., labor supply).[19] All these insights present an opportunity for a new type of cash-plus model – one that provides recipients with cash in addition to options for psychological support.

Social empowerment and self-affirmation are also key components of a successful cash transfer program. One tool to address this is to use social norms throughout the program, as well as other design features that help facilitate positive social interactions. Evidence from Madagascar highlights the success of mother leader groups, where mother leaders (who are themselves program beneficiaries) led monthly wellness sessions discussing the benefits of good family practices for early childhood development.[20] These groups rely on the role of norms and support of other mothers. Similar results can be seen in another program in Nicaragua.[21] Witnessing local success stories of upward mobility from mother leaders to whom beneficiaries look up motivated and encouraged beneficiaries to themselves productively use their cash. Evidence shows that those who interacted with local leaders had multiplier effects of their own transfers that were sustained two to three years after the interventions finished.[22]

Whether a program has conditions attached to the disbursement of cash or not is a design feature of cash transfer programs that is heavily debated, particularly because of their impact on mental health. Whether to include conditions in a cash transfer program often involves arguments about their negative impact on recipient psychological well-being. Evidence suggests that trust is a crucial component of program success.[23] Conditions may bring about feelings of distrust in the recipient's ability to spend the money wisely, and they might cause the added stress of having to fulfill the program's conditions. Unconditional cash transfers, in contrast, may signal trust in recipients to independently decide how to spend their money and that the organization has faith that they will allocate the funds appropriately. This might in turn improve self-esteem and self-assurance. Although conditions evidently affect behaviors and remain a somewhat unresolved topic, it is important to factor mental health considerations into the discussion.

THE WAY FORWARD

In this chapter, we aimed to provide some motivation on the use of behavioral science in the design of cash transfer programs and other welfare programs. Although these programs have slowly begun integrating behavioral interventions, there is vast progress to be made that has the potential to greatly improve the efficacy of cash transfers. We have introduced some examples of existing work done toward achieving this goal, but numerous other organizations are continuing to factor in behavioral science when designing cash transfer programs. Given how important the mental health space is, and how it has been neglected in prior program iterations, future work needs to focus on how to use behavioral science to improve well-being and mental health outcomes.

Various open questions remain. First, future research should focus on providing more evidence on design features of cash transfer programs that can help recipients achieve program outcomes. For example, behavioral science can help untangle the best timing of transfers, who should receive transfers, or how to integrate cash transfer program schemes with other interventions. Second, behavioral science can be helpful from both the beneficiary and the management perspective. Although most of our examples addressed cash transfer programs from the beneficiary's perspective, a plethora of ways exist in which the management side can be improved using behaviorally informed interventions. There could, for example, be improvements in the training of social workers to enhance their face-to-face interactions with beneficiaries, including how to reduce biases and prejudices that can often lead to low program take-up. On a more general note, behavioral science can help identify sludge and administrative inefficiencies and simplify the work of those who run the program.

In answering some of these questions, we advocate for continuous experimentation and evidence gathering in the design phase of cash transfer programs. We believe that there are many efficient ways of collecting evidence on the role of design features in outcomes, from integrating surveys and experiments to interviews with expert informants or a content analysis of past cash transfer programs. More important, we call for a different mindset on the part of program designers and administrators – one that critically examines various design features of programs in their specific context and using iterative approaches to understand their effects on the behavior of recipients and program outcomes.

Lifting people out of extreme poverty is a fundamental question for development policy. Despite advancements in the past few decades, the growing evidence suggests that it is not just about the capital. It is critical to understand the constraints on decision making that come from situations of extreme poverty. These include the impact of scarcity on decisions; the need to build assets, savings, and investments; and how to make those assets and investments productive. Behavioral science aims to do exactly that. This involves factoring in the poverty context in which the recipient lives, integrating considerations of how participating in the cash transfer program may psychologically affect their behavior, and designing effective behavioral interventions to make cash transfers more effective. Integrating such considerations into cash transfer programs is not a luxury, it is essential.

NOTES

1 Fiszbein, A., Schady, N., Ferreira, F.H.G., Grosh, M., Keleher, N., Olinto, P., & Skoufias, E. (2009). *Conditional cash transfers: Reducing present and future poverty*. World Bank.

2 For examples, see Organisation for Economic Co-operation and Development. (2017). *Behavioural insights and public policy: Lessons from around the world*. OECD Publishing. https://doi.org/10.1787/9789264270480-en.

3 See Soman, D. (2020). *Sludge: A very short introduction*. University of Toronto, Rotman School of Management, Behavioural Economics in Action at Rotman. https://www.rotman.utoronto.ca/-/media/Files/Programs-and-Areas/BEAR/White-Papers/BEARxBIOrg-Sludge-Introduction.pdf.

4 For challenges associated with successful scaling, see List, J.A. (2022). *The voltage effect*. Penguin Business; and Mažar, N., & Soman, D. (2022). *Behavioral science in the wild*. University of Toronto Press.

5 Thaler, R.H., & Sunstein, C.R. (2008). *Nudge: Improving decisions using the architecture of choice*. Yale University Press.

6 Fiszbein et al. (2009).

7 Banerjee, A., Duflo, E., Goldberg, N., Karlan, D., Osei, R., Pariente, W., Shapiro, J., Thuysbaert, B., & Udry, C. (2015). A multifaceted program causes lasting progress for the very poor: Evidence from six countries. *Science, 348*(6236), Article 1260799. https://doi.org/10.1126/science.1260799.

8 See Arriagada, A.-M., Perry, J., Rawlings, L., Trias, J., & Zumaeta, M. (2018). *Promoting early childhood development through combining cash transfers and parenting programs* (Working Paper No. 8670). World Bank Policy Research. https://ssrn.com/abstract=3299141; Premand, P., & Barry, O. (2020). *Behavioral change promotion, cash transfers and early childhood development: Experimental evidence from a government program in a low-income setting* (Policy Research Working Paper No. 9368). World Bank Group. http://hdl.handle.net/10986/34385; Paxson, C., & Schady, N. (2010). Does money matter? The effects of cash transfers on child development in rural Ecuador. *Economic Development and Cultural Change, 59*(1), 187–229. https://doi.org/10.1086/655458; Fernald, L.C.H., Gertler, P.J., & Neufeld, L.M. (2008). Role of cash in conditional cash transfer programmes for child health, growth, and development: An analysis of Mexico's *Oportunidades*. *Lancet, 371*(9615), 828–37. https://doi.org/10.1016/s0140-6736(08)60382-7; Fernald, L.C., Kagawa, R.M., Knauer, H.A., Schnaas, L., Guerra, A.G., & Neufeld, L.M. (2017). Promoting child development through group-based parent support within a cash transfer program: Experimental effects on children's outcomes. *Developmental Psychology, 53*(2), 222–36. https://doi.org/10.1037/dev0000185; Barry, O., Maidoka, A.M., & Premand, P. (2017). *Promoting positive parenting practices in Niger through a cash transfer program.* CALP Network. https://www.calpnetwork.org/wp-content/uploads/2020/03/ecm1712nigerbarry-1.pdf.

9 Schultz, T.P. (2004). School subsidies for the poor: Evaluating the Mexican Progresa Poverty Program. *Journal of Development Economics, 74*(1), 199–250. https://doi.org/10.1016/j.jdeveco.2003.12.009.

10 Attanasio, O., Sosa, L.C., Medina, C., Meghir, C., & Posso-Suárez, C.M. (2021). *Long term effects of cash transfer programs in Colombia* (Working Paper No. 29056). National Bureau of Economic Research. https://doi.org/10.3386/w29056.

11 Carneiro, P.M., Kraftman, L., Mason, G., Moore, L., Rasul, I., & Scott, M. (2020). *The impacts of a multifaceted pre-natal intervention on human capital accumulation in early life* (IZA Discussion Paper No. 13955). IZA Institute of Labor Economics. https://doi.org/10.2139/ssrn.3751848.

12 Bates, M.A., Glennerster, R., Gumede, K., & Duflo, E. (2012). The price is wrong. *Field Actions Science Reports, 4*. http://journals.openedition.org/factsreports/1554.

13 Troller-Renfree, S.V., Costanzo, M.A., Duncan, G.J., Magnuson, K., Gennetian, L.A., Yoshikawa, H., Halpern-Meekin, S., Fox, N.A., & Noble, K.G. (2022). The impact of a poverty reduction intervention on infant brain activity. *Proceedings of the National Academy of Sciences, 119*(5), e2115649119. https://doi.org/10.1073/pnas.2115649119.

14 Kaur, S., Mullainathan, S., Oh, S., & Schilbach, F. (2021). *Do financial concerns make workers less productive?* (Working Paper No. 28338). National Bureau of Economic Research. https://doi.org/10.3386/w28338.

15 Blattman, C., Jamison, J.C., & Sheridan, M. (2015). *Reducing crime and violence: Experimental evidence from cognitive behavioral therapy in Liberia* (Working Paper No. 21204). National Bureau of Economic Research. https://doi.org/10.3386/w21204.

16 Rahman, A., Malik, A., Sikander, S., Roberts, C., & Creed, F. (2008). Cognitive behaviour therapy-based intervention by community health workers for mothers with depression and their infants in rural Pakistan: A cluster-randomised controlled trial. *Lancet, 372*(9642), 902–9. https://doi.org/10.1016/s0140 -6736(08)61400-2.

17 Bolton, P., Bass, J., Neugebauer, R., Verdeli, H., Clougherty, K.F., Wickramaratne, P., Speelman, L., Ndogoni, L., & Weissman, M. (2003). Group interpersonal psychotherapy for depression in rural Uganda. *JAMA, 289*(23), 3117. https://doi .org/10.1001/jama.289.23.3117.

18 See Mozer, E. (2008). Psychotherapeutic intervention by telephone. *Clinical Interventions in Aging, 3,* 391–6. https://doi.org/10.2147/cia.s950; and Varker, T., Brand, R.M., Ward, J., Terhaag, S., & Phelps, A. (2019). Efficacy of synchronous telepsychology interventions for people with anxiety, depression, posttraumatic stress disorder, and adjustment disorder: A rapid evidence assessment. *Psychological Services, 16*(4), 621–35. https://doi.org/10.1037/ser0000239.

19 Patel, V., Burns, J.K., Dhingra, M., Tarver, L., Kohrt, B.A., & Lund, C. (2018). Income inequality and depression: A systematic review and meta-analysis of the association and a scoping review of mechanisms. *World Psychiatry, 17*(1), 76–89. https://doi.org/10.1002/wps.20492.

20 World Bank Group. (2019, May 21). *In Madagascar, cash transfers provide more than money.* Retrieved April 22, 2022, from https://www.worldbank.org/en/news /feature/2019/05/21/cash-transfers-provide-more-than-money.

21 Macours, K., & Vakis, R. (2014). Changing households' investment behaviour through social interactions with local leaders: Evidence from a randomised transfer programme. *Economic Journal, 124*(576), 607–33. https://doi.org/10.1111 /ecoj.12145.

22 Macours, K., & Vakis, R. (2016). *Sustaining impacts when transfers end: Women leaders, aspirations, and investment in children* (Working Paper No. 22871). National Bureau of Economic Research. https://doi.org/10.3386/w22871.

23 Gennetian, L.A., Shafir, E., Aber, J.L., & de Hoop, J. (2021, June 29). *Behavioral insights into cash transfers to families with children.* Behavioral Science and Policy Association. https://behavioralpolicy.org/articles/behavioral-insights-into-cash -transfers-to-families-with-children/.

CHAPTER FIVE

What Do We Know about Basic Income – and How Can Experiments Help?

Evelyn L. Forget

In 1971, Senator David Croll chaired a Special Senate Committee on Poverty in Canada that called for the immediate implementation of a guaranteed annual income as "a first firm step in the war against poverty" because "the poor could not be asked to wait years for the help they so urgently need."[1] For the next 50 years, committee after committee made similar recommendations. In 1985, the Royal Commission on the Economic Union and Development Prospects for Canada (the Macdonald Commission) endorsed a similar policy,[2] and in 2009 the Subcommittee on Cities of the Senate Standing Committee on Social Affairs, Science and Technology, repeated the call.[3] In 2019, the *Final Report of the National Inquiry into Missing and Murdered Indigenous Women and Girls* called for a guaranteed livable income for all Canadians,[4] and in 2020 50 senators wrote an open letter to the prime minister calling for a guaranteed livable income that would ensure all residents of Canada have enough to live above the poverty line, set at the market basket measure by the federal government.[5]

Again and again, policy makers recognized the inadequacy of a piecemeal approach to addressing poverty that forced those in desperate straits to turn to the provinces and territories for programs of last resort. They proposed, instead, a form of basic income that guarantees all residents of the country a guaranteed minimum income.

Fifty years after Senator Croll tabled his report, Canada has adopted many of the features of basic income to offer income supports to low-income older adults and families with children aged younger than 18 years. Most recently, there have been efforts in some provinces and federally to offer similar programs for people with permanent and severe disabilities. Yet, low-income residents of Canada between ages 18 and 64 years who are deemed capable of working for pay continue to subsist on provincial income assistance programs, all of which pay residents a benefit well below the poverty line and impose a variety of work requirements.

There is every reason to believe that basic income would offer residents the opportunity to live healthier lives in stronger and more resilient communities. Basic income experiments of varying quality have already been conducted around the world in low-, middle-, and high-income countries, and they have yielded promising results. Some, like the Finnish Basic Income Experiment in 2017–2018 or the Utrecht Trust Experiment, modified existing social assistance or employment assistance programs to raise the rates and remove job search requirements. They documented increased trust in social institutions among recipients, better self-rated health, and no significant reduction in hours worked.[6] Others effectively designed smaller, foundation-funded programs for people in low-income countries with few supports in place. They, too, documented better health and nutrition, increased school attendance, and, in some cases, improved employment or small business creation.[7] Can well-designed basic income experiments offer more compelling evidence to support the design of an evidence-based basic income policy?

DEFINING BASIC INCOME IN A CANADIAN CONTEXT

In Canada, *basic income* has come to be defined as an income-tested benefit that guarantees recipients an income, paid in the form of money, that is adequate to live a modest but dignified life. It does not replace goods and services offered by the provinces, such as health care, pharma care, affordable housing, job training, equipment and services for people with disabilities, and so on. It does replace provincial income or social assistance that individuals receive in the form of money. Basic income is a cash transfer that ensures that everyone has enough money that they can spend however they like to make their own decisions about how they want to live. In Canada, basic income is generally conceived as an income-tested benefit: as income from other sources increases, the size of the benefit is gradually reduced so that it disappears altogether for middle- and upper-income earners.

Unlike provincial income assistance, basic income is not conditional on being available and willing to work for pay or on demonstrating a disability that makes work for pay impossible. All provincial income assistance programs impose regulations that require those deemed capable of working for pay to actively seek employment and those deemed incapable of work to demonstrate both that they have a diagnosed disability and that the disability makes work for pay a significant hardship.

Political and social support for basic income has waxed and waned over the past 50 years, but both the international financial crisis of 2008–2009 and, more recently, the COVID-19 pandemic have increased the support for basic income worldwide. In Canada, groups as varied as Canadian senators, the Chamber of Commerce, the National Farmers Union, the Steelworkers Union, advocates for artists, women's groups, food security advocates, and many others have called for a basic income that would raise incomes to the level of the market basket measure.[8]

Political support for a basic income, however, is not universal, and it is the unconditionality of basic income that accounts for much of the criticism. If everyone is entitled to support whether they work or not, there is a broadly held belief that some people might choose not to work for pay, instead choosing to volunteer, work as an artist, spend time caring for their community, or sit under a tree and daydream. That freedom raises the ire of critics, even though there is a good deal of evidence to suggest that a well-designed basic income will not reduce work hours in any significant way: the Parliamentary Budget Office, in a report estimating the impact of a guaranteed basic income, suggested that it might reduce the number of hours worked by as much as 1.5 per cent nationally.[9] Yet the report of the BC Panel on Basic Income rejected a basic income, recommending instead significant expansions of conditional supports, claiming, "Throughout our recommendations we have sought to encourage work ... The result will be the dignity and self-respect provided by work for those encouraged to work, and economic and fiscal gains for society."[10]

Those who reject basic income because of its purported work disincentives assume not only that there is a job, and not just a job but a job that confers dignity and self-respect, for anyone who wants to work, but also that anyone not diagnosed with a disability is ready and able to work within the constructs of the formal paid labor market. Does an individual who cannot, or chooses not to, work for pay have a right to live a dignified life? Or should financial support take the form of conditional support because, as the BC panel argued, "We believe that all of this should be done with careful concern for building public trust – not just among those who most need support but also among those who will see themselves mostly as paying into the system."[11] The BC panel report elicited significant controversy, with critics raising many of the points discussed here.[12]

It is, of course, in the context of hard cases that policy disputes are most challenging. Conditionality matters, but it especially matters in the case of working-age adults. Consequently, it is not a surprise that the highest poverty rates and the greatest resistance to the principles of basic income occur in the context of adults aged between ages 18 and 64 years. Indeed, since 1971 Canada has adopted unconditional federal income support policies that resemble basic incomes for children aged younger than 18 years and people aged 65 years and older, and similar unconditional income supports are beginning to emerge at both the provincial and the federal levels for people with permanent and severe disabilities.

BENEFITS OF BASIC INCOME

The slow but steady emergence of income support programs for children, older adults, and, most recently, people with profound disabilities has demonstrated the benefits of unconditional cash transfers that resemble basic income. Basic income experiments, in Canada and around the world, as well as the analysis of basic-income-like programs, have also generated support for the implementation of basic income for all Canadians.

In Canada, the first large-scale basic income experiment was called *mincome* and paid some families in Winnipeg, Dauphin, and a few smaller rural communities in Manitoba a basic income between 1975 and 1978. Families with no other means of support received benefits marginally greater than they would have received from income assistance if they had been eligible. Low-wage workers also received partial benefits; the benefit was reduced by $0.50 for every dollar earned until it disappeared entirely for middle- and upper-income earners. The outcomes were encouraging. Poverty rates declined, physical and mental health improved, and high school completion rates increased.[13] Crime, and especially family violence, declined.[14] Participants reported less stress and greater community involvement; women, in particular, reported greater autonomy.[15]

People who were working when mincome was introduced continued to work; there was no change in labor force participation, and very little change in the number of hours worked. Only two groups reduced their work hours significantly: young men aged between 15 and 24 years worked fewer hours because, instead of leaving school at age 16 to take a full-time job, they stayed in high school longer, and new mothers, who expected a maternity leave of only four weeks, used some of the stipend to extend parental leave when they gave birth.[16] The short-term results were strong, but imagine for a moment how different life would be over the next four decades for someone who graduated from high school in 1975 and someone who left school early to become financially independent.

These results are far from unique. Similar findings emerged from experiments conducted in high-, middle- and low-income countries. Ontario launched a basic income experiment in 2017, which was canceled shortly after the provincial election in early 2018. Although participants continued to receive money until March 2019, no systematic analysis of the results was permitted. A survey, which suffered from all the limitations of voluntary surveys as well as the unusual circumstances of data collection after a disrupted experiment, did yield some interesting results.[17] The authors found that self-reported mental and physical health improved and stress levels declined. Participants reported that the quality of the jobs they held had improved; basic income allowed them to search for better jobs than the short-term, poorly paid jobs they held before the experiment. At one of the experimental sites, food bank use declined.[18]

Similar results have been found in other high-income countries. Finland released a report on its basic income experiment that focused on long-term unemployed persons.[19] Once again, stress levels declined, mental and physical health improved, and, by the end of the experiment, even those participants with significant employment barriers were beginning to move into permanent jobs at a rate higher than the control group. Several cities in the Netherlands conducted a series of "trust" experiments at about the same time.[20] These experiments did not increase the amount of money that recipients were eligible to receive; instead, they focused on a different aspect of basic income. Participants were eligible to receive their benefits without reporting to a caseworker, and they received their benefits without conditions. Work requirements were removed. Help with job searches was available to those who sought it, but these supports were not mandated. By the end of the experiment, those who were not coerced to work were more likely to be working full time in permanent jobs than those who faced a work requirement. Stress levels declined, self-reported health improved, social engagement increased, and trust in government and society improved.

These results are consistent with other experimental results. In almost all low-income countries, nutrition and basic health improved.[21] Young mothers in Kenya were more likely to take their children to clinics and send them to school. In almost all high-income countries, mental health and self-reported health improved.[22] Adolescent girls in Malawi were more likely to attend school and less likely to engage in transactional sex work.[23] Mental and physical health improved, poverty rates declined, and financial security and reported well-being increased.

Experimental results from around the world are consistent with what is known from the analysis of basic-income-like programs that exist in Canada. Food security and general health among low-income seniors improves as soon as they turn age 65 years and become eligible for Old Age Security (OAS) and the Guaranteed Income Supplement (GIS) that, together, operate like a basic income for older adults.[24] Young families in Canada have access to the Canada Child Benefit (CCB), which provides an unconditional cash transfer to families with children aged younger than 18 years. Kourtney Koebel and Tammy Schirle report that there was no general flight from the labor market; married mothers worked marginally less, but single mothers worked more.[25]

The benefits seem clear enough: a basic income is associated with better physical and mental health, investment in education, improved financial security, and stronger and more resilient communities, without reducing the number of hours that recipients are prepared to work for pay. Research results consistently invalidate many of the fears that critics express.

BASIC INCOME AND PROVINCIAL INCOME ASSISTANCE

Since 1971, there has been a general move toward a basic income in Canada. The GIS, which enhances the earnings of low-income seniors eligible for OAS, was first introduced as a temporary measure in 1967 but has subsequently been enhanced and made permanent. As a consequence, the poverty rate among older adults in 2018 was 3.5 per cent, whereas that of working-aged adults was 10.5 per cent.[26] Similarly, the CCB has been substantially expanded over time, reducing the poverty rate among children. Both of these benefits are income-tested and paid in the form of money; as income increases, the size of the benefit declines. Several provinces, notably Saskatchewan and Alberta, have moved toward creating similar income-tested benefits for those with severe and permanent disabilities, and a federal disability benefit modeled on the GIS was a Liberal promise during the 2021 federal election. At the provincial level, these programs pay more than provincial income assistance and do not require repeated medical reports to demonstrate a continuing inability to work. Other provinces, however, continue to offer support to people with disabilities through provincial income assistance, with lower levels of support and greater caseworker and ongoing medical scrutiny.

Adults aged between 18 and 64 years who are deemed capable of work, however, continue to be subject to the income assistance programs of last resort offered by the provinces. Those who can work are expected to make every effort to do so. Those who cannot work are required to demonstrate the extent and details of their disability. Those who can find some other means of support are expected to do so.

Some of the advantages that are expected to accompany a basic income come about because the proposed benefit level is significantly higher than provincial income assistance. Others occur because some provincial income assistance programs reduce benefits dramatically as soon as recipients earn a small income, whereas basic income generally allows recipients to keep a larger portion of earned income without losing access to the entire basic income. However, the additional benefits that emerge from the unconditionality of basic income cannot be achieved by raising the support levels associated with the highly conditional provincial income assistance.

Other critics point to additional in-kind benefits recipients receive (such as dental insurance or pharma care) with income assistance, which are not part of most basic income plans, and suggest that recipients would actually be much worse off under a basic income than they would be with income assistance. However, these extended health benefits are a necessary support in high-income countries and should be made dependent on a family's level of income rather than its source. There is no logical reason to tie such benefits to any form of income replacement of any kind. Someone who works and earns a low income is in just as much need of dental insurance as someone with a very similar income who receives provincial income assistance. Separating services from income maintenance is a necessary modification of all social welfare programs, and, in fact, this separation has been underway in high-income countries since the early 1970s.[27] Pharma care is already delivered independently of the income assistance program in several provinces, including Manitoba and British Columbia. And yet, the principle needs to be further extended. One of the barriers to exiting provincial disability support programs is that so many necessary services are tied to income maintenance that anyone offered a job may well choose to turn it down rather than risk leaving a program that offers supports they might need in the future and being required to undergo a lengthy, intrusive, and uncertain qualification process all over again. The fact that some existing programs tie services to income maintenance is an argument for adopting a more just and efficient system by implementing a basic income and severing the link between income maintenance and services. It is not a justification of the status quo.

These arguments, however, neglect the real reason that the benefits of basic income cannot be achieved by modifying existing income assistance plans. Income assistance is a conditional payment that rests on a highly bureaucratized program of coercion and control,[28] whereas basic income is automatic and unconditional. It depends only on reported income.

Basic income is, by definition, an unconditional cash transfer, whereas income assistance takes the form of a conditional transfer. When conditions are imposed on the receipt of income recipients desperately need, the voices of recipients go unheard; they lose control over what services they want and need and are, instead, presented with supports chosen by others. Conditionality is designed to make receipt of cash benefits contingent on positive steps to improve well-being and to create incentives for desired behavior, where both "positive steps" and "desired behavior" are chosen by the people who designed the system rather than those who need financial support. Work requirements (or "incentives") are the condition most commonly imposed by Canadian income assistance programs, usually justified by claims that "dignity and self-respect" will follow.

Work requirements, however, can have negative effects on recipients and on the rest of society. There is little evidence that work requirements associated with income supports actually improve labor market outcomes and at least some evidence that long-run outcomes are harmed.[29] Some recipients, most notably people leaving violent relationships and formerly incarcerated people, are often not ready to work in the paid labor market.[30] Artists of all types are underappreciated and underpaid in our society, and yet social well-being depends on such activities.[31] More than eight million Canadians act as unpaid caregivers for friends and family members; many of these caregivers are working-aged adults who curtail work hours to provide needed care.[32]

Conditionality in existing income assistance programs, however, goes far beyond work requirements. Adults who live alone and depend on provincial income assistance may find their rent paid directly to their landlords by the province because they are deemed at risk of homelessness. One consequence is that such tenants lose what little power they had to demand that landlords initiate needed repairs or care for the property.

Parents who depend on provincial income assistance often find themselves caught between two bureaucracies – one associated with income assistance and another associated with child and family services. Although any parent can come into contact with the child welfare system, parents who rely on income assistance are vulnerable to surveillance that other parents may escape.[33] Their young children may be left to care for themselves because childcare services are rarely responsive to the needs of workers with unpredictable working hours. Children may appear at school without lunches or inadequately clothed, not because they are neglected but because their families have too little money. Not all teachers, who are required to report concerns to child welfare, can distinguish between poverty and neglect. Involvement with child welfare authorities might entail required attendance at childcare classes or requirements to ensure school attendance. If the worst happens and children are taken into care, income support provided to parents will be reduced, which can lead to a downward spiral of adverse events that can leave children vulnerable to an uncertain foster system while making it virtually impossible for parents to reunite their families.[34]

People with disabilities face even more intrusive surveillance. Qualifying for provincial income assistance when one has a disability generally requires two reports: one report providing a medical diagnosis and prognosis and a second detailing the impact of the diagnosis on the person's ability to work and activities of daily living. Qualifying for support often depends at least as much on the skill of the person completing the form as on the medical condition of the applicant. People with conditions that change over time face particular challenges in accessing support. If successful, a recipient will receive more money than an applicant without a disability, although levels of support in most provinces are still far below the poverty line. However, they are often required to requalify for support on an ongoing basis, proving that their condition still merits support.[35]

All of these cases demonstrate a key difference between basic income, which is an unconditional cash transfer, and provincial income assistance. The first provides cash to recipients only on the basis of their reported income and trusts recipients to make decisions about the services that they believe they need and want. By contrast, the second grudgingly provides inadequate levels of support as a last resort to individuals who can demonstrate to the satisfaction of an intrusive bureaucracy that they need help, can find no one else to support them, and are prepared to demonstrate the "positive" behavior these systems are designed to incentivize.

HOW CAN MORE AND BETTER EXPERIMENTS HELP?

It has become commonplace for basic income advocates to argue that more temporary experiments are not necessary. After all the unconditional and conditional cash transfer experiments that have taken place around the world, and after the two large-scale experiments that have taken place in Canada, they argue, we already understand both the likely outcomes of basic income and the limitations of experimental methodology.[36] Others argue that experiments are, by their nature, temporary, and the behavior of people who receive a temporary basic income might not mirror the effects of permanent program changes and that experiments cost a lot and take time to conduct and analyze.[37] Still others wonder whether the urge to experiment might not be a convenient way of distracting supporters until the political climate changes, thereby delaying any substantive policy change.

Implementing large-scale social experiments is challenging at the best of times. Different ethical frameworks in different countries impose limitations on researchers' capacity to randomize. Most basic income experiments occur within the context of social policies that already exist. Policy change does not stop for the three or four years of an experiment, which sometimes contaminates results or makes interpretation challenging.[38] Government-led experiments are vulnerable to political change, which can undermine or even cancel experiments midstream.[39] Systematic reviews invariably note that the quality of many of the studies that have been conducted is variable and that it is difficult to compare outcomes.[40]

Yet, there is much to learn from well-conducted basic income experiments. In a high-income country such as Canada, any basic income that is implemented must inevitably coexist with a broad range of publicly provided services. These services, which include everything from subsidized housing to public transportation to health care, are necessary and will continue to exist even if a basic income is in place. Most, but not all, public services operate at the level of provinces or municipalities, whereas a basic income might very well be a federal undertaking. The tension between levels of government will complicate the friction between service delivery and basic income. Will a basic income reduce recipients' access to rent subsidies or subsidized transit passes? How can these programs work together? A well-designed basic income experiment can explore the interaction between public services and basic income. It can, in fact, go much further: are there services that do not currently exist that would enhance the positive outcomes of a basic income? Much has been made of the fact that approximately 10 per cent to 12 per cent of Canadians do not file income tax returns, and these non-filers are disproportionately low-income, Indigenous, and racialized people.[41] That claim is based on data from 2016, just as the much-enhanced CCB was being introduced, and one might expect many of the previous non-filers to file now that such a large benefit is delivered through the income tax system. Several programs have been introduced across the country to increase the rate of tax filing among those with low income. One of the challenges that should be investigated in Canada is what kinds of financial education and financial access programs would most benefit those receiving a basic income and how they should be designed to meet the needs of recipients. Similarly, are there existing services that might be redesigned or eliminated altogether? Investigating service use by participants in an experimental setting through the collection of good qualitative and quantitative evidence can help to identify service gaps and design flaws.

Are there factors that either enhance or act as barriers to necessary cooperation between levels of government? These results are not necessarily generalizable between times and places, but in some ways designing the experiment generates as much or even more knowledge than analyzing its outcomes. As provinces redesign income supports in the wake of the COVID-19 pandemic, some are seeking partnerships with the federal government that would allow them to explore the feasibility of offering a basic income. Prince Edward Island has indicated an interest in doing so,[42] as has Nunavut. Province-wide trials, such as the one called for in Prince Edward Island, present opportunities to examine the interaction between federal and provincial programs, to identify gaps and overlaps, and to rethink how the various levels of government can work together to ensure coordinated delivery.

The quality of the evidence provided by experiments depends on many factors, one of which is the size of the sample. Most basic income experiments conducted to date have focused on relatively diverse populations, but some of the most pressing questions about basic income relate to very specific subgroups of the population. Are there specific groups of residents whose needs would not be met by a basic income? What are their particular needs, and what is the appropriate level of support? The federal government has indicated an interest in designing a basic income for people with long-term disabilities, and it is actively engaging with people who are experiencing disability and have engaged with existing support systems. Several provinces are reexamining provincial income support for people with disabilities. One of the obvious questions is what level of support is appropriate and which levels of government should be involved in delivery, but there are other issues associated with the interaction of existing programs and the ways that support services might be made available with a basic income.

Critics of basic income have asked whether there are people who would be harmed by unconditional income.[43] Focused experiments are surely one way to gather evidence.[44]

If COVID-19 forced everyone to recognize how the impact of both the infection and the public health measures put in place to address it varied by socioeconomic status, it also made us all very aware of the limitations of the social safety net. This is the time to reflect seriously on what everyone needs to survive and have the opportunity to thrive in this very fortunate society we share.

NOTES

1 See pp. xi and viii of Canada, Parliament, Senate, Special Committee on Poverty. (1971). *Poverty in Canada: report of the Special Senate Committee on Poverty* (D. Croll, Chair). Information Canada.
2 Canada, Privy Council Office. (1985). *Royal Commission on the Economic Union and Development Prospects for Canada* (Vol. 1, D.S. MacDonald, Chair). https://publications.gc.ca/site/eng/472251/publication.html.
3 Canada, Standing Committee on Social Affairs, Science and Technology, Subcommittee on Cities (2009, December). *From the margins: A call to action on poverty, housing and homelessness.* https://sencanada.ca/content/sen/Committee/402/citi/rep/rep02dec09-e.pdf.
4 National Inquiry into Missing and Murdered Indigenous Women and Girls. (2019). *Reclaiming power and place: The final report of the National Inquiry into Missing and Murdered Indigenous Women and Girls.* https://www.mmiwg-ffada.ca/final-report/.
5 UBI Works. (2020, April 21). *50 Canadian senators call for a minimum basic income* [Press release]. https://www.ubiworks.ca/post/50senators.
6 See Kangas, O., Jauhaiainen, S., Simanainen, M., & Ylikäbbö, N. (2021). *Experimenting with unconditional basic income: Lessons from the Finnish BI experiment 2017–2018.* Edward Elgar; and Verlaat, T., de Kruijk, M., Rosenkranz, S., Groot, L., & Sanders, M. (2020). *Onderzoek: Weten wat werkt: samen werken aan een betere bijstand* [Study: Knowing what works: Working together on better assistance]. Utrecht University. An English-language summary of Verlaat et al. is available at https://www.uu.nl/en/publication/final-report-what-works-weten-wat-werkt.
7 Many of these programs have taken place. Some were permanent, such as Bolsa Familia in Brazil, and others were temporary experiments. Some are conditional cash transfers, such as Bolsa Familia; some are trials that combine conditional and unconditional cash transfers, such as an experiment in Malawi; and others are unconditional cash transfers. Several systematic reviews have been conducted, and the best to begin with are these two: Pega, F., Liu, S.Y., Walter, S., Pabayo, R., Saith, R., & Lhachimi, S.K. (2017). Unconditional cash transfers for reducing poverty and vulnerabilities: Effect on use of health services and health outcomes in low- and middle-income countries. *Cochrane Database of Systematic Reviews, 3.* https://doi.org/10.1002/14651858.CD011135.pub3; Pinto, A.D., Perri, M., Pedersen, C.L., Aratangy, T., Hapsari, A.P., & Hwang, S.W. (2021). Exploring different methods to

evaluate the impact of basic income interventions: A systematic review. *International Journal for Equity in Health*, 20(1), Article 142. https://doi.org/10.1186/s12939-021-01479-2.

8 Many of these letters of support have been posted by the Basic Income Canada Network (https://basicincomecanada.org/), the Basic Income Canada Youth Network (https://www.basicincomeyouth.ca/), and the Ontario Basic Income Network (https://www.obin.ca/).

9 Office of the Parliamentary Budget Officer. (2021). *Distributional and fiscal analysis of a national guaranteed basic income.* https://distribution-a617274656661637473.pbo-dpb.ca/71f12c2a896208681dcd59ff69f19e1a6c024d00a60c2e2c195f56293f8fff1c.

10 See Executive Summary, p. 6, in Green, D.A., Kesselman, J.R., & Tedds, L.M. (2020). *Covering all the basics: Reforms for a more just society* (Final Report of the Expert Panel on Basic Income). https://bcbasicincomepanel.ca/wp-content/uploads/2021/01/Final_Report_BC_Basic_Income_Panel.pdf.

11 Ibid., Executive Summary, p. 4.

12 See, for example, this article by Senator Yen Pau Woo: Woo, Y.P. (2021, July 10). *The basic income study that wasn't.* Georgia Straight. https://www.straight.com/news/yuen-pau-woo-basic-income-study-that-wasnt.

13 Forget, E.L. (2011). The town with no poverty: The health effects of a Canadian guaranteed annual income field experiment. *Canadian Public Policy/Analyse de politique*, 37(3), 283–305. https://doi.org/10.3138/cpp.37.3.283.

14 Calnitsky, D., and Gonalons-Pons, P. (2020). The impact of an experimental guaranteed income on crime and violence. *Social Problems*, 68(3), 78–98. https://doi.org/10.1093/socpro/spaa001.

15 Fisher, K. (Director). (2018). *The Manitoba story: A basic income film* [Film]. Truth Be Told Production.

16 Hum, D., & Simpson W. (1991). *Income maintenance, work effort, and the Canadian mincome experiment.* Economic Council of Canada.

17 Ferdosi, M., McDowell, T., Lewchuk, W., & Ross, S. (2020). *Southern Ontario's basic income experience.* Hamilton Roundtable for Poverty Reduction, McMaster University, & Hamilton Community Foundation. https://labourstudies.socsci.mcmaster.ca/documents/southern-ontarios-basic-income-experience.pdf.

18 Benns, R. (2019, May). Food bank use soars after cancellation of basic income; donations needed. *Lindsay Advocate.* https://lindsayadvocate.ca/food-bank-use-swells-after-cancellation-of-basic-income-donations-needed/.

19 See pp. 187ff. of Kangas, O., Jauhianen, S., Simanainen, M., & Ylikännö, M. (2020). *Suomen perustulokokeilun arviointi. Sosiaali-ja terveysministeriö* [Evaluation of Finland's basic income experiment. Social and Health Ministry. https://julkaisut.valtioneuvosto.fi/bitstream/handle/10024/162219/STM_2020_15_rap.pdf?sequence=1&isAllowed=y; and Kangas et al. (2021).

20 Verlaat et al. (2020).

21 See Haushofer, J., & Shapiro, J. (2016). The short-term impact of unconditional cash transfers to the poor: Experimental evidence from Kenya. *Quarterly Journal of Economics*, 131(4), 1973–2042; Pega et al. (2017); Akresh, R., De Walque, D., & Kazianga, H. (2016). *Evidence from a randomized evaluation of the household welfare impacts of conditional and unconditional cash transfers given to mothers or fathers* (World Bank Policy Research Working Paper 7730). World Bank Group; Davala, S., Jhabvala, R., Standing, G., & Kapoor Mehta, S. (2015). *Basic income: A transformative policy for India.* Bloomsbury Academic; and Woolard, I., & Leibbrandt, M. (2010). *The evolution and impact of unconditional cash transfers in South Africa* (Southern Africa Labour and Development Research Unit Working Paper No. 51). SALDRU, University of Cape

Town. https://www.opensaldru.uct.ac.za/bitstream/handle/11090/66/2010_51
.pdf?sequence=1.

22 See Pinto et al. (2021); and Standing, G. (2017, January 17–20). *An insight, an idea with Guy Standing* [Speech audio recording]. World Economic Forum Annual Meeting, Davos-Klosters, Switzerland. https://www.weforum.org/events/worldeconomic
-forum-annual-meeting-2017/sessions/an-insight-an-idea-with-guy-standing.

23 Baird, S., Garfein, R., McIntosh, C., & Ozler, B. (2012). Effect of a cash transfer programme for schooling on prevalence of HIV and herpes simplex type 2 in Malawi: A cluster randomised trial. *Lancet, 379*(9823), 1320–9. https://doi.org
/10.1016/S0140-6736(11)61709-1.

24 See McIntyre, L., Kwok, C., Emery, J.H., & Dutton, D.J. (2016a). Impact of a guaranteed annual income program on Canadian seniors' physical, mental and functional health. *Canadian Journal of Public Health, 107*(2), e176–82. https://doi
.org/10.17269/cjph.107.5372; and McIntyre, L., Dutton, D.J., Kwok, C., & Emery, H.J. (2016b). Reduction of food insecurity among low-income Canadian seniors as a likely impact of a guaranteed annual income. *Canadian Public Policy/Analyse de politique, 42*(3), 274–86. https://doi.org/10.3138/cpp.2015-069.

25 Koebel, K., & Schirle, T. (2016). The differential impact of universal child benefits on the labour supply of married and single mothers. *Canadian Public Policy/Analyse de politique, 42*(1), 49–64. https://doi.org/10.3138/cpp.2015-049.

26 Forget, E.L. (2020). *Basic income for Canadians: From the COVID-19 emergency to financial security for all*. Lorimer.

27 Handler, J.F. (1973). *The coercive social worker: British lessons for American social services*. Rand McNally.

28 See pp. 1–26 of Martinez-Vazquez, J., & Winer, S.L. (Eds.). (2014). *Coercion, welfare, and the study of public finance*. Cambridge University Press; and Zwolinski, M. (2015). Property rights, coercion, and the welfare state: The libertarian case for a basic income for all. *Independent Review, 19*(4), 515–29.

29 See Han, J. (2021). The impact of SNAP work requirements on labor supply. *Labour Economics, 74*, Article 102089. https://doi.org/10.1016/j.labeco.2021.102089; and David, H., & Houseman, S.N. (2010). Do temporary-help jobs improve labor market outcomes for low-skilled workers? Evidence from "Work First." *American Economic Journal: Applied Economics, 2*(3), 96–128.

30 See Forget, E., & Owczar, H. (2021). *Radical trust: Basic income for complicated lives*. ARP Books; and National Inquiry into Missing and Murdered Indigenous Women and Girls. (2019).

31 Berggold, C., Verjee, Z., Windatt, C. (2020, July 16). *A public letter from the arts community for a basic income guarantee*. https://www.obin.ca/a_public_letter_from
_the_arts_community_for_a_basic_income_guarantee

32 Stanfors, M., Jacobs, J.C., & Neilson, J. (2019). Caregiving time costs and trade-offs: Gender differences in Sweden, the UK, and Canada. *SSM – Population Health, 9*, Article 100501. https://doi.org/10.1016/j.ssmph.2019.100501

33 See Alphonso, G.M. (2021). Political-economic roots of coercion: Slavery, neoliberalism, and the racial family policy logic of child and social welfare. *Columbia Journal of Race and Law, 11*(3), 471–500; and Pelton, L.H. (2016). Separating coercion from provision in child welfare. *Child Abuse & Neglect, 51*, 427–34. https://doi.org/10.1016/j.chiabu
.2015.08.007.

34 Forget (2020).

35 Forget & Owczar (2021).

36 Widerquist, K. (2018). *A critical analysis of basic income experiments for researchers, policymakers, and citizens*. Springer International.

37 Green et al. (2020).

38 Kangas et al. (2021).

39 See Forget (2011) and Ferdosi et al. (2020).

40 See Pega et al. (2017) and Pinto et al. (2021).

41 Robson, J., & Schwartz, S. (2020). Who doesn't file a tax return? A portrait of non-filers. *Canadian Public Policy/Analyse de politiques*, *43*(3), 323–39. https://doi.org/10.3138/cpp.2019-063.

42 *Special Committee on Poverty in PEI* (Final Report). (2020, November 27). Charlottetown. https://docs.assembly.pe.ca/download/dms?objectId=ebb58bb4-b7db-43b9-9c69-fa59f27aac51&fileName=FINAL%20REPORT%20-%20Special%20Committee%20on%20Poverty%20in%20PEI%20-%20November%2027,%202020.pdf.

43 Broadbent Institute. (2020, May 14). *Lift the floor: Would a UBI guarantee a good life for all Canadians?* [Video]. https://www.broadbentinstitute.ca/would_a_universal_basic_income_guarantee_a_good_life_for_all_canadians.

44 Dwyer, R.J., Palepu, A., Williams, C., & Zhao, J. (2021). *Unconditional cash transfers reduce homelessness*. PsyArXiv. https://doi.org/10.31234/osf.io/ukngr.

PART TWO

Behavioral Science in Design and Delivery

CHAPTER SIX

The Effect of Design Features on the Effectiveness of Cash Transfer Programs: A Behavioral Perspective

*Daniella Turetski, Xiao (Mimosa) Zhao, Oceana Ding,
Waleed Hussain, Sherry Ning, and Dilip Soman*

INTRODUCTION

Despite decades of economic prosperity and well-being, poverty is still a major problem in many parts of the world. Estimates suggest that more than 700 million people live with less than US$2 per day,[1] and (even in developed nations) poverty rates range from 5 per cent to 26 per cent.[2] The COVID-19 pandemic has further increased poverty and worsened economic hardship. Several academics and policy commentators have called for governments to use poverty alleviation programs such as basic income or cash transfers.[3] Although these programs have been widely prevalent, our purpose is to develop a behaviorally informed approach to studying the design features of these programs and a better understanding of how to optimize their impact.

The most common poverty alleviation program is a cash transfer program. A typical cash transfer program (of which basic income is a special case) consists of a cash payment disbursed by a government or non-governmental organization to eligible recipients. The payment is supplementary income designed to alleviate poverty, spur economic activities, or improve specific social outcomes,[4] such as education, health, safe drinking water, food security, or even entre-preneurial activity.[5] Much of the research on such programs has focused on (1) needs analysis (identifying and encouraging social outcomes), (2) their cost–benefit evaluation, and (3) program evalu-ations. In particular, research in development economics treats cash transfer programs as a "black box" and studies the effects of aggre-gate factors (e.g., program costs, number of participants, program length, total reach) on their overall effectiveness and impact. How-ever, treating complex programs as a single entity with an aggre-gate outcome measure does not allow for a nuanced understanding of their behavioral effects (e.g., participation in health check-ups, school attendance) on beneficiaries.[6]

Much of the policy thinking on poverty alleviation treats pov-erty purely as a financial construct, loosely defined as the absence of financial resources. However, behavioral research on the psy-chological effects of scarcity suggests that poverty is not simply a financial construct but rather a cognitive one. In particular, pov-erty imposes significant cognitive constraints that impair decision making.[7] Sludge, or frictions that can cause cognitive, psychologi-cal, or information barriers to engage with products and services,[8] could prevent people from consuming services to which they are entitled.[9] Simply put, poor people might not accept cash transfers, not because they are unaware of them or because they believe that the dollar amounts are too little, but because (among other reasons) they might not have the bandwidth to process all the complex infor-mation about the program, they are deterred by the administrative hurdles that they have to jump through to receive the cash transfer, or they are embarrassed or feel socially stigmatized about receiving such payments.

To obtain a more complete understanding of the effectiveness of poverty alleviation programs, these behavioral elements must there-fore be incorporated into research. This approach is in its infancy. The incidence of poverty and calls to use cash transfer programs to sup-port citizens have grown over the past years, but there is still very little research providing a nuanced understanding of how such pro-grams should be designed, keeping beneficiaries' behaviors in mind.

In this chapter, we build on prior work on cash transfer programs and the behavioral sciences in the following two ways. First, following the delivery system proposed by the World Bank,[10] instead of treating a program as one entity, we break it into four distinct phases, each with an outcome measure. These phases are (1) access (making prospects aware of the program), (2) enrollment (assessing eligibility and formally enrolling recipients), (3) provision (the actual transfer of cash and any other associated services), and (4) management (maintaining the program, checking for compliance, and monitoring outcomes). One way of measuring the aggregate effects of these four phases is conversion – how well recipients can convert assistance into outcomes. Second, we identify five design features that may affect behaviors and hence program effectiveness (see also Chapter 6 for an empirical review of cash transfer programs). These features are (1) the conditionality of the program (whether the receipt of cash is conditional on the recipient performing certain actions),[11] (2) its scope (whether the program is designed to have specific goals, e.g., education, health, schooling, or a general goal, e.g., a basic income program at its extreme),[12] (3) the provision of additional services (whether the program offers additional non-mandatory services to support recipients, e.g., coaching), (4) the payment mode (whether payments are made in a lump sum or are recurring), and (5) the payment method (whether payments are made via check or electronic transfer and how visible the disbursements are). All of these factors have been studied separately in the context of behavioral economics as having effects on individual behaviors. Through a literature review and a series of in-depth exploratory interviews, our goal is to develop a series of propositions on the effect of each of the five design features on the four program phases.

The rest of this chapter is organized in four parts. First, we provide a brief overview of relevant literature in the cash transfer and behavioral science areas. Second, we present a framework and discuss our approach to the interviews. Third, we discuss our findings and present propositions. Fourth, we conclude with a discussion and the implications of our results.

CONVERTING THE CASH TRANSFER PROGRAM BLACK BOX INTO A GLASS BOX

Policy makers and practitioners tend to view welfare programs as a single entity. In particular, they may ask questions about whether such programs work, and they might have a tendency to measure the efficacy of programs at the aggregate level. Such a black-box approach has its obvious limitations. If instead we had a glass-box view of programs in which we could identify specific pathways by which these programs work and associated outcomes, we would be able to develop a nuanced understanding of not just whether programs work, but why and at what stages are they particularly efficacious. A World Bank sourcebook identifies four stages in the delivery chain of social assistance programs (see Table 6.1).[13] Rather than thinking about the efficacy of programs overall, we can now study the effects of design features on each of these four stages.

Why might the design features we identified earlier influence programs' efficacy? Literature in the areas of behavioral science and cash transfer programs provides initial insights into the role of design features in influencing the delivery, implementation, and outcomes of cash transfers.

Scope

How do recipients of cash transfers decide what to spend the money on? Programs that have well-defined behavioral goals can provide suggestions to recipients on what to spend the cash. Research on mental accounting suggests that labeling a cash transfer as, say, education money increases the likelihood that it will be spent on education.[14] In contrast, programs with a broader scope can offer flexibility in mental accounting, which allows for greater discretion and increases the program's overall attractiveness.[15] This added flexibility, however, may have opposite effects – it could afford the benefit of allowing the recipient to spend on their greatest needs, but it may also increase decision difficulty.

Table 6.1. Delivery chain of social assistance programs

Delivery chain	Description
Access	Outreach
	Intake and registration
	Assessment of needs and conditions
Enroll	Eligibility and enrollment decisions
	Determination of benefits and service package
	Notification and onboarding
Provide	Provision of benefits, services, or both
Manage	Beneficiaries' compliance, updating, and grievances
	Exit decisions, notifications, and case outcomes

Additional Services

Prior studies have shown that support services (such as coaching) increase confidence and promote more efficient decision making.[16] They have also shown that coupling cash transfers with supervision and training,[17] technical assistance,[18] additional grants,[19] or insurance[20] positively affects beneficiaries by allowing them to spend money in an efficient manner. These non-mandatory services are complementary to the cash transfer and should not impede beneficiaries' qualifications to receive support from other social assistance programs.

Conditionality

Cash transfer programs can range from being completely unconditional to being conditional through varying levels of surveillance and enforcement mechanisms. Research on the psychology of poverty indicates that chronic poverty causes stress, creates high cognitive loads, and consumes scarce mental resources.[21] As such, conditional cash transfers might impose costly distractions on people who are trying to do the best thing for their families under situations of severe scarcity.[22] In that sense, unconditional cash transfers foster competency and autonomy and show trust in beneficiaries' behaviors and financial decisions.[23] Although trust and reduced anticipated sludge increase willingness to participate from the beneficiary's perspective, it is worth noting that conditions allow for better monitoring, delivery, and confidence for program managers.[24]

Payment Mode

Mental accounting research has shown that the way in which payments are structured (e.g., transfer frequency) has the potential to increase engagement and improve prudent spending.[25] Frequent regular payments allow for better matching and facilitate consumption smoothing, whereas one-time payments might result in rags-to-riches spending patterns.[26] The timing of payments particularly matters in situations in which there is seasonality in income but consumption and expenditure streams are uniform over time. Seasonal liquidity constraints in agricultural households not only undermine those households' ability to smooth consumption over the cropping cycle but have been shown to have other effects. In particular, liquidity-constrained farmers sell family labor off-farm to meet short-run cash needs.[27] Therefore, in making cash transfers, a transfer schedule that allows recipients to match income to expenses might result in better outcomes. Recent research (and resulting products) from the private sector also show that the timing of payment matters significantly for the financial well-being of recipients.[28]

   In particular, in the Fink et al. study,[29] a large agricultural firm in Malawi allowed its employees to receive their wages at a later date as a deferred lump sum. Given that agriculture wages are usually highly seasonal, this allowed employees to smooth wages over time such that they matched expenses. Results showed that after two years of the intervention, treated workers were more likely to have made permanent improvements to their homes and were generally in a better financial position. In a similar vein, the growth of a new class of products called on-demand wage platforms and apps allows workers to withdraw wages that are already due to them before their formal payday and thereby reduces lumpiness in wages and better matching of expenses with wages.[30]

Payment Method

A review of the literature on payment method (i.e., visibility) shows that electronic payment methods can reduce the time spent on and cost of collecting the transfer,[31] which could increase the time available to engage in more productive activities (e.g., employment,

Table 6.2. Design features and their levels

Design feature	Low level	High level
Scope	CTP with a single goal (e.g., housing, or children's education)	CTP with multiple goals (e.g., health and education of children) or higher-level goals (e.g., overall poverty alleviation).
Additional services	CTP with a cash transfer only and no services	CTP with a cash transfer accompanied by additional services
Conditionality	CTP has a relatively tightly specified set of conditions	CTP is completely unconditional
Payment mode	CTP offers a one-time lump sum payment (e.g., US$1,200 for a one-year program)	CTP offers recurring payments (e.g., US$100/month for each of 12 months)
Payment method	CTP payouts are done in a visible manner (e.g., cash or checks disbursed at bank branches, food stamps)	CTP payouts are done invisibly (e.g., via direct deposit to bank account)

Note: CTP = cash transfer program.

cultivation). Moreover, electronic transfers may address key logistical challenges in implementing cash transfer programs in developing countries, especially those with limited road and financial infrastructure.[32] For beneficiaries, visible payments (e.g., publicly queueing at payment stations) may cause stigma and shame, whereas invisible payments reduce such embarrassment.[33] The use of different payment methods (e.g., prepaid card vs. cash) can also influence spending decisions. Cash and check payments lead consumers to better remember the expense, resulting in a temporary reluctance to spend more. Payments by card, however, are less memorable and may therefore result in a greater likelihood of spending more.[34]

CONCEPTUAL DEVELOPMENT: A FRAMEWORK

To be able to improve the effectiveness of cash transfer programs through better program design and delivery, we are interested in understanding how changing design features may affect behaviors and, subsequently, program outcomes. Table 6.2 defines the levels of each of the five design features, and Table 6.3 captures the basic structure of our conceptual framework.

Table 6.3. Impact of design features on delivery stages

	Delivery stage			
Design feature	Access	Enroll	Provide	Manage
Scope				
Additional services				
Conditionality				
Payment mode				
Payment method				

METHODOLOGY

To develop testable propositions, we conducted a series of 12 semi-structured interviews with 16 academics and practitioners for an average of 30 minutes each. Two of the interviews involved multiple experts. Experts were instructed to answer several preset open-ended questions in our interview guide, which was sent to them before the interview. We started each interview by explaining the conceptual framework and ensuring that the experts understood the four-stage delivery chain and five design features. After confirming their understanding, we asked them to identify which design features would have the most meaningful effects on a delivery stage, followed by further predictions of how other design features could affect each of the delivery stages. Probing questions were used to encourage responses providing practical examples, academic references, and additional interaction effects between design features. We closed the interviews with final questions seeking the experts' general comments on the design and implementation of cash transfer programs. We then conducted thematic analyses based on the interview transcripts and compiled the interview findings into a matrix similar to the one presented in Table 6.3.

All the interviewees were expert academics or experienced practitioners. They came from different regions, including North America, the United Kingdom, the Middle East, and Africa. Approximately half were academic researchers or professors with a background in behavioral science and economics. The other half were practitioners from organizations such as the World Bank, ideas42, Busara Center, and Nudge Lebanon who had extensive experience in applying

Table 6.4. Interview findings on the effects of design features on delivery stage

Design feature	Delivery stage			
	Access	Enroll	Provide	Manage
Scope	Scope has a positive effect on access.	No consensus among experts	No prediction	No consensus among experts
Additional services	The presence of additional services affects access.	The presence of additional services has a positive impact on enrollment.	No consensus among experts	The presence of additional services has a positive impact on management.
Conditionality	Conditionality has a negative impact on access.	Conditionality has a negative impact on enrollment.	No consensus among experts	No consensus among experts
Payment mode	Impact is a function of multiple moderators.	Impact is a function of multiple moderators.	No consensus among experts	No prediction
Payment method	Impact is a function of multiple moderators.	No consensus among experts	No consensus among experts	No prediction

behavioral insights in designing cash transfer programs and solving policy challenges. Presented in Table 6.4, the interview findings contribute to a better understanding of the substantive context of cash transfer programs and beneficiaries' perception and experiences. In the next sections, we explicitly discuss the findings in each row from the beneficiaries' perspective.

EFFECTS OF SCOPE

Overview

Scope refers to whether a program is designed to have specific goals (e.g., education, health, food security) or a general goal (e.g., universal basic income [UBI]). For program administrators and field staff, specific cash transfer programs with a narrow scope are easier to manage, whereas general programs require more resources and coordination among multiple stakeholders. For beneficiaries, specific programs deliver transfers to a more targeted population, whereas general programs provide broader access to prospective beneficiaries. Our hypothesis is that specific programs have positive effects on conversion for high-scarcity beneficiaries (i.e., people struggling with severe lack of key resources). We also predict that general programs have positive effects on conversion for low-scarcity beneficiaries (i.e., people experiencing mild levels of resource scarcity) and positive effects on all beneficiaries for access and enrollment.

Findings

Policy decisions regarding program scope often discuss the trade-off between inclusion and exclusion. Depending on the context, either a specific or a general program may be optimal. Interview findings indicate that general cash transfer programs with a broad scope promote inclusivity, whereas specific programs encourage behavioral change and outcomes associated with targeted goals.

General programs are more likely to increase public awareness because the program mandate identifies multiple goals that may be attractive to a broader population. Given that specific cash transfer programs are more targeted, they may restrict access.

The experts had different views on the impact of program scope on the enrollment stage. One perspective is that general programs may increase participation because multiple goals will attract different groups. In an extreme case, a UBI program provides a fixed amount of cash to everyone, regardless of income level. In that sense, everyone is auto-enrolled for UBI. However, there is the paradox-of-choice (i.e., more is less) argument. Multiple goals tend to increase the perceived complexity of the programs, which may have a negative impact on enrollment. For example, the complexity involved in understanding multiple goals may demotivate prospective beneficiaries from enrolling. Another benefit of specific programs (as opposed to general programs) is that they promote self-selection and informed decision making: prospective beneficiaries can self-select or self-unselect depending on whether there is a fit between program goals and their personal interests or needs.

Specific programs provide targeted transfers aligned with predetermined goals. So, there is clear evidence that specific goals contribute to more targeted behavioral change. For example, if a program is specifically designed to improve child nutritional status, one would expect to see improvements in nutrition intake and dietary diversity compared with other health behaviors that the program was not designed to address. Moreover, a single goal is more straightforward and specific for beneficiaries with limited cognitive bandwidth. When the program has only one specific goal, it is easier for beneficiaries to complete the program and feel satisfaction from accomplishing the goal. For a similar reason, general programs with multiple goals may have a negative impact on behavioral change and outcomes because of their perceived complexity. Experts have emphasized the importance of effective program communication (e.g., program brochure, messaging) as a solution to clarify confusion and prompt expected behaviors, especially when a general program entails multiple, complex goals.

EFFECTS OF ADDITIONAL SERVICES

Overview

Provision of additional services refers to offering additional non-mandatory services to support beneficiaries (e.g., coaching or training, financial literacy, skills development). Such services are complementary interventions provided alongside the standard cash transfer. For program administrators and field staff, the provision of additional services requires more resource allocation and program planning. Beneficiaries are provided with both financial and non-financial support. Our hypothesis is that the presence of additional support services has a positive impact on enrollment and conversion, whereas it may make program provision and management more difficult.

Findings

Recognizing that cash transfers alone are not the silver bullet, international best practice has been to complement cash payments with other support services, including educational sessions, nutritional supplements, workshops, and so forth.[35] Interview findings indicated that, in general, the presence of additional services can increase attraction and keep beneficiaries more engaged with cash transfer programs.

Additional services can be used as a selling point to attract beneficiaries. However, this extra support would only have a positive impact on the access stage if the support is appealing to the beneficiaries.

In general, the provision of additional services has a positive impact on the enrollment stage. If a larger variety of additional services is offered, the program may attract a broader audience. As well, it is important to note that these optional additional services are offered to beneficiaries for free. Given that people are biased toward free offerings and may change their behavioral patterns when something free comes along,[36] the complimentary services can attract individuals and boost enrollment. Furthermore, given the non-mandatory nature of additional services, beneficiaries may feel trusted because they have the freedom to select services that are most helpful to them rather than being required to participate in mandatory sessions. Nevertheless, the willingness to enroll depends on how personally valuable beneficiaries perceive the services to be.

Most experts agreed that the presence of additional services has positive effects on the provision stage. One common problem in programs is that beneficiaries usually spend their transfer on the most salient uses or short-term issues rather than on longer-term goals (e.g., education). The provision of additional services may help beneficiaries allocate and budget their transfer in a more optimal way. Coupled with cash transfers, additional services provide a solution to the cognitive overload that sometimes prevents them from making the best use of their transfer. For example, coaching services can help individuals make better decisions on how to spend money, and Short Message Service (text) reminders can help people reduce procrastination and stick to desired behaviors (especially in the case of conditional cash transfers). It is important from a management perspective to ensure that the associated costs do not outweigh the marginal benefit arising from additional support. For example, one-on-one coaching is effective but comes at a high cost, whereas text reminders are a low-cost option but may not change behaviors. Offering additional services can also improve beneficiary engagement. For example, beneficiaries may stay more engaged with the program when participating in training sessions, communicating with service providers, and taking up vocational courses. However, one expert expressed the concern that beneficiaries may need to invest more time in the program when additional support is provided, even though the support is non-mandatory. Such time commitments may reduce time spent on other labor or leisure activities that are even more important for achieving the program's goal.

The positive impact on beneficiaries is expected to be stronger when cash transfers are provided in combination with additional services. Such services can provide useful guidance to beneficiaries. For example, educational sessions can make parents feel more capable when allocating resources to send kids to school, financial planning can help beneficiaries improve business outcomes, and flyers or messages can communicate social norms to modify beliefs and influence behaviors. Similarly, prior studies have highlighted the positive effects on educational and health outcomes and on livelihood and productivity.[37] As a note of caution, the positive effects can reverse if the additional services are perceived as mandatory (even though by definition they are not).

EFFECTS OF CONDITIONALITY

Overview

Conditionality refers to whether the receipt of cash is conditional on beneficiaries performing certain actions. For program administrators and field staff, conditional programs involve monitoring and enforcement arrangements, which may allow for easier tracking of

case outcomes. For beneficiaries, conditions are behavioral requirements they must fulfill to receive cash payments. Our hypothesis is
that unconditional programs have positive effects on access, enrollment, and conversion (potentially moderated by scarcity), whereas
conditional programs have positive effects on delivery and management from the program operation perspective.

Findings

Much of the discussion has focused on comparing conditional and
unconditional cash transfer programs in terms of program effectiveness and social outcomes. A study by the World Bank indicated that
conditional programs outperform unconditional programs on inter-
mediate participation indicators (e.g., school enrollment or visits
to health centers) and health and education outcomes.[38] However,
arguments against conditional programs point out that beneficiaries
should have the autonomy to decide how to spend their aid money
instead of relying on aid organizations and donors thousands of
miles away, who may not understand their specific and unique
needs, to choose for them.[39] From interview findings, experts agreed
that conditions can negatively affect access and enrollment stages,
but they diverged in their predictions on the impact of conditions on
provision and management stages.

All experts agreed that conditions have a negative impact on the
access stage. Conditional cash transfer programs have a narrower
reach than unconditional programs because conditions may make
potential beneficiaries perceive the program as difficult to accomplish. Such psychological barriers appear to stem from (1) perceived
difficulty of the conditions, (2) poor or unclear communication of
the conditions, and (3) predicted inability to follow through with
conditions. All of these contribute to barriers to public outreach in
comparison with unconditional cash transfer programs, which may
appear more straightforward.

The aforementioned negative perceptions may spill over and
further affect the enrollment stage. Conditions, particularly hard
conditions, deter potential beneficiaries from joining a cash transfer
program, even if they need it and would highly benefit from the

program's offerings. In most cases, potential beneficiaries are faced with resource scarcity, so adding conditions would only further exhaust their already limited cognitive bandwidth and discourage them from enrollment. For example, on top of their original plan for how to spend the money, conditionality adds other requirements for them to consider – a consideration without which they will not be eligible to enroll. Inclusion is a major concern because whenever there are rules that limit individuals, fewer will be interested and fewer will be qualified. This is exacerbated if potential beneficiaries think that the effort or cost of fulfilling the conditions outweighs the benefits they would receive. Prior studies have noted that conditional cash transfer programs may exclude the most vulnerable and poverty-stricken populations. For example, for some households living in remote communities the level of transfer may not be sufficient to compensate for the transportation costs of attending schools or visiting clinics as required by the program's specific conditions.[40]

In conditional cash transfer programs, non-compliers do not receive their transfer, thereby limiting the program's reach and lessening the level of impact it could have. Conditions also convey distrust because they may imply that programs do not trust the beneficiaries to use the money properly unless they accomplish certain behavioral requirements. One of the experts emphasized that unconditional programs communicate trust, which gives beneficiaries a certain psychological power in addition to the provision of financial support.

There are, however, also notable circumstances in which conditionality has a positive impact on the provision stage. Conditions may help beneficiaries mentally account for the use and goal of their transfer and can assist in locking in the money for this specific use. One expert also mentioned that if the transfer is conditional, beneficiaries are not under social pressure to lend money to families or neighbors from the same community because others will better understand why they get the money and on what they are expected to spend the money. If transfers are unconditional, however, the money may be viewed as an amount that can be spent in a broader number of contexts. Furthermore, conditionality may serve as a commitment device and help beneficiaries stick to longer-term goals (e.g., education) rather than spending the money on other salient or tempting purposes. Behavioral economics research has shown that people have fallen victim to the tendency to value immediate rewards disproportionately more than future benefits.[41]

Management is the last stage for which individual compliance and case outcomes are considered. For any conditional cash transfers, the response to noncompliance is punitive, where, in the worst-case scenario, beneficiaries who do not comply with the behavioral requirements are faced with immediate suspension of the cash transfer. This may blunt the program outcome and work against the objectives of welfare programs. Interview findings also show that any additional hoops or barriers that beneficiaries must jump through will ultimately limit the program's impact, especially when conditions make beneficiaries feel as though they are not trusted. If there are mandatory conditions, it is recommended that they be soft conditions such as nudges that encourage parents to invest in human capital development through financial planning and buying educational materials rather than hard conditions that enforce strict attendance for kids going to school.

Conditions may, however, have positive effects on the management stage because they can largely encourage expected behaviors from beneficiaries and effectively promote positive behavioral change. This finding is consistent with the evidence from the literature that making transfers conditional on certain behaviors or actions (e.g., health visits) can positively affect the outcomes related to the conditions on which the transfers are conditioned.[42]

EFFECTS OF PAYMENT MODE

Overview

Payment mode refers to whether payments are made in a lump sum or are recurring. For program administrators and field staff, recurring payments may cause more logistical challenges. For beneficiaries, recurring payments may provide gratification on a regular basis. However, the attraction of lump sum payments is that beneficiaries can withdraw the entire transfer at one time. Our hypothesis is that lump sum (vs. recurring) payments will have positive effects on conversion for high-scarcity beneficiaries, but less so for low-scarcity beneficiaries.

Findings

Payment mode determines transfer frequency, which essentially dictates the timing of transfers. According to our experts, when considering the impact of payment mode on the delivery chain, it is important to account for mediating factors that may change the direction and size of effects.

In the access stage, lump sum payments seem to be appealing because people tend to be motivated by absolute amounts. Clear communication about payment mode (e.g., size and frequency of transfer) is important because it influences beneficiaries' expectations and accommodates different interests. For example, beneficiaries with a plan to invest or save may prefer a lump sum payment, and beneficiaries with dependents may favor predictable monthly payments.

The effect of payment mode (i.e., frequency) on enrollment changes with the complexity of receiving the transfer. For example, beneficiaries who do not have access to banking services cannot enroll in a program if an account is required to receive the payment, and beneficiaries who may not yet trust newer technologies (e.g., mobile apps) may not participate if the transfer will be made via mobile payment. The effect also depends on the enrollment schedule. Recurring payments may have a positive effect on enrollment depending on whether the program onboards people together as a cohort or people are allowed to join the program on a continuous basis. For example, potential beneficiaries are more likely to enroll if they know the recurring payment will be available to them by the next payment date, instead of by the next cohort round when the program restarts. However, if beneficiaries are allowed to join the program over the entire length of the program, they may feel less urgency to enroll if the payment is lump sum.

Payment frequency will influence how beneficiaries choose to spend the money, therefore encouraging varied behaviors and leading to different social outcomes. Recurring payments will have a positive impact on outcomes such as food security because they require less self-control and planning, whereas lump sum payments better serve investment purposes such as purchasing equipment or technologies. Most experts indicated that the effect of payment mode may change depending on the purpose of the transfer. In general, recurring payments are more effective for sustaining consumption, human development, early childhood care, and preparing for risks, and the impact on productive investment is more pronounced if the payment is made in lump sum. From the beneficiary's perspective, lump sum payments provide more flexibility in that recipients can use their discretion in regular spending and financial decisions. However, the advantage of recurring payments is that beneficiaries can rely on the consistent nature of the transfer and limit financial volatility. A potential downside of recurring payments is that, compared with one-off lump sums, frequent transfers will involve more steps for operations and management, which may spill over and create more frictions for the beneficiaries.

EFFECTS OF PAYMENT METHOD

Overview

Payment method refers to how payments are delivered (e.g., via checks or electronic transfers), which determines how visible the disbursements are. For program administrators and field staff, visible payments require more manual distribution efforts and physical interactions with beneficiaries than invisible payments, in which the transfer usually happens between bank accounts. For beneficiaries, visible payments deter engagement because of social stigma. Our hypothesis is that visible (vs. invisible) payment delivery methods will have negative effects on enrollment and provision.

Findings

With the rise of modern technologies, many cash transfer programs (e.g., M-Pesa in Kenya) have implemented mobile or electronic transfers (invisible payments) as opposed to manual cash delivery (visible payments) to reach beneficiaries. As indicated by interview findings, visible payments tend to evoke social stigma and shame, as well as other negative emotions, that can have a negative impact on enrollment and provision.

The effect of payment method (i.e., visibility) on the access stage depends on the level of perceived convenience of the transfer delivery. For example, potential beneficiaries will be less interested if an invisible payment requires multiple procedures, such as downloading a mobile app, uploading digital copies of IDs, or two-step verification, compared with a more streamlined, sludge-free process.

Experts had different perspectives on the impact of payment method on the enrollment stage. Visible payments may carry social stigma that will deter people from enrolling. However, an opposing view is that more visible payments can facilitate enrollment in that people living in the same community will see their friends and neighbors receiving the cash transfer and hence become interested themselves.

Most experts agreed that visible payments have a negative impact on the provision stage. First, visible payments (e.g., publicly lining up for food stamps) can put vulnerable beneficiaries in the spotlight, which is especially concerning in certain cultural contexts in which poverty is a taboo or embarrassing topic. In addition, families, friends, and neighbors in the same community may propose spending decisions or borrow money from the beneficiaries if the payment is visible, resulting in the beneficiaries having less independence in making their own financial decisions. Moreover, one expert mentioned that human emotions may play a critical role when payments are visible. For example, when witnessing others getting paid, non-beneficiaries or those currently on waiting lists may feel envy, annoyance, resentment, and sadness, all leading to negative spillover effects. Even among beneficiaries, there may be social comparison between different levels of transfer if payment amounts are visible. From the management perspective, visible payments are difficult and time-consuming to execute compared with invisible payments such as e-transfer, mobile payment, and direct deposit.

Nevertheless, some experts considered visibility to be whether the payment is visible to beneficiaries themselves. In that sense, visible payments are beneficial in that they will increase salience and help beneficiaries spend responsibly.

One expert emphasized the importance of ease of access when considering the effect of visibility on transfer delivery. In remote or isolated areas, sacrificing privacy to improve accessibility is understandable. For example, in rural villages of Northern Ghana, payments were a somewhat public affair with openness and transparency.[43] There were cash payment stations set up in locations familiar to beneficiaries, and all beneficiaries arrived at the payment points around the same time to collect the cash.

CONCLUSION AND THE WAY FORWARD

Our goal in this chapter was to decompose the delivery of cash transfer programs into discrete stages, identify design features of programs that might behaviorally influence the outcomes at each stage, and, therefore, present a nuanced framework that would help in better designing and evaluating such programs. As the results of interviews with experts suggest, there is a fair amount of consensus on how design features affect some features and outcomes. However, there are also some areas of disagreement. In particular, our experts diverged in their predictions in several cells of Table 6.4. Table 6.5 summarizes key findings and suggestions for best practices based on interview findings.

Although our goal was exploratory – to provide a framework for further practice and research to build on – we want to highlight a few key discussion points:

Table 6.5. Key findings and suggestions for best practices

Design features	Key findings	Suggestions for best practices
Scope	General CTPs with a broad scope promote inclusivity. Specific CTPs encourage behavioral change and outcomes associated with targeted goals.	Clear program communication is needed for general CTPs that entail multiple, complex goals.
Additional services	Overall, the presence of additional services can increase attraction and keep beneficiaries more engaged with CTPs.	The costs of providing additional services should not outweigh their subsequent benefits.
Conditionality	Conditions can negatively affect the access and enrollment stages.	Because conditional CTPs might not communicate trust in the same way as unconditional CTPs, it is important to make beneficiaries feel trusted and empowered through other means.
Payment mode	Recurring payments have a positive impact on outcomes such as food security. Lump sum payments better serve investment purposes.	When choosing payment mode, it is important to consider the external factors and context that may positively or negatively affect the beneficiaries and select options that fit best with the program.
Payment method	Visible payments tend to evoke social stigma and shame, as well as other negative emotions that can have a negative impact on enrollment and provision.	Accessibility is a key factor to be considered when deciding on payment method.

1. **The importance of context:** Research in the behavioral sciences is replete with the idea that context affects the results of behavioral interventions. Elements of context include the situation in which programs are delivered (the actual interface, the logistics involved in recruiting and paying out cash, languages used, or even the nature of interaction with recipients) and individual or cultural differences of recipients. Perhaps one source of disagreement between experts had to do with the fact that each was making predictions on the basis of experiences in one context, and these contexts might be different across the experts. This

would suggest moderating effects of background variables that future research will need to explore. This also highlights the important point that it would be prudent to avoid designing a cash transfer program simply by anchoring on a previous program and modifying it from an operational perspective. This is because the previous program – even though it might have been successful – might have been optimized to work in one particular context, whereas the current context might be different. Our framework, we hope, provides designers with the basic tools and approach to think about how each of the design features of the program could affect multiple outcomes.

2. **The need for empirical testing:** As discussed, our goal in this chapter was modest – to break down success factors and design features, to use the literature to make predictions about what the effects might be, and to validate these predictions with expert interviews. We encourage researchers and practitioners alike to start empirically documenting some of these effects going forward. This could be done through a careful evaluation of existing programs (but using the framework proposed in Table 6.3) or by conducting additional randomized controlled trials or even laboratory experiments designed to test programs' basic features. This empirical effort will also allow us to better understand why we had agreement across experts in some domains but not all.

3. **The design of communications:** Although the focus of this chapter is on the effects of five design features of cash transfer programs summarized in Table 6.5, there are several additional elements relating to the communication and delivery of these programs in which design choices might play a key role. The nature of communication might be particularly important – prior research shows that digital (rather than in-person) communication can reduce social frictions such as embarrassment,[44] resulting in greater take-up of products and services. Likewise, even in the domain of digital interfaces, research suggests that interfaces that are seen as less "human-like" (e.g., chatbots) are more likely to result in engagement and adoption.[45] We therefore advocate further empirical research on how the design of

communication and outreach at the last mile helps with the take-up of cash transfer programs.

4. **Incorporating behavioral science in program design:** Our work was motivated by the simple observation that most designers of cash transfer programs construct the program with a view toward optimizing the supply and delivery of the program, not through a careful consideration of how certain design features of the program could affect the end user. Converting the black box of how programs work into a glass box allows designers and policy makers to take a much more nuanced approach to design programs that could be optimized for various stages in the distribution pipeline. A thoughtful design can help greatly reduce the sludge that impedes progress at the various stages.

NOTES

1 World Bank. (2018, September 19). *Decline of global extreme poverty continues but has slowed* [Press release]. https://www.worldbank.org/en/news/press-release/2018/09/19/decline-of-global-extreme-poverty-continues-but-has-slowed-world-bank.

2 Organisation for Economic Co-operation and Development. (2021). *Poverty rate (indicator).* https://doi.org/10.1787/0fe1315d-en.

3 Johnson, A.F., & Roberto, K.J. (2020). The COVID-19 pandemic: Time for a universal basic income? *Public Administration and Development, 40*(4), 232–5. https://doi.org/10.1002/pad.1891.

4 Lindert, K., Karippacheril, T.G., Caillava, I.R., & Chávez, K.N. (Eds.). (2020). *Sourcebook on the foundations of social protection delivery systems.* World Bank.

5 Bastagli, F., Hagen-Zanker, J., Harman, L., Barca, V., Sturge, G., Schmidt, T., & Pellerano, L. (2016, July 27). *Cash transfers: What does the evidence say?* ODI. https://odi.org/en/publications/cash-transfers-what-does-the-evidence-say-a-rigorous-review-of-impacts-and-the-role-of-design-and-implementation-features/.

6 Mullainathan, S., & Shafir, E. (2013). *Scarcity: Why having too little means so much.* Macmillan.

7 Mani, A., Mullainathan, S., Shafir, E., & Zhao, J. (2013). Poverty impedes cognitive function. *Science, 341*(6149), 976–80; Hall, C.C., Zhao, J., & Shafir, E. (2014). Self-affirmation among the poor: Cognitive and behavioral implications. *Psychological Science, 25*(2), 619–25.

8 Thaler, R.H., & Sunstein, C.R. (2021). *Nudge: The final edition.* Penguin.

9 Soman, D., & Yeung, C. (Eds.). (2020). *The behaviorally informed organization.* University of Toronto Press.

10 Lindert et al. (2020).

11 Baird, S., Ferreira, F.H., Özler, B., & Woolcock, M. (2014). Conditional, unconditional and everything in between: A systematic review of the effects of cash transfer programmes on schooling outcomes. *Journal of Development Effectiveness, 6*(1), 1–43.

12 Gentilini, U., Grosh, M., Rigolini, J., & Yemtsov, R. (Eds.). (2019). *Exploring universal basic income: A guide to navigating concepts, evidence, and practices*. World Bank.
13 Lindert et al. (2020).
14 Soman, D., & Cheema, A. (2011). Earmarking and partitioning: Increasing saving by low-income households. *Journal of Marketing Research, 48*(SPL), S14–22.
15 Soman, D. (2004). Framing, loss aversion, and mental accounting. In D.J. Koehler & N. Harvey (Eds.), *Blackwell handbook of judgment and decision making* (pp. 379–98). Blackwell.
16 Anderson, V., & Wallin, P. (2018). Instructional coaching: Enhancing instructional leadership in schools. *National Teacher Education Journal, 11*(2), 53–9.
17 Blattman, C., Green, E.P., Jamison, J., Lehmann, M.C., & Annan, J. (2016). The returns to microenterprise support among the ultrapoor: A field experiment in postwar Uganda. *American Economic Journal: Applied Economics, 8*(2), 35–64.
18 Sadoulet, E., Finan, F., de Janvry, A., & Vakis, R. (2004). Can conditional cash transfer programs improve social risk management? *Lessons for education and child labor outcomes* (Social Protection Discussion Paper No. 0420). World Bank. https://web .worldbank.org/archive/website01047/WEB/IMAGES/0420.PDF.
19 Macours, K., & Vakis, R. (2009). *Changing households' investments and aspirations through social interactions: Evidence from a randomized transfer program* (World Bank Policy Research Working Paper No. 5137). World Bank.
20 Karlan, D., Osei, R., Osei-Akoto, I., & Udry, C. (2014). Agricultural decisions after relaxing credit and risk constraints. *Quarterly Journal of Economics, 129*(2), 597–652.
21 Haushofer, J., & Fehr, E. (2014). On the psychology of poverty. *Science, 344*(6186), 862–7.
22 Fiszbein, A., & Schady, N.R. (2009). *Conditional cash transfers: Reducing present and future poverty*. World Bank.
23 Gennetian, L.A., Shafi, E., Aber, J.L., & De Hoop, J. (2021). Behavioral insights into cash transfers to families with children. *Behavioral Science & Policy, 7*(1), 71–92.
24 Dunning, D., Fetchenhauer, D., & Schlösser, T. M. (2012). Trust as a social and emotional act: Noneconomic considerations in trust behavior. *Journal of Economic Psychology, 33*(3), 686–94; Soman, D. (2020). *Sludge: A very short introduction*. University of Toronto, Rotman School of Management, Behavioural Economics in Action at Rotman and Behaviourally Informed Organizations. https://www .rotman.utoronto.ca/-/media/Files/Programs-and-Areas/BEAR/White-Papers /BEARxBIOrg-Sludge-Introduction.pdf; Baird, S., McIntosh, C., & Özler, B. (2011). Cash or condition? Evidence from a cash transfer experiment. *Quarterly Journal of Economics, 126*(4), 1709–53.
25 Soman, D. (2001). Effects of payment mechanism on spending behavior: The role of rehearsal and immediacy of payments. *Journal of Consumer Research, 27*(4), 460–74.
26 Huffman, D., & Barenstein, M. (2004). *Riches to rags every month? The fall in consumption expenditures between paydays* (IZA Discussion Paper No. 1430). IZA Institute of Labor Economics. https://www.iza.org/publications/dp/1430/riches -to-rags-every-month-the-fall-in-consumption-expenditures-between-paydays
27 Fink, G., Jack, B.K., & Masiye, F. (2020). Seasonal liquidity, rural labor markets, and agricultural production. *American Economic Review, 110*(11), 3351–92. https://doi .org/10.1257/aer.20180607.
28 Brune, L., Chyn, E., & Kerwin, J. (2021). Pay me later: Savings constraints and the demand for deferred payments. *American Economic Review, 111*(7), 2179–212. https:// doi.org/10.1257/aer.20191657.
29 Fink et al. (2020).
30 See, for example, www.wagestream.com, www.zayzoon.com, and www.dayforcewallet .com; see also Rolfe, K. (2021, July 7). Payday disrupted: New platforms help

stretched employees tap their earnings in real time. *Financial Post*. https://
financialpost.com/fp-finance/payday-disrupted-new-platforms-help-stretched
-employees-tap-their-earnings-in-real-time; and Perlman, W. (2021, December 7).
Council post: Is on-demand pay right for your company? *Forbes*. https://www
.forbes.com/sites/forbestechcouncil/2021/12/07/is-on-demand-pay-right-for
-your-company/?sh=65748ba121a3.

31 Aker, J.C., Boumnijel, R., McClelland, A., & Tierney, N. (2011). *Zap it to me: The short-
term impacts of a mobile cash transfer program* (Working Paper 268). Center for Global
Development.

32 Aker, J. C., Boumnijel, R., McClelland, A., & Tierney, N. (2016). Payment mechanisms
and antipoverty programs: Evidence from a mobile money cash transfer experiment
in Niger. *Economic Development and Cultural Change, 65*(1), 1–37.

33 Soman (2020).

34 Soman (2001).

35 Bastagli et al. (2016).

36 Ariely, D., & Jones, S. (2008). *Predictably irrational*. Harper Audio.

37 Fiszbein & Schady (2009); Gilligan, D.O., Hoddinott, J., & Taffesse, A.S. (2009). The
impact of Ethiopia's Productive Safety Net Programme and its linkages. *Journal of
Development Studies, 45*(10), 1684–706.

38 Artuc, E., Cull, R., Dasgupta, S., Fattal, R., Filmer, D., Giné, X., Jacoby, H., Jolliffe, D.,
Kee, H.L., Klapper, L., Kraay, A., Loayza, N., McKenzie, D., Özler, B., Rao, V., Rijkers,
B., Schmukler, S., Toman, M., Wagstaff, A., & Woolcock, M. (2020). *Toward successful
development policies: Insights from research in development economics* (Policy Research
Working Paper 9133). World Bank.

39 GiveDirectly. (2021). https://www.givedirectly.org/about/.

40 Adato, M., Roopnaraine, T., Smith, N., Altinok, E., Çelebioğlu, N., & Cemal, S. (2007).
*An evaluation of the conditional cash transfer program in Turkey: Second qualitative and
anthropological study* (Final report submitted to the General Directorate of Social
Assistance and Solidarity, Prime Ministry, Republic of Turkey). International Food
Policy Research Institute.

41 Soman, D. (2015). *The last mile: Creating social and economic value from behavioral
insights*. University of Toronto Press.

42 Gentilini et al. (2019).

43 UNICEF. (2015, December 14). *It's payday! What a cash transfer looks like in Ghana*.
https://blogs.unicef.org/blog/its-payday-what-a-cash-transfer-looks-like-in
-ghana/.

44 See An, J., Kim, M., & Soman, D. (2016). *Financial behaviour online: It's different*.
University of Toronto, Rotman School of Management, Behavioural Economics in
Action at Rotman. https://www.rotman.utoronto.ca/-/media/Files/Programs-and
-Areas/BEAR/White-Papers/BEAR-FinancialBehaviourOnline-(1).pdf?la=en&has
h=D399B712877FC5758E0CF4D388FBD24F5C08D317; and Goldfarb, A., McDevitt,
R.C., Samila, S., & Silverman, B.S. (2015). The effect of social interaction on economic
transactions: Evidence from changes in two retail formats. *Management Science,
61*(12), 2963–81.

45 Jin, J., Walker, J., & Walker Reczek, R. (2022). *Preference for and inferences about chatbots
when purchases activate self-presentation concerns* (Working Paper). Ohio State University.

CHAPTER SEVEN

Don't Waste Recipients' Time: How to Save and Give Time in Cash Transfer Programs

Colin West and Ashley Whillans

Although poverty alleviation programs provide critical goods, services, and resources, they often simultaneously impose burdensome time costs on their recipients. For instance, many cash transfer programs require people to travel long distances, wait in lines, and fill out complex paperwork. Using the cash often requires further time and effort because of restrictions designed to prevent misappropriation. Also, to maintain eligibility, people must undergo frequent, onerous means-testing and renewal processes. As a result, many cash transfer programs provide one resource at the expense of another: recipients' time.

A critical overlooked benefit of cash transfers is their time efficiency. Innovations in financial technology have made it possible to provide cash transfers to even the poorest and most remote recipients with minimal time costs. However, many cash transfer programs do not realize these time-saving benefits. In this chapter, we analyze the role of time in cash transfer programs. First, we examine how cash transfer programs can be designed, implemented, and evaluated to maximize time savings for recipients. Second, we propose a new model for poverty alleviation programs that involves combining simultaneous cash transfers and time transfers, thereby freeing up two fundamental resources that people can use to over-come poverty traps.

When policy makers decide how to allocate economic assistance – be it food, goods, or cash – recipients' time constraints are rarely considered. This is partly because time efficiency does not evoke an especially compelling or empathetic narrative. Policy makers are well aware that voters and donors are motivated more by emotional stories than by quantitative metrics on impact and efficiency.[1] For instance, in-kind aid programs – providing goods such as food, livestock, and fertilizer or services such as job training – are still the most common forms of economic assistance in developing countries, and they usually impose large time costs on their recipients. These programs are often selected and designed on the basis of their narrative, rather than on evidence of impact. Furthermore, administrators are reluctant to test their programs against cash transfers, which have the potential to be highly efficient in terms of both cost and time.[2] Indeed, giving food directly to impoverished households offers a more emotional narrative compared with sending cash. In this decision process, recipients' resources of time are not an important consideration, if they are considered at all.

Another reason why time constraints are ignored is a widespread assumption that people living in material poverty have an abundance of time.[3] So, policy makers are rarely concerned about imposing time costs on recipients of economic aid, for example, during means-testing and in how aid is disbursed. As a result, time costs often accumulate unchecked in the administration of economic aid programs, and very rarely do these programs invest any substantial resources to save time for their recipients. Spending money just to save recipients time or to make aid disbursement more convenient is viewed as a frivolous waste of charitable or taxpayer dollars. However, these attitudes are based on inaccurate assumptions about how people living in poverty actually spend their time. Rigorous time-use survey data show that people living in poverty usually do not have an abundance of time. Rather, financial poverty and time poverty often coincide, especially for working women in developing countries.[4] For instance, working women in Kibera, an urban informal settlement in Nairobi, earn an average of US$14 per week while doing 44 hours of paid labor and 41 hours of unpaid labor.[5] Compared with the average working woman in the United States, working women in Kibera do slightly more paid labor and approximately twice as much unpaid labor.

Policy makers should be aware of the time constraints facing their constituents and account for these constraints in how they design economic aid programs. This begins with measuring the time costs that policy makers themselves are imposing on recipients of economic aid and then making specific changes and investments to reduce these time burdens. We argue that the extent to which a poverty alleviation program costs or saves recipients time will play a significant role in its ultimate impact.

In the next section, we review how time costs accumulate in administration of cash transfer programs, including how these programs (1) target, means-test, and enroll recipients; (2) disburse cash; and (3) evaluate their impact. We then propose specific changes to the design of cash transfer programs to reduce time costs and maximize their potential to save time for people living in poverty.

TIME COSTS IMPOSED ON RECIPIENTS DURING TARGETING AND MEANS-TESTING

Who should receive economic assistance, and who should be excluded? This is a fundamental question facing cash transfer programs, and it often provokes strong reactions to any perceived unfairness. Indeed, policy makers, voters, and donors will frequently reject programs that would produce greater benefits for all stakeholders out of a concern for fairness.[6] This has led to an intense focus on targeting in the design of cash transfer programs. *Targeting* refers to the process of determining which individuals are eligible for a given economic assistance program, how these individuals will be identified, and how they will be enrolled.[7] Cash transfer programs usually target recipients using one or more of the following five methods: (1) formal income data targeting, (2) categorical targeting, (3) proxy means-testing (PMT), (4) community-based targeting (CBT), or (5) self-targeting (i.e., "ordeal targeting").

Table 7.1. Time costs in each targeting method

Targeting method	Pros	Cons	Time costs
Income data targeting: eligibility is determined using formal income data from taxes or bank accounts. This is the most common targeting method in advanced economies.	This is a straightforward method that measures income directly. It is transparent and usually accurate.	This method does not account for monthly income fluctuations, which are becoming increasingly common.[a] Recipients can be excluded if they experience temporary income spikes.	Recipients typically undergo frequent, time-consuming renewal processes in which they must reverify their income.
Categorical targeting: eligibility is determined on the basis of category membership (e.g., age, parenthood, health, employment status)	This method allows programs to select for groups of people who are especially vulnerable or most likely to benefit from a given program.	Administrators often use a complex combination of categorical requirements, making it difficult for people to know whether they are eligible.	Application processes are usually long and require a lot of paperwork to ensure that recipients meet all categorical requirements.
Proxy means-testing: eligibility is determined using proxy measures that are indicative of household wealth (e.g., assets, housing material). This method is common in developing countries where formal income data are unattainable.	Proxy indicators can often accurately predict wealth in remote communities and among households without formal bank accounts.	Measuring proxies can be costly because enumerators must go door to door observing potential recipients' homes and assets and conducting surveys.	Proxy means-testing often involves long, time-consuming household surveys.

(Continued)

Table 7.1. Continued

Targeting method	Pros	Cons	Time costs
Community-based targeting: eligibility is determined by an elected committee of community members. The committee decides either who should receive cash transfers or which targeting criteria to use.	Committee members often have insight into economic constraints and disadvantages that are difficult or costly to measure. For instance, the selection process can consider estimates of earning potential, rather than just static wealth.	This method is susceptible to corruption among committee members. Also, it creates an incentive for people to hide their wealth so as to increase their chances of being selected, which could have negative ancillary effects on the local economy.	Time burdens fall on the small number of committee members, but the recipients themselves need not face any substantial time costs.
Self-targeting: programs impose "ordeal costs" to discourage wealthier recipients from applying. Ordeals include complex application processes and long wait times.	Self-targeting methods have been shown to be effective at screening out richer individuals.[b]	Ordeal costs may inadvertently screen out people who are especially time poor, such as working mothers or those with inflexible work schedules.	In this method, imposing time costs is intentional. The aim is to impose time costs that are just high enough to discourage richer individuals.

[a] See Organisation for Economic Co-operation and Development. (2019). *The future of work: OECD Employment Outlook 2019.* https://doi.org/10.1787/9ee00155-en; Morduch, J., & Schneider, R. (2017). *The financial diaries: How American families cope in a world of uncertainty.* Princeton University Press; Morduch, J., & Siwicki, J. (2017). In and out of poverty: Episodic poverty and income volatility in the US financial diaries. *Social Service Review, 91*(3), 390–421; and Dynan, K., Elmendorf, D., & Sichel, D. (2012). The evolution of household income volatility. *BE Journal of Economic Analysis and Policy, 12*(2), 1–44.

[b] Alatas, V., Banerjee, A., Hanna, R., Olken, B.A., & Tobias, J. (2012). Targeting the poor: Evidence from a field experiment in Indonesia. *American Economic Review, 102*(4), 1206–40.

Most of these targeting methods impose substantial time costs that could inadvertently lead to the exclusion of individuals who are especially time poor (e.g., as a result of the high burden of unpaid labor) and undermine the overall impact of the program. Yet, little attention is given to time costs when designing targeting strategies in cash transfer programs.

Income Data Targeting and Categorical Targeting

Major cash assistance programs in the United States use a combination of formal income data targeting and categorical targeting – these programs include Supplemental Security Income; Supplemental Nutrition Assistance Program (SNAP); Special Supplemental Nutrition Program for Women, Infants, and Children; Temporary Assistance for Needy Families (TANF); and General Assistance. There are combinations of categorical eligibility requirements at the federal, state, and county levels, which makes it difficult for people to know whether they meet the criteria. Furthermore, most jurisdictions do not offer a simple centralized mechanism to check eligibility, so people must determine for themselves whether they meet the criteria and then complete an arduous application involving complex paperwork as well as frequent renewal processes to prove their continued eligibility. For example, the TANF eligibility process takes 45 days, on average, and applicants must submit documentation on their income, expenses, other benefits they are receiving, and employment status (if they are unemployed, they must demonstrate that they have been actively seeking work). These time costs likely contribute to the fact that only 23 per cent of families living in poverty in the United States receive cash assistance via the TANF program.[8] Indeed, TANF participation among eligible recipients has been declining since the program's inception in 1996, largely as a result of increasingly complex eligibility criteria and paperwork burdens.[9] In contrast, SNAP participation rates have been improving since 2002: the share of eligible low-income households participating in SNAP rose from 42 per cent in 2002 to 75 per cent in 2016.[10] This improvement has been largely attributed to concerted efforts to reduce the time costs associated with applying to and renewing SNAP.[11]

Proxy Means-Testing

PMT can also impose significant time costs on recipients, depending on the proxies that are chosen and how they are measured. Time costs tend to accumulate when policy makers are overly focused on minimizing inclusion errors (providing economic assistance to an individual or household that is not poor). Voters and donors are outraged anytime cash transfers are given to people who are not especially poor, and, as a result, policy makers will often use highly complex and administratively burdensome PMT procedures to reduce inclusion errors. For instance, cash transfer programs often collect and weight a large number of proxy indicators to more accurately predict household wealth. Such proxies include the education level of the head of household, literacy, number of children, asset ownership, housing materials, number and type of livestock owned, and land ownership, as well as community-level indicators such as the quality of the roads, access to clean water, access to electricity, and cost of electricity. Using a larger number of proxy variables in the PMT formula will improve its performance in predicting household wealth and reducing inclusion errors, but it is also costly with respect to recipients' time.[12] This trade-off between predictive performance and time cost is rarely considered when choosing the "best" set of proxies. PMT methods have been so focused on increasing targeting accuracy that time costs can accumulate, unrecognized or unchecked, despite the potential negative downstream consequences for the program's overall impact.

Community-Based Targeting

CBT imposes minimal time costs. This method takes advantage of local knowledge about which individuals are most in need of cash assistance; therefore, program administrators do not need to impose time costs to collect formal income data, determine categorical eligibility, or measure proxy indicators of wealth. Furthermore, surveys have found that CBT tends to be very popular among recipients themselves – people report that they mostly trust locally elected committees to allocate cash transfers fairly and appreciate the transparency of this process.[13] However, in practice, CBT is rarely used, and there is little empirical research comparing the targeting accuracy of CBT with that of more common methods such as PMT.[14] It is also susceptible to corruption among committee members, and there are challenges in scaling this approach for national and international cash transfer programs. However, the time efficiencies relative to other targeting methods should not be undervalued – more research should examine the targeting accuracy of CBT and best practices for scaling this approach.

Self-Targeting

Self-targeting is method in which time costs are not a by-product but a deliberate tactic to influence the behavior of program applicants. Program administrators intentionally impose time costs such as long travel times, wait times, and paperwork to discourage richer individuals from applying. The rationale is that richer individuals will self-select out of the program because of the time and effort involved. The initial evidence suggests that this tactic is effective. For example, a conditional cash transfer program in Indonesia tested the effects of self-targeting in a randomized controlled trial (RCT). In collaboration with the Indonesian government, researchers randomized 400 villages to have either an automatic application or a self-targeting application. For villages assigned to the automatic application, enumerators traveled to all households and conducted a proxy means-test (observing household material and assets). If a household passed the test, it was automatically enrolled in the program and sent US$130 per year for six years. In the "self-targeting" villages, in order to enroll in the program, people were required to travel to a central registration site, wait in line, and complete an eligibility form. When researchers reviewed who ultimately enrolled, they found a substantially poorer group of beneficiaries in the self-targeting villages, indicating that these additional time costs did effectively discourage relatively wealthier individuals from applying.[19] However, these time costs might lead to other unintended selection effects, such as screening out people who have inflexible working schedules, many dependents, or a heavy burden of unpaid labor (i.e., people who are especially time-poor).

Targeting and Means-Testing: Design Insights to Reduce Time Costs

The time costs associated with targeting in cash transfer programs can be reduced in several ways. The first, most obvious, and most disruptive approach is to remove targeting altogether. Such universal cash transfer programs – those that provide a fixed amount of money to everyone regardless of income level, assets, or socioeconomic characteristics – are rare, but there have been an increasing number of experimental trials in recent years and there are some early indications that doing away with means-testing altogether may be the best option in some cases.[15] A second option is to simply means-test recipients less frequently, that is, to have longer eligibility periods so that recipients are subjected to fewer time-consuming renewal processes. Less frequent means-testing would inevitably lead to more inclusion errors because it would allow some individuals to continue receiving benefits even after they have escaped poverty, but the benefits may outweigh these costs. A third option is to account for recipients' time costs when selecting a targeting method. We explore this third option in more detail here.

Among the targeting methods outlined earlier, CBT usually involves the lowest time costs for recipients. More cash transfer programs should consider using CBT as a primary or secondary targeting technique. For instance, programs could use a hybrid targeting approach, selecting villages that are known to have a high rate of poverty (e.g., using past census data or satellite imaging, discussed shortly) and then relying on CBT to select households within these villages.

When using PMT, policy makers should consider not only the predictive accuracy of a given proxy, but also the time costs associated with its measurement. This could be done quantitatively, for instance, using stepwise regression techniques or machine learning models that select the best set of proxies on the basis of predictive accuracy, administrative costs, and estimated time costs.

Policy makers should also consider new targeting methods that can reduce or eliminate time costs. For example, some cash transfer programs have experimented with geographic targeting: providing cash transfers to entire regions or villages that are assessed to be poor, on average, without doing any individual-level or household-level targeting. An experiment in Siaya County, in rural Kenya, provided US$1,000 cash transfers to more than 10,500 households across 653 villages in which there are high levels of poverty.[16] In aggregate, these cash transfers amounted to a 15-percentage-point increase in the local gross domestic product, and the results showed significant benefits for households in the villages that received cash as well as spillover benefits for households in nearby villages as a result of the boost to the local economy.

There are also potential time efficiencies in novel targeting methods using satellite imaging and mobile phone data in machine learning models. In some regions, satellite and mobile phone data can be used to create geospatial maps of poverty without imposing any time costs on recipients.[17] For example, an emergency cash transfer program in Togo (Novissi) relied on a contactless targeting method to quickly identify recipients using satellite data in a machine learning model trained on past census data. The model learned which types of geographic patterns are indicative of poverty, tracing indicators such as building density, size of farm plots, paved versus unpaved roads, and roofing materials. After applying this approach to identify the poorest villages in Togo, mobile phone data were used to target the poorest individuals in these villages. Even the poorest people in rural Togo have access to a cell phone, so researchers could capture cell phone metadata that are correlated with poverty, such as the duration of phone calls, total volume of mobile data used, and mobile money transactions. By combining satellite geospatial data with mobile phone metadata, the Novissi program was able to accurately target poor individuals who were then prompted via text message to enroll and immediately receive cash via a mobile money transfer.[18] Similar targeting methods using mobile phone metadata are being planned in cash transfer programs in Uganda and Bangladesh.[19]

It is important to note that many of the time-saving ideas that we have proposed would inevitably result in more inclusion errors. When designing a targeting strategy, there is often an unavoidable trade-off between minimizing inclusion errors and minimizing time costs for recipients. To date, many cash transfer programs have been so focused on reducing inclusion errors that they have not explicitly addressed this trade-off. One must keep in mind that the central goal of cash transfer programs is to reduce poverty, and improving targeting accuracy is only beneficial insofar as it contributes to this goal. Therefore, it is critical to measure the costs of targeting – including time costs – so that cash transfer programs can evaluate whether these costs are justified by greater reductions in poverty.

TIME COSTS IN CASH DISBURSEMENT: HOW CASH IS SENT AND RECEIVED

In principle, cash transfer programs are very straightforward: send money to those who need it. However, the ways in which cash is disbursed can influence the program's overall effectiveness. For instance, cash transfer programs must make critical design choices related to their cash disbursement method, the conditions they will impose (if any) on how the cash can be used, and how they will communicate with their recipients. Currently, these design choices are made with little attention to recipients' time constraints. Cash transfer programs tend to focus narrowly on their recipients' financial constraints, which is understandable but ultimately a mistake because people living in financial poverty often face simultaneous deficits of time. In this section, we review current practices and propose specific design insights to save time.

Payment Mechanisms

Sending money to those who need it is not always as simple as it seems, especially in developing economies and in rural areas with little financial infrastructure. Currently, there are three overarching methods for sending cash transfers: (1) direct transfers, (2) paypoint

Table 7.2. Time costs in each cash disbursement method

Cash disbursement method	Example programs	Time costs
Direct transfers: money is sent directly to recipients via checks in the mail, bank transfers, or prepaid debit cards.	Direct bank deposit is a common method for large-scale social welfare programs in the United States (e.g., Social Security Income), Canada, the United Kingdom, and many other advanced economies around the world. Related programs, such as SNAP and TANF in the United States, typically provide cash transfers via prepaid debit cards.	Direct bank transfers and checks involve minimal time costs. However, prepaid debit cards can impose time costs when they are restricted to specific merchants and ATMs.
Paypoint transfers: recipients travel to a specific location (i.e., paypoint) to pick up physical cash. Paypoints include local program offices, bank branches, or networks of designated ATMs.	In regions with limited financial technology infrastructure or low rates of financial inclusion, paypoint transfers are the most common cash disbursement method. Examples include programs in Ethiopia (Productive Safety Net Programme), Eritrea (Results-based Financing Conditional Cash Transfer Program), Kenya (Cash Transfer for Orphans and Vulnerable Children Program), Malawi (Social Cash Transfer Programme), and Ghana (Livelihood Empowerment Against Poverty program). Typically, recipients are notified of the paypoint location 1–2 days in advance, and they must show up at a designated time to check in with administrators, complete paperwork, and receive their cash.	Paypoint methods are administratively burdensome and extremely time-consuming. Recipients must often travel long distances, wait in line, and sometimes even the spend the night at the paypoint because of limited transportation options.
Mobile money transfers: payments are sent and received via mobile phone applications.	Kenya is the leader in mobile money: 90% of adults have a mobile money account, digital money is accepted at most local shops, and there is a wide network of more than 300,000 mobile money agents who facilitate conversion to cash.[a] This reach has made it possible for several large-scale cash transfer programs in Kenya to reach extremely poor recipients via mobile money.[b] In most other countries, mobile money adoption remains quite low and, therefore, providing cash transfers via this mechanism would likely exclude people at the bottom of the income spectrum.[c]	Mobile money transfers are usually highly time-efficient because the money is received instantly. However, there are some small, one-off time costs required to set up an account. Also, when local merchants do not accept mobile money, people must go to local agents to convert it to physical cash.

[a] Andersson-Manjang, S.K., & Naghavi, N. (2021). *State of the industry report on mobile money 2021*. GSM Association.

[b] See Haushofer, J., & Shapiro, J. (2016). The short-term impact of unconditional cash transfers to the poor: Experimental evidence from Kenya. *Quarterly Journal of Economics, 131*(4), 1973–2042; Haushofer, J., & Shapiro, J. (2018). *The long-term impact of unconditional cash transfers: Experimental evidence from Kenya*. Busara Center for Behavioral Economics; and Banerjee, A., Faye, M., Krueger, A., Niehaus, P., & Suri, T. (2020). *Effects of a Universal Basic Income during the pandemic* (Technical Report). University of California, San Diego.

[c] See Pénicaud, C., & Katakam, A. (2019). State of the industry 2013: Mobile financial services for the unbanked. *Gates Open Research, 3*, 1429; and Evans, D.S., & Pirchio, A. (2014). An empirical examination of why mobile money schemes ignite in some developing countries but flounder in most. *Review of Network Economics, 13*(4), 397–451.

Notes: SNAP = Supplemental Nutrition Assistance Program; TANF = Temporary Assistance for Needy Families.

transfers, and (3) mobile money transfers. Here, we examine the time costs involved in each of these methods and explore specific interventions to save time.

Direct transfer methods are used in large-scale social welfare programs around the world, and they are usually quite efficient with respect to recipients' time. Bank deposits are received within 24 hours, and they impose virtually no time costs. Checks are similarly efficient, except for the time costs and delays involved with sending physical mail. Prepaid debit cards can impose some time costs when their use is restricted to specific ATMs and merchants. For example, in California, TANF cash transfers are distributed via prepaid cards, but money can only be withdrawn (without a fee) at specific bank branches and ATMs. Many recipients do not live close to any of these designated branches or ATMs; therefore, they must either waste time traveling or incur a withdrawal fee (which can be substantial).[20]

Paypoint transfer methods are used in places where it is not possible to send money via direct transfer. Paypoint cash disbursement often imposes large time costs. For instance, Ethiopia's Productive Safety Net Programme (PSNP) provides monthly cash transfers for six months of the year via paypoints across Tigray, Amhara, Oromia, and the Southern Nations, Nationalities, and Peoples' Region. This program measured the amount of time recipients spent collecting cash transfers (one of the few programs to do so) and found that 97 per cent of recipients traveled to the paypoints on foot, which took 60–120 minutes, and 19 per cent of recipients had to spend the night at the paypoint.[21]

Some alternative paypoint methods can reduce these time costs. For instance, Kenya's Hunger Safety Net Programme (HSNP) provides cash transfers of KSh2,700 (US$24) every two months to poor households via a network of ATMs. During the enrollment process, recipients register a bank account and receive a designated bank card that can be used to withdraw the cash transfers at any branch or ATM or with program agents based at local shops. An evaluation of the HSNP found that most people can travel to their closest paypoint on foot in less than an hour, and they typically wait for less than 30 minutes at the paypoint to collect their cash.[22] By providing a broader network of paypoints and allowing recipients to come at a time of their choosing, Kenya's HSNP imposes much lower time costs on recipients than Ethiopia's PSNP.

However, by far the most time-efficient cash disbursement method in developing economies is mobile money. These Short Message Service (text)–based applications allow cash transfers to be sent with minimal transaction fees and minimal time costs. As mobile money systems continue to develop and proliferate, time costs will decrease even further. For instance, when mobile money was first introduced in Kenya, it had very limited functionality and could only be used for simple peer-to-peer transfers. If people wanted to use their mobile money at local merchants, they first had to convert it into physical cash at a local bank branch or ATM or with a mobile money agent in their community. All of these conversion options involved time costs, to a greater or lesser extent, depending on their accessibility in the local area. However, mobile money has developed rapidly in Kenya, such that it can now be used for a wide range of financial transactions without ever having to be converted to cash. Mobile money is now accepted at most merchants (especially in urban areas), it can be deposited into directly into digital savings accounts, and it can be used as collateral to take loans. As other countries follow these developments in Kenya, mobile money will become an increasingly time-efficient and frictionless method of sending cash transfers.

Conditions on Cash Transfers

As cash transfers have become increasingly popular as a tool for poverty alleviation, there has been a growing debate about the ethics and effectiveness of enforcing conditions.[23] Conditional cash transfers (CCTs) require recipients to comply with certain conditions to maintain their eligibility, such as keeping their children in school, ensuring that they receive regular health checkups, or participating in job training programs. Unconditional cash transfers (UCTs), however, provide money with no stipulations whatsoever. There is an ongoing debate about the relative impact and ideology of CCTs versus UCTs that we do not address here, except to note that enforcing conditions almost always requires imposing time costs. These time costs must be justified by increased welfare benefits. Currently, most CCT programs do not even measure the time costs associated with monitoring conditions. The financial and administrative costs of monitoring conditions are rigorously evaluated,[24] but the time costs are unmeasured and unaccounted for in cost–benefit analyses. Although imposing conditions might be effective in motivating important behaviors, such as school attendance and health checkups, it is unclear whether the associated time costs undercut these benefits. As a first step, CCT programs should rigorously measure the time costs they impose as well as the overall effects of the program on recipients' time use.

Communicating with Recipients

Another important element of cash disbursement is communications with recipients. Cash transfer programs must explain to recipients why they are receiving the transfer, how to register, the payment mechanism, amounts and timing, and conditions. Miscommunication and confusion are common, often leading to wasted time and distortionary effects.[25] Many cash transfer programs do not invest sufficient resources into improving their communication procedures, perhaps underestimating the importance of effective messaging, or not appreciating the diversity of attitudes, perspectives, and obstacles facing their target population. Recently, some cash transfer programs have started to think more carefully about their communication strategy, conducting research using qualitative methods from human-centered design and quantitative methods from behavioral economics to better understand the psychological, social, and cultural dynamics that might influence how recipients respond to cash transfers.

Cash Disbursement: Design Insights to Reduce Time Costs

Cash transfer programs can save time for their recipients in four key ways: (1) by changing to their payment mechanism, (2) by redesigning their conditions and restrictions, (3) by providing planning and budgeting tools, and (4) by improving their communication with recipients.

First, in developing countries, cash transfer programs should consider switching from paypoint cash disbursement to mobile money. Infrastructure constraints often make it difficult or costly to make this switch. For instance, mobile money adoption might be low in the target region, or there might not be an sufficient network of bank branches, ATMs, or agents to facilitate conversion to physical cash. However, the benefits of switching to mobile money might justify up-front capital expenditures to overcome some of these barriers. Such expenditures might include providing cell phones, placing more ATMs, or hiring mobile money agents. Typically, cash transfer programs do not consider such infrastructure expenditures as within their scope, but the returns could be substantial. Not only will the switch to mobile money save recipients time, but it would also be safer (digital money is much more difficult to steal) and more transparent (transaction records make mobile money transfers less susceptible to corruption), and it can accelerate financial inclusion (access to credit, insurance, and other financial products). To date, few studies have empirically tested the effects of switching from paypoint disbursement to mobile money.[26] Future research should investigate whether the benefits outweigh the up-front capital costs, including estimating the total time-savings that can be realized over the duration of the program.

When it is not possible to use mobile money, cash transfer programs should measure and account for recipients' time costs when designing alternative payment mechanisms. For instance, when using paypoints, program administrators could invest resources to offer a larger number of locations with more flexible pick-up hours, thereby providing recipients more control over their time. Again, the welfare benefits of such time-saving investments should be evaluated in RCTs to determine whether the costs are justified.

Second, CCT programs should account for recipients' time when selecting their conditions and how they are monitored. In some cases, soft conditions or "nudges" could be used in place of traditional conditions, which usually involve time-intensive enforcement and monitoring.[27] The core purpose of conditions is to force recipients to invest more money into human capital, usually on children's schooling or health care. However, it may be possible to encourage similar human capital expenditures using non-coercive methods.[28] As an example, a cash transfer program in Morocco tested the effects of labeled cash transfers (LCTs) in an RCT. Parents of school-aged children received a standard CCT (conditional on their children's school attendance), an LCT (labeled as "designed to facilitate education investment"; there were no conditions of any kind on this cash transfer), or neither (control). The results showed that the LCT was most effective in increasing school attendance. Among children of parents who received the LCT, school attendance was 7.3 percentage points higher than in the control group and 2 percentage points higher than in the CCT group.[29] In addition to increasing school attendance, LCTs may have psychological and economic benefits for parents because of the time savings relative to the burdensome monitoring of CCTs.

Future research should go beyond LCTs to investigate non-coercive interventions such as earmarking and partitioning cash transfers. For instance, past research suggests that partitioning cash transfers into multiple payments or depositing them into separate labeled "accounts" could further increase the likelihood that they are spent as intended.[30] Some mobile money systems now have the option to create labeled savings accounts.[31] Cash transfer programs aiming to increase human capital investment could deposit payments directly into education or health savings accounts with commitment elements, such as self-imposed fees for early withdrawal.

Third, cash transfer programs could provide people with budgeting tools to help them stick to their intentions and get the most out of their cash transfers. For example, beneficiaries could indicate how they intend to spend the money ahead of time, and administrators could then deposit cash transfers into multiple accounts earmarked with their chosen goals, recognizing that once money has been earmarked for a specific purpose, people are less likely to spend it on temptations or other goods.[32] These types of digital tools take advantage of both the flexibility of UCTs – for instance, funds can still be redirected in the event of an emergency – and recent innovations in financial technology that can help people to pursue their financial goals, stick to their commitments, and save time.

Fourth, program administrators should pay careful attention to how they communicate with recipients. Although cash transfer programs are intended to be simple, they can quickly become burdensome when the communication strategy is poorly designed or fails to understand recipients' concerns and constraints. Gaps in communication can lead to wasted time and fears about whether the cash transfers will be terminated or reallocated. Furthermore, the messaging accompanying cash transfers can influence recipients' psychological well-being and allocation decisions. For instance, messaging can be explicitly or implicitly stigmatizing, reinforcing the narrative that one is receiving cash transfers because one is personally deficient, vulnerable, or incapable. Such stigmatizing messaging can undermine recipients' self-efficacy or lead them to forego the program altogether,[33] whereas messaging focused on empowerment can afford dignity to recipients and may even increase the overall effectiveness of the program.[34] Cash transfer programs should conduct field research to inform the design of their communications and then test alternative messaging strategies in randomized controlled trials.

TIME COSTS IN THE EVALUATION OF CASH TRANSFER PROGRAMS

Measuring Time Costs in Cash Transfer Programs

We argue that evaluations of cash transfer programs need to be revamped, beginning with more rigorous measurement of recipients' time use. Most impact evaluations do not collect any measurements of recipients' time, partly because time as a resource is undervalued by policy makers, and partly because time is a difficult resource to measure, both practically and conceptually. From a practical standpoint, measuring time use typically requires in-depth surveys in which respondents are provided with a list of activities and asked to estimate the amount of time they spent on each activity over the past week.[35] This method is costly to administer, time consuming, and subject to memory biases.[36] Alternative methods capture snapshots of time use that serve as a proxy for time use more generally. For example, the day reconstruction method (DRM) asks respondents to fill out a structured time diary for the previous day, and the experience sampling method (ESM) asks respondents what they are doing and feeling in the moment (respondents receive multiple timed "pings" to complete a one-minute survey).[37] Implementing DRM or ESM time tracking makes it possible to estimate the effects of a given economic assistance program on recipients' time use. At the very least, cash transfer programs should measure time costs associated with the program itself, including the time it takes to enroll, to receive each cash transfer, and to maintain eligibility.

We also recommend that cash transfer programs measure *subjective time poverty*, defined as the extent to which people have a chronic feeling of having too many things to do and not enough time to do them.[38] Subjective time poverty can be measured in surveys or incorporated into DRM or ESM time tracking, using items such as "I feel pressed for time today" (0 = *do not agree at all*, 6 = *completely agree*),[39] "I often feel rushed" (1 = *every day*, 6 = *never*),[40] and "I never seem to have enough time to get everything done" (0 = *do not agree at all*, 6 = *completely agree*).[41] These measures are only moderately correlated with total hours of paid and unpaid labor (in our own time-use survey conducted among working mothers in Kibera, Kenya, we found a correlation between subjective and objective time poverty of .33).[42] That is, the extent to which someone feels time-poor can be influenced by factors other than simply how much work they must do, including the type of work they do, their work schedule (e.g., predictability and volatility of working hours), autonomy over their time, and local norms related to busyness, leisure, and status.

It is useful to measure both objective and subjective time poverty because they are both important leading indicators of downstream psychological and economic well-being. For instance, subjective time poverty has been linked to future risk of depression, decreased productivity and performance at work, less creativity, and lower overall life satisfaction.[43] Given that most cash transfer programs only run for a period of months or a few years, it is difficult to measure their

effects on these types of long-term life outcomes. Leading indicators, such as measures of time poverty, can help researchers to estimate the future effects of a cash transfer program.

Analyzing Time Use and Time Poverty Data

Several methods can be used to incorporate time use and time poverty data into empirical evaluations of cash transfer programs. We
suggest incorporating these data in four ways: (1) analyze hetero-
geneous treatment effects, (2) analyze causal pathways, (3) evaluate
specific time-saving design features, and (4) conduct cost–benefit
analyses.

First, baseline time use and time poverty are important variables
to consider when analyzing the heterogeneity of treatment effects.
These analyses can help to address the question, "How effective
are cash transfers among people who are especially time-poor?"
Although some people living in material poverty are simultaneously time-poor (e.g., working mothers in urban areas in developing
countries), other people have too much idle time (a problem that has
been documented among some agricultural workers during lean
seasons).[44] Cash transfers may have differential effects depending
on the preexisting time constraints of the target population.

Second, cash transfer programs should conduct causal pathway
analyses to examine the extent to which time savings or changes in
time use led to any observed downstream benefits. Cash transfers
may help to free up time resources or change how people choose
to spend their time. For instance, cash transfers may enable people
to outsource certain tasks, take on additional paid work, or spend
more time socializing. When cash transfers are evaluated in RCTs,
collecting longitudinal data on time use (before, during, and after
the intervention) will allow researchers to conduct causal pathway
analyses (e.g., using structural equation modeling) that can help
determine whether recipients' time use plays an important role in
explaining treatment effects.

Third, specific time-saving design features should be evaluated
in RCTs. To date, many RCTs have tested the overall impact of
cash transfer programs, but there is comparatively little evidence

on the welfare effects of specific design features that cost or save time. For instance, RCTs should test the effects of switching to more time-efficient targeting methods (see Premand & Schnitzer, 2021,[45] for example of such an experiment), reducing means-testing (e.g., longer eligibility periods, shorter means-testing processes), and changing cash disbursement methods (e.g., increasing the number of paypoints or switching from paypoint methods to mobile money). To run these RCTs, programs could independently manipulate one of these design features to examine treatment effects on poverty reduction and then follow up with causal pathway analyses to investigate whether time savings were, in fact, the cause of any observed improvements in psychological or economic well-being.

Fourth, policy makers should incorporate recipients' time into cost–benefit analyses. Many social welfare programs conduct rigorous cost–benefit analyses, but beneficiaries' time is rarely factored into their models. To do so, policy makers first need to determine how to value beneficiaries' time. This is a complex endeavor that raises several critical questions: should all individuals' time be valued at the same rate? Should individual differences in earning potential or differences in value to the local community be factored in? How can we account for differences in the value that individuals place on their own time? Fortunately, there is a useful precedent for addressing these complex questions. Since the 1970s, policy makers have calculated measures such as the value of a statistical life (VSL) and the value of a quality-adjusted life-year (QALY) to assess the costs and benefits of policies such as environmental and health regulations.[46] For example, the Environmental Protection Agency values a human life at US$7.4 million (in 2006 dollars), and therefore the benefits of a new environmental policy that reduces the risk of mortality by 1 per cent can be valued at US$74,000 per person affected. Similarly, cash transfer programs could calculate the value of a statistical hour (VSH) to account for time costs or savings realized by beneficiaries of a given program. There are a variety of ways in which a VSH could be calculated. For instance, a VSH could be determined using an estimate of the hourly earning potential for affected persons or by measuring how people value their own time (e.g., reservation wages). Another straightforward method would be to simply divide the value placed on a human life by the average life expectancy in hours. Using the figure of $7.4 million as the value of a statistical life and an average global life expectancy of 73 years (according the World Health Organization), the corresponding VSH would be US$11.57 (in 2006 dollars). Establishing the VSH could help to empirically evaluate whether the time costs involved in targeting methods, means-testing, or conditions in cash transfer programs are justified.

CASH TRANSFERS PLUS TIME TRANSFERS

We have proposed that time costs may be an important factor in determining whether cash transfer programs are effective in lifting people out of poverty. When people are extremely time-constrained, they may not be able to take full advantage of cash transfers. For instance, they might not be able to spend the cash productively on building new income streams. More generally, if recipients have extremely limited time, they may be less able to make substantial changes to their income-earning, spending, and saving behaviors.

Cash transfer programs can take two overarching approaches to save time for their recipients. First, they can reduce the time costs that they themselves impose. Thus far, we have focused on this first approach. We have proposed several specific changes to the design of cash transfer programs to reduce time costs. A second approach is to provide people with direct time transfers. Next, we outline a new model for economic assistance that combines cash transfers with simultaneous time transfers to help overcome poverty traps and generate more sustainable improvements in economic well-being. Time transfers can include (1) investing in infrastructure that saves people time, (2) providing labor-saving goods or appliances, or (3) providing access to services that save time on chores. In this section, we provide the rationale and evidence supporting this proposal and offer some insights into how to design a program that provides cash transfers plus time transfers.

Rationale for Cash Transfers Plus Time Transfers

Evaluations of cash transfers have shown that they have a reliably positive impact on short-term, proximate outcomes such as asset accumulation, income, consumption, and food security, but the evidence is mixed with respect to their effects on long-term, second-order outcomes such as new income generation, nutrition, children's education attainment, and health.[47] In some impact evaluations, researchers find that the economic, psychological, and health benefits of cash transfers diminish quite quickly after people stop receiving payments, leading some critics to argue that cash transfers do not have transformative effects.[48]

What might prevent cash transfers from having more lasting effects? It may be that people living in poverty are not only cash poor but also constrained by psychological and structural barriers that make it difficult to use cash injections productively. Some psychological barriers might include chronic stress and increased risk of depression.[49] There are also myriad structural barriers that might undermine the effectiveness of cash transfers, including inadequate infrastructure, market failures, crime and corruption, risk exposure, and heavy burdens of unpaid labor. Recognizing some of these constraints, policy makers and researchers have tested several variations of "cash-plus" programs, which provide cash transfers in combination with other goods, services, information, or nudges in an effort to unlock the full benefits of the cash. For example, to address psychological barriers, some programs have combined cash payments with mental health services. However, these cash-plus-mental-health programs have had mixed results. In Liberia, a program combining cash and cognitive–behavioral therapy led to more lasting decreases in violent and criminal behavior among young men compared with cash alone and cognitive–behavioral therapy alone.[50] In contrast, a program in Kenya found no such complementarity effects – both cash and therapy were beneficial for economic and psychological well-being, but combining them provided no extra benefits.[51]

Cash-plus programs have also sought to address structural barriers. For example, several programs have tested cash plus nutritionally fortified foods (that are not available in local markets).[52] Others have tested cash plus management training (in Senegal) and cash plus health insurance (in Rwanda, Burundi, and South Korea), with mixed results.[53]

To date, no poverty alleviation program has tested an intervention that provides cash plus time. We have made the case that deficits of time may play an important role in the effectiveness of cash transfer programs. Specifically, people may be unable to start a new job or generate new income streams without both discretionary money and time. For instance, people might need spare money and spare time to move locations, undergo formal or informal job training, and incur a temporary income loss. Similarly, microentrepreneurs and agricultural workers may not be able to take advantage of productive new technologies if they cannot incur up-front financial and temporal costs. In addition, having more discretionary time to invest in social relationships, community, leisure, and rest may help people to extract greater benefit from cash transfers. Furthermore, in many developing countries, it is difficult to buy time. Therefore, cash transfers alone may not be able to address recipients' time constraints. For instance, time-poor individuals cannot use cash transfers to remove time constraints caused by poor infrastructure. Also, time-saving goods and services are often unavailable or exorbitantly expensive in local markets. As an example, in the Kibera informal settlement in Nairobi, outsourcing a single load of laundry costs KSh500, on average – three times the average daily wage for local working women.[54] This represents a market failure that cannot be solved by cash transfers alone.

Although cash plus time has never been directly tested, some preliminary evidence suggests that it could be especially effective. First, a large-scale multifaceted poverty alleviation program combined cash transfers with four other elements: (1) a productive asset grant (e.g., livestock), (2) job training, (3) access to a savings account, and (4) health services. This program was tested in Ethiopia, Ghana, Honduras, India, Pakistan, and Peru. The impact evaluation showed significant welfare improvements that lasted up to 36 months.[55] These lasting benefits may have been produced, in part, by the fact that this program enabled beneficiaries to spend more time working. Compared with the control group, beneficiaries spent an average of 17.5 additional minutes per day working (primarily on agricultural activities). A drawback of this program was the high cost of administration per household. However, it was designed to be temporary: "a big push over a limited period of time, with the hope of unlocking a poverty trap"[56]

To the best of our knowledge, only one study has experimentally tested a poverty alleviation program directly aimed at saving time.[57] This study was a longitudinal field experiment in Nairobi with a sample of 1,550 working mothers, a population that is especially likely to be time-poor. Participants were randomly assigned to receive weekly time transfers (laundry or prepared meal services) that reduced their burden of unpaid labor by four to six hours per week for three consecutive weeks. The effect of these time transfers was compared with that of equivalently valued UCTs that increased their income by 33 per cent relative to baseline earnings and a survey-compensation-only control condition that increased incomes by 14 per cent. Surprisingly, the results showed similar increases in psychological well-being (reduced stress, increased net affect, and lower relationship conflict) across all three conditions. Pathway analyses revealed that the cash transfers and time-saving services produced these benefits via distinct mechanisms. For instance, people who received UCTs had more cash on hand (i.e., liquid resources) and felt a sense of financial safety that led to a subsequent decrease in perceived stress. In contrast, time transfers reduced stress by lessening recipients' burden of unpaid labor, indicating that freeing up resources of time may provide an alternative pathway toward poverty alleviation. Furthermore, this study found that time transfers were especially beneficial for microentrepreneurs. By the end of this program, microentrepreneurs who received time transfers generated more revenue than those in the cash transfer condition and the control condition.

This preliminary evidence suggests that time transfers may be an effective complement to cash transfers. Providing a temporary boost of both money and time may help people to gain more control over their lives, make more meaningful changes to their economic circumstances, and escape poverty traps.

How to Design a Program that Combines Cash Transfers and Time Transfers

The first critical question in designing such a program is how to transfer time. There are three approaches: (1) investing in time-saving infrastructure, (2) providing time-saving technologies, and (3) providing time-saving services.

Infrastructure improvements are an expensive but highly effective method of transferring time. For instance, improving roads and public transportation can drastically reduce commute times, which fall disproportionately on poor individuals because they tend to live farther away from work than wealthier individuals. A study of 40 million households in the United States found that upward economic mobility was negatively correlated with commute time. Specifically, poor people living around cities with greater urban sprawl, and therefore longer commutes, were less likely to move up a wealth quintile.[58]

Time-saving technologies are a more immediate method of providing time transfers to people living in poverty. Such technologies include more efficient cookstoves and other household appliances, water collection technologies, and agricultural tools. For example, an NGO in rural India, OneProsper, builds rainwater harvesting tanks to reduce the number of trips that people take to their nearest water source. These tanks cost US$520 and can save up to five hours per day for a person living in a remote village north of Jodhpur.[59] Another example includes agriculture technology designed to save time for farmers and help them increase their yield. In Kenya, a machine-sharing company called Hello Tractor allows farmers to share or rent expensive agricultural equipment with their neighbors, saving time and money. Another Kenyan company, Digifarm, saves time for farmers through a mobile phone application that provides immediate access to financial services (e.g., credit and crop insurance), educational content (e.g., peer-to-peer knowledge sharing about best practices in planting and cultivation), and a digital marketplace to sell their produce.

Finally, a direct way to transfer time is to provide services that allow people to outsource routine unpaid labor. In the experiment with working mothers in Kibera, those who received laundry vouchers were able to eliminate an arduous chore (saving five to seven hours per week), and those who received meal vouchers were able to take a night or two off from cooking (saving two to four hours per week).[60] Future research should evaluate the viability of other time-saving services such as grocery delivery, water delivery, cleaning services, and subsidized childcare.

Policy makers should also consider time transfers specifically designed for microentrepreneurs – a subset of the working poor who may be able to use additional time most productively. For instance, economic assistance programs could provide cash transfers combined with time transfers in the form of business services, such as outsourced bookkeeping. Past research has shown that cash transfers for microentrepreneurs are effective in increasing revenues, but other forms of business assistance, such as management training, have been largely unsuccessful.[61] Perhaps cash transfers plus time transfers would enable microentrepreneurs to accelerate the growth of their businesses.

Overall, when selecting a time transfer method, there are a few guiding principles that we think policy makers should follow. First, time transfers should be evaluated on cost-efficiency. This includes estimating how much time is saved per dollar spent and evaluating the downstream welfare benefits in RCTs that compare different time transfer methods and benchmarking them against equivalently valued UCTs. Second, policy makers should be careful not to remove chores that have important ancillary benefits. For instance, in some communities, walking to collect water is an important opportunity for socializing. Policy makers should be aware of these social and psychological dimensions before removing particular chores. Third, cash transfers and time transfers should be provided simultaneously and consistently so that recipients can take advantage of complementarity effects and make plans for how they will allocate upcoming transfers. These plans could then be supported by providing budgeting tools, time planners, and commitment devices to help people follow through on their intentions.

CONCLUSION

Cash transfer programs cannot ignore their recipients' time. How people spend their time, the control they feel over time, and their ability to plan for the future – these are central to their well-being and aspirations. It is difficult to imagine a better future and take the first steps toward realizing that future when daily life is filled with excessive unpaid labor, commuting, and waiting. For cash transfers to have a lasting impact, policy makers need to better understand the effects they are having on their recipients' time use and take steps to reduce the time constraints that often coincide with financial constraints. Avoiding exacerbating these time constraints should be a first principle in the design of cash transfer programs.

We have outlined several steps that cash transfer programs can take to save time for their recipients. Start by identifying the time costs imposed in the targeting and enrollment process. How many hours of travel and administrative work are being imposed on the people you are seeking to help? Consider sacrificing some degree of targeting accuracy to reduce these time burdens. Also, take advantage of novel data sources for targeting, such as satellite imaging and cell phone metadata.

Change the way cash is delivered to recipients. How can the cash be made more accessible so that recipients' lives are disrupted as little as possible? Be careful in assuming that the cash is so valuable to beneficiaries that it justifies any inconvenience. Keep in mind that small time costs in cash disbursement can accumulate into a large burden over the duration of the program.

Consider soft conditionality, nudges, and budgeting tools instead of strict conditions and monitoring. For instance, if you want to ensure that recipients are investing in their children's education and health, consider labeled cash transfers, reminders, and commitment devices rather than top-down enforcement.

Perhaps most important: measure recipients' time use and subjective feelings of time poverty using techniques such as DRM or ESM. You may find that the program is having a profound effect on how people spend their time and how time-poor they feel. Furthermore, these metrics will allow rigorous evaluation of the cost-effectiveness of time-saving interventions.

Last, consider investing in time transfers along with cash transfers. Time and money are two fundamental resources that people need to escape poverty. A program that provides a temporary boost in both of these resources may empower people to overcome barriers to economic mobility and make lasting improvements to their personal and working lives.

NOTES

1 See Andreoni, J., & Payne, A.A. (2013). Charitable giving. In A.J. Auerbach, R. Chetty, M. Feldstein, & E. Saez (Eds.), *Handbook of public economics* (Vol. 5, pp. 1–50). Elsevier; Dickert, S., Kleber, J., Västfjäll, D., & Slovic, P. (2016). Mental imagery, impact, and affect: A mediation model for charitable giving. *PloS One, 11*(2), Article e0148274; and Andreoni, J., Rao, J.M., & Trachtman, H. (2017). Avoiding the ask: A field experiment on altruism, empathy, and charitable giving. *Journal of Political Economy, 125*(3), 625–53; Small, D.A., Loewenstein, G., & Slovic, P. (2007). Sympathy and callousness: The impact of deliberative thought on donations to identifiable and statistical victims. *Organizational Behavior and Human Decision Processes, 102*(2), 143–53; and Bloom, P. (2017). *Against empathy: The case for rational compassion.* Random House.

2 See Garcia, M., & Moore, C.M.T. (2012). Design and implementation of cash transfers in Sub-Saharan Africa: Trends, lessons, and knowledge gaps. In M. Garcia & C.M.T. Moore (Eds.), *The cash dividend: The rise of cash transfer programs in Sub-Saharan Africa* (pp. 75–214). World Bank Group. https://doi.org/10.1596/978-0-8213-8897-6; Davis, B., Handa, S., Hypher, N., Rossi, N.W., Winters, P., & Yablonski, J. (Eds.). (2016). *From evidence to action: The story of cash transfers and impact evaluation in sub Saharan Africa.* Oxford University Press; and Millán, T.M., Barham, T., Macours, K., Maluccio, J.A., & Stampini, M. (2019). Long-term impacts of conditional cash transfers: Review of the evidence. *World Bank Research Observer, 34*(1), 119–59.

3 Giurge, L.M., Whillans, A.V., & West, C. (2020). Why time poverty matters for individuals, organisations and nations. *Nature Human Behaviour, 4*(10), 993–1003.

4 Hirway, I. (2017). *Mainstreaming unpaid work: Time-use data in developing policies.* Oxford University Press.

5 Whillans, A., & West, C. (2022). Alleviating time poverty among the working poor: A pre-registered longitudinal field experiment. *Scientific Reports, 12*(1), 1–17.

6 See Fehr, E., & Schmidt, K.M. (1999). A theory of fairness, competition, and cooperation. *Quarterly Journal of Economics, 114*(3), 817–68; Fehr, E., & Schmidt, K.M. (2001). Theories of fairness and reciprocity-evidence and economic applications. In M. Dewartripont, L. Hansen, & S. Turnovsky (Eds.), *Advances in economics and econometrics: Theory and applications, Eighth World Congress* (Econometric Society Monographs, pp. 208–57). Cambridge University Press; and Alesina, A., & Angeletos, G.M. (2005). Fairness and redistribution. *American Economic Review, 95*(4), 960–80.

7 Slater, R., & Farrington, J. (2009). *Cash transfers: Targeting.* Overseas Development Institute.

8 Floyd, I., Pavetti, L., & Schott, L. (2017, July 20). *Lessons from TANF: Initial unequal state block-grant funding formula grew more unequal over time.* Center on Budget and Policy Priorities. https://www.cbpp.org/research/family-income-support/lessons-from-tanf-initial-unequal-state-block-grant-funding-formula

9 See Ribar, D.C. (2014). How to improve participation in social assistance programs. *IZA World of Labor, 104.* https://doi.org/10.15185/izawol.104; and Office of the Assistant Secretary for Planning and Evaluation. (2014). *Strategies for increasing TANF work participation rates.* Retrieved December 15, 2022, from https://aspe.hhs.gov/strategies-increasing-tanf-work-participation-rates.

10 U.S. Department of Agriculture. (2018, January). *Design issues in USDA's Supplemental Nutrition Assistance Program: Looking ahead by looking back* (Economic Research Report No. 243). Economic Research Service. https://www.ers.usda.gov/webdocs/publications/86924/err-243.pdf?v=0.

11 Center on Budget and Policy Priorities. (2019, June 6). *SNAP caseload and spending declines have accelerated in recent years*. https://www.cbpp.org/research/food-assistance/snap-caseload-and-spending-declines-have-accelerated-in-recent-years.

12 Brown, C., Ravallion, M., & van de Walle, D. (2016). A poor means test? Econometric targeting in Africa. *Journal of Development Economics, 134*, 109–24.

13 Alatas et al. (2012).

14 Hillebrecht, M., Klonner, S., Pacere, N.A., & Souares, A. (2020). Community-based versus statistical targeting of anti-poverty programs: Evidence from Burkina Faso. *Journal of African Economies, 29*(3), 271–305.

15 Universal cash transfer programs have been implemented or tested in a temporary trial in Alaska, California, Brazil, Finland, Spain, Canada, and Kenya, among other places.

16 Egger, D., Haushofer, J., Miguel, E., Niehaus, P., & Walker, M.W. (2019). *General equilibrium effects of cash transfers: Experimental evidence from Kenya* (Working Paper No. 26600). National Bureau of Economic Research.

17 Steele, J.E., Sundsøy, P.R., Pezzulo, C., Alegana, V. A., Bird, T.J., Blumenstock, J., Bjelland, J., Engø-Monsen, K., de Montjoye, Y.-A., Iqbal, A.M., Hadiuzzaman, K.N., Lu, X., Wetter, E., Tatem, A.J., & Bengtsson, L. (2017). Mapping poverty using mobile phone and satellite data. *Journal of the Royal Society Interface, 14*(127), Article 20160690.

18 See Blumenstock, J. (2020). Machine learning can help get COVID-19 aid to those who need it most. *Nature*. Advance online publication. https://doi.org/10.1038/d41586-020-01393-7; Aiken, E., Bellue, S., Karlan, D., Udry, C.R., & Blumenstock, J. (2021). *Machine learning and mobile phone data can improve the targeting of humanitarian assistance* (Working Paper No. 29070). National Bureau of Economic Research; and Blumenstock, J.E. (2016). Fighting poverty with data. *Science, 353*(6301), 753–4.

19 Marchenko, A., & Chia, H.S. (2021, April 13). *How MobileAid & machine learning-based targeting can complement existing social protection programs*. Medium. https://medium.com/center-for-effective-global-action/how-precision-aid-and-machine-learning-based-targeting-can-complement-existing-social-protection-de3bc3211fd2.

20 See Sprague, A. (2015). *Leveraging public assistance to promote financial inclusion: A new approach for TANF*. https://static.newamerica.org/attachments/12121-leveraging-public-assistance-to-promote-financial-inclusion/Asset-Building-Leveraging-Public-Assistance-TANF-2.4b5d041e89094ebaa86488ef8d54eab0.pdf.

21 Hirvonen, K., & Hoddinott, J. (2021). Beneficiary views on cash and in-kind payments: Evidence from Ethiopia's Productive Safety Net Programme. *World Bank Economic Review, 35*(2), 398–413.

22 Otulana, S., Hearle, C., Attah, R., Merttens, F., & Wallin, J. (2016). *Evaluation of the Kenya Hunger Safety Net Programme Phase 2: Impact Evaluation Qualitative Research Study 1*. Oxford Policy Management. https://reliefweb.int/sites/reliefweb.int/files/resources/1518601483.HSNP2%20Qualitative%20Summary%20Report%202017.pdf

23 See Freeland, N. (2007). Superfluous, pernicious, atrocious and abominable? The case against conditional cash transfers. *IDS Bulletin, 38*(3), 75–8; Gaarder, M. (2012). Conditional versus unconditional cash: A commentary. *Journal of Development Effectiveness, 4*(1), 130–3; and Baird, S., Ferreira, F.H.G., Özler, B., & Woolcock, M. (2014). Conditional, unconditional and everything in between: A systematic review of the effects of cash transfer programmes on schooling outcomes. *Journal of Development Effectiveness, 6*(1), 1–43.

24 See De Janvry, A., & Sadoulet, E. (2006). Making conditional cash transfer programs more efficient: Designing for maximum effect of the conditionality. *World Bank Economic Review, 20*(1), 1–29; and Garcia, S., & Saavedra, J.E. (2017). Educational

impacts and cost-effectiveness of conditional cash transfer programs in developing countries: A meta-analysis. *Review of Educational Research, 87*(5), 921–65.

25 See Bastagli, F., Hagen-Zanker, J., Harman, L., Barca, V., Sturge, G., & Schmidt, T. (2019). The impact of cash transfers: A review of the evidence from low-and middle-income countries. *Journal of Social Policy, 48*(3), 569–94; and Bryan, G., Chowdhury, S., Mobarak, A.M., Morten, M., & Smits, J. (2022). *Encouragement and distortionary effects of conditional cash transfers.* Retrieved April 13, 2023, from https://elischolar .library.yale.edu/cgi/viewcontent.cgi?article=2084&context=egcenter-discussion -paper-series.

26 Aker, J.C., Boumnijel, R., McClelland, A., & Tierney, N. (2016). Payment mechanisms and antipoverty programs: Evidence from a mobile money cash transfer experiment in Niger. *Economic Development and Cultural Change, 65*(1), 1–37.

27 Davis, B., Gaarder, M., Handa, S., & Yablonski, J (2012). Evaluating the impact of cash transfer programmes in Sub-Saharan Africa: An introduction to the special issue. *Journal of Development Effectiveness, 4*(1), 1–8.

28 De Brauw, A., & Hoddinott, J. (2011). Must conditional cash transfer programs be conditioned to be effective? The impact of conditioning transfers on school enrollment in Mexico. *Journal of Development Economics, 96*(2), 359–70.

29 Benhassine, N., Devoto, F., Duflo, E., Dupas, P., & Pouliquen, V. (2015). Turning a shove into a nudge? A "labeled cash transfer" for education. *American Economic Journal: Economic Policy, 7*(3), 86–125.

30 Soman, D., & Cheema, A. (2011). Earmarking and partitioning: Increasing saving by low-income households. *Journal of Marketing Research, 48*(SPL), S14–S22; West, C., Ulkumen, G., Arundel, P., & Fox, C. (2023). *The choice architecture of personal budgeting tools.* Retrieved April 14, 2023, from https://www.colinwest.org/s/20220531 -MANUSCRIPT-Budgets-as-Choice-Architecture.pdf.

31 Jack, W., & Habyarimana, J. (2018). *High hopes: Experimental evidence on saving and the transition to high school in Kenya* (Working Paper No. 4). Georgetown University Initiative on Innovation, Development and Evaluation. https://repository.library .georgetown.edu/bitstream/handle/10822/1048254/WP004_Habyarimana.Jack _v3.pdf?sequence=8

32 Heath, C., & Soll, J.B. (1996). Mental budgeting and consumer decisions. *Journal of Consumer Research, 23*(1), 40–52.

33 Walker, R., Kyomuhendo, G.B., Chase, E., Choudhry, S., Gubrium, E. K., Nicola, J. Y., Lødemel, I, Mathew, L., Mwiine, A., & Ming, Y.A. (2013). Poverty in global perspective: Is shame a common denominator? *Journal of Social Policy, 42*(2), 215–33; Hall, C.C., Zhao, J., & Shafir, E. (2014). Self-affirmation among the poor: Cognitive and behavioral implications. *Psychological Science, 25*(2), 619–25.

34 Thomas, C.C., Otis, N.G., Abraham, J.R., Markus, H.R., & Walton, G.M. (2020). Toward a science of delivering aid with dignity: Experimental evidence and local forecasts from Kenya. *Proceeding of the National Academy of Sciences, 117*(27), 15546–53.

35 Hamermesh, D.S. (2019). *Spending time: The most valuable resource.* Oxford University Press.

36 Kahneman, D., Krueger, A.B., Schkade, D.A., Schwarz, N., & Stone, A.A. (2004). A survey method for characterizing daily life experience: The day reconstruction method. *Science, 306*(5702), 1776–80.

37 See Csikszentmihalyi, M., & Larson, R. (2014). Validity and reliability of the experience-sampling method. In *Flow and the foundations of positive psychology: The collected works of Mihaly Csikszentmihalyi* (pp. 35–54). Springer; and Kahneman et al. (2004).

38 Giurge et al. (2020).

39 Whillans, A.V., Dunn, E.W., Smeets, P., Bekkers, R., & Norton, M. I. (2017). Buying time promotes happiness. *Proceedings of the National Academy of Sciences*, *114*(32), 8523–7.

40 Strazdins, L., Welsh, J., Korda, R., Broom, D., & Paolucci, F. (2016). Not all hours are equal: Could time be a social determinant of health? *Sociology of Health & Illness*, *38*(1), 21–42.

41 Roxburgh, S. (2004). "There just aren't enough hours in the day': The mental health consequences of time pressure. *Journal of Health and Social Behavior*, *45*(2), 115–31.

42 Whillans & West (2022).

43 Giurge et al. (2020).

44 See Fink, G., Jack, B.K., & Masiye, F. (2014). *Seasonal credit constraints and agricultural labor supply: Evidence from Zambia* (Working Paper No. 20218). National Bureau of Economic Research; Gollin, D., Lagakos, D., & Waugh, M.E. (2014). The agricultural productivity gap. *Quarterly Journal of Economics*, *129*(2), 939–93; Gollin, D., Lagakos, D., & Waugh, M.E. (2014). Agricultural productivity differences across countries. *American Economic Review*, *104*(5), 165–70; Lagakos, D., Mobarak, A.M., & Waugh, M.E. (2018). *The welfare effects of encouraging rural-urban migration* (Working Paper No. 24193). National Bureau of Economic Research; and Lagakos, D. (2020). Urban-rural gaps in the developing world: Does internal migration offer opportunities? *Journal of Economic Perspectives*, *34*(3), 174–92.

45 Premand, P., & Schnitzer, P. (2021). Efficiency, legitimacy, and impacts of targeting methods: Evidence from an experiment in Niger. *World Bank Economic Review*, *35*(4), 892–920.

46 See Kniesner, T.J., & Visusi, W.K. (2005). Value of a statistical life: Relative position vs. relative age. *American Economic Review*, *95*(2), 142–6; Diamond, P.A., & Hausman, J.A. (1994). Contingent valuation: Is some number better than no number? *Journal of Economic Perspectives*, *8*(4), 45–64.

47 See Millán et al. (2019); Rodríguez-Oreggia, E., & Freije, S. (2012). *Long term impact of a cash-transfers program on labor outcomes of the rural youth* (CID Working Paper No. 23). Harvard University, Center for International Development; and Attah, R., Barca, V., Kardan, A., MacAuslan, I., Merttens, F., & Pellerano, L. (2016). Can social protection affect psychosocial wellbeing and why does this matter? Lessons from cash transfers in sub-Saharan Africa. *Journal of Development Studies*, *52*(8), 1115–31.

48 See Slater, R. (2011). Cash transfers, social protection and poverty reduction. *International Journal of Social Welfare*, *20*(3), 250–9; and Molyneux, M., Jones, W.N., & Samuels, F. (2016). Can cash transfer programmes have "transformative" effects? *Journal of Development Studies*, *52*(8), 1087–98.

49 See Ridley, M., Rao, G., Schilbach, F., & Patel, V. (2020). Poverty, depression, and anxiety: Causal evidence and mechanisms. *Science*, *370*(6522), Article eaay0214; and Haushofer, J., & Fehr, E. (2014). On the psychology of poverty. *Science*, *344*(6186), 862–7.

50 Blattman, C., Jamison, J.C., & Sheridan, M. (2017). Reducing crime and violence: Experimental evidence from cognitive behavioral therapy in Liberia. *American Economic Review*, *107*(4), 1165–206.

51 Haushofer, J., Mudida, R., & Shapiro, J.P. (2020). *The comparative impact of cash transfers and a psychotherapy program on psychological and economic well-being* (Working Paper No. 28106). National Bureau of Economic Research.

52 Langendorf, C., Roederer, T., de Pee, S., Brown, D., Doyon, S., Mamaty, A.A., Touré, L.W.-M., Manzo, M.L., & Grais, R.F. (2014). Preventing acute malnutrition among young children in crises: A prospective intervention study in Niger. *PLoS Medicine*, *11*(9), e1001714.

53 Ambler, K., De Brauw, A., & Godlonton, S. (2020). Cash transfers and management advice for agriculture: Evidence from Senegal. *World Bank Economic Review, 34*(3), 597–617; See Devereux, S., Roelen, K., Sabates, R., Stoelinga, D., & Dyevre, A. (2015). *Concern's Graduation Model Programme in Burundi: Final evaluation report.* Institute of Development Studies, Centre for Social Protection; Devereux, S., & Sabates, R. (2016). *Enhancing the productive capacity of extremely poor people in Rwanda: Final evaluation report.* Institute of Development Studies, Centre for Social Protection; and Blouin C., Bhushan, A., Murphy, S., & Warren, B. (2007). *Trade liberalisation: Synthesis papers* (Research Paper No. 4). World Health Organization, Globalisation and Health Knowledge Network
54 Whillans & West (2022).
55 Banerjee, A., Duflo, E., Goldberg, N., Karlan, D., Osei, R., Parienté, W., & Udry, C. (2015). A multifaceted program causes lasting progress for the very poor: Evidence from six countries. *Science, 348*(6236), 1260799.
56 Ibid., p. 1.
57 Whillans & West (2022).
58 Chetty, R., Hendren, N., Kline, P., Saez, E., & Turner, N. (2014). Is the United States still a land of opportunity? Recent trends in intergenerational mobility. *American Economic Review, 104*(5), 141–7.
59 Ferdjani, H., Lefebvre, A., & Perié, A. (2019). *Taanka: A rainwater harvesting tank.* McGill University.
60 West & Whillans (2022).
61 Martínez, C., Puentes, E., & Ruiz-Tagle, J. (2013). *Micro-entrepreneurship training and asset transfers: Short term impacts on the poor* (Working Paper No. wp380). University of Chile, Department of Economics.

CHAPTER EIGHT

A Behavioral Perspective on the Decision to Seek Formal and Informal Financial Help

Ania Jaroszewicz

INTRODUCTION

A 2017 survey by the Consumer Financial Protection Bureau found that approximately one in five Americans felt that they probably or definitely could not come up with US$2,000 in the next 30 days to pay for an unexpected need.[1] That same survey found that two in five respondents found it somewhat or very difficult to cover their expenses and pay all their bills in a typical month.

Such statistics underscore the incredible pervasiveness of financial insecurity in the United States. In this chapter, I use a behavioral economic lens to examine how people facing such insecurities decide to seek financial help. *Help* can broadly be categorized as being either formal (provided by an organization or professional) or informal (provided by an individual acting in a personal capacity).[2] I focus on one particularly vital type of financial help from each of these categories: from formal help, I examine social welfare program benefits; from informal help, I examine financial loans or gifts from friends and family. Although distinct in many ways, both of these forms of help can be incredibly valuable in addressing financial needs.[3]

I begin by presenting a general framework that outlines how a person may decide to seek help. I then apply that framework separately to the two types of help, each time reviewing prior literature on factors that affect people's (un)willingness to seek that help.[4] Finally, I discuss policy implications, arguing that an understanding of both formal and informal help-seeking processes is crucial for informing policies intended to help financially vulnerable populations. To focus the chapter, I primarily examine the US context.

HELP-SEEKING FRAMEWORK

How might a person choose whether to seek financial help? In this section, I present a three-stage help-seeking framework adapted from prior models.[5] The framework is primarily intended to be an organizing tool to group together common themes in the extant literature rather than a precise depiction of the help-seeking process.

I take as a starting point that the person in need recognizes their financial problem.[6] I then model their decision-making process as following three stages that they must progress through in order to seek help. These stages are (1) awareness of the help, (2) evaluations of the desirability of being helped if no action were required to get the help, and (3) evaluations of the costs of taking action to seek the help. Within each stage, a range of factors can make a person either more or less likely to move forward. Figure 8.1 illustrates the three stages, as well as example factors falling within each stage. Some factors may fall into more than one stage.[7]

In the first stage, awareness of help, a person must determine whether help might be available to them – specifically, whether a program or potential helper exists at all and whether they might be able to receive help from that source. Awareness of or attention to a particular help source can be thought of as a prerequisite to evaluating the desirability of being helped.[8] If a person is simply unaware of a social welfare program or of a person who might be able to help, they obviously will not seek help from that source. Similarly, if they believe that help is available generally, but they themselves would not be able to access it (e.g., because of the eligibility criteria), they

Figure 8.1. A help-seeking framework with examples of factors that could prevent a person from seeking formal help (left) and informal help (right)

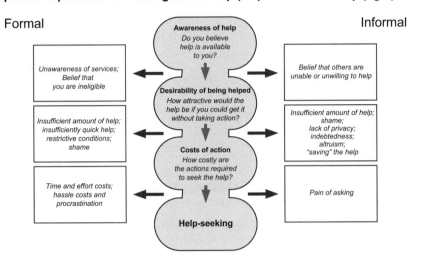

Formal   Informal

Awareness of help
Do you believe
help is available
to you?

Unawareness of services;
Belief that
you are ineligible

Belief that others are
unable or unwilling to help

Desirability of being helped
How attractive would the
help be if you could get it
without taking action?

Insufficient amount of help;
insufficiently quick help;
restrictive conditions;
shame

Insufficient amount of help;
shame;
lack of privacy;
indebtedness;
altruism;
"saving" the help

Costs of action
How costly are
the actions required
to seek the help?

Time and effort costs;
hassle costs and
procrastination

Pain of asking

Help-seeking

would not progress beyond this stage. Later, in the "Factors Affecting the Decision to Seek Formal Help" and "Factors Affecting the Decision to Seek Informal Help" sections, I describe the evidence for the role of awareness in the help-seeking process.

Simply being aware of a help source does not, however, necessarily mean a person will seek it out.[9] Before a person will seek help, they must also evaluate how desirable it would be to be helped if they did not need to do anything to get the help, and they must evaluate the costs of seeking the help. Although most models of help-seeking group these two evaluations together,[10] distinguishing between them is important for developing precise policy and practice interventions.[11] For this reason, this help-seeking framework places them into two separate stages.

In particular, the framework proposes that if a person is aware of the fact that help might be available to them, they will move onto the second stage of the framework, at which point they must determine whether they would in theory want to be helped if they did not need to do anything to get it. That is, if they simply experienced the end state of having been helped without taking any actions to get to that state, would they be better or worse off? If they determine that they would be better off, they would be described as wanting to be helped (and would move onto the next stage). If they determine that they would be worse off, they would be described as not wanting to be helped (and would not move onto the next stage). Although it may at first blush appear strange for a person to not want additional resources, there are a range of documented reasons why this may occur, such as the person feeling ashamed of being helped or not wanting to be indebted to someone else. This research is also described in the "Factors Affecting the Decision to Seek Formal Help" and "Factors Affecting the Decision to Seek Informal Help" sections.

Finally, even when a person determines that they would in theory want to be helped, they must still typically take costly action to seek it, for instance by submitting applications (in the case of formal help) or having a conversation with a potential helper (in the case of informal help). The evaluation of these perceived costs of action is the subject of the third and final stage of the framework. The "Factors Affecting the Decision to Seek Formal Help" and "Factors Affecting the Decision to Seek Informal Help" sections also describe the evidence for how the costs of taking action affect help-seeking.

The framework implies that bottlenecks in any of the three stages can prevent a person from seeking help, and a person will only seek help if they can progress through all three stages. Although for simplicity I model the person as progressing through the stages in order, this is not always the case.[12] In deciding whether to seek help, a person may be considering the help-seeking factors in each of the three stages in isolation or jointly.[13] At the same time, they may also be comparing multiple sources of help.[14] For instance, a person may simultaneously be choosing among applying for a social welfare program, asking a cousin for help, and asking a neighbor for help.

It is also important to note that although I refer to both social welfare program benefits and loans from friends or family as help, whether the person in need perceives them as help is a different question. This is, moreover, more than just a point about semantics. Perceptions of what qualifies as help are somewhat malleable. Framing can affect whether a given resource is perceived as help, which can in turn affect a person's willingness to pursue that resource.[15] The framework presented here should be applied to situations in which the person in need perceives that the resource at hand constitutes help.

In the next two sections, I use this framework to describe how a person might decide to seek social welfare program benefits and help from friends and family. For each type of help, I first provide some background on its characteristics and usage, then describe a (non-exhaustive) set of factors affecting people's decisions to seek it. The factors are organized by the three stages described earlier.

FORMAL FINANCIAL HELP

What Is Formal Financial Help?

As mentioned, *formal help* is defined broadly as help from an organization (e.g., the government, an employer, or an education institute) or an individual acting in a professional capacity.[16] To focus the discussion, in this section I examine one particularly important type of formal financial help: social welfare program benefits.

Social welfare program benefits are cash or in-kind resources provided by a governmental entity, usually on the basis of low-income means-tested eligibility criteria.[17] Seeking these benefits often requires completing an application, which can be extensive and demand proof of need. It may also require phone calls, in-person visits to the organization's office, or both. Once submitted, applications and other materials are typically reviewed according to a set of predetermined and non-negotiable rules – rules that govern whether the request is granted and, if so, the level of resources given, the duration, and the conditions of receipt.

Paradigmatic examples of such programs in the United States include the Earned Income Tax Credit, Supplemental Nutrition Assistance Program, and Medicaid. Although I do not review evidence for this, many of the conclusions presented here are likely to apply to other types of formal help – such as university financial aid and benefits from non-governmental organizations – as well as to other countries. For brevity, I henceforth use the terms *social welfare program benefits* and *formal help* interchangeably.

Formal Help Usage

The extent to which a social welfare program is used can be measured in several ways.[18] One of the more common metrics is a take-up rate, which captures the percentage of people eligible for a particular benefit who are receiving it. A low take-up rate typically reflects a failure to apply for benefits, and is sometimes called *primary non–take-up*. There may also be situations in which eligible people are denied, for instance if they do not have appropriate documentation (secondary non–take-up). There may also be lags between when a person applies and when they begin receiving benefits (temporary non–take-up).[19] Although important for understanding why there is incomplete take-up, these latter, administrative-side factors are largely unrelated to a person's decision to (not) seek help and thus are outside the scope of this chapter. Throughout, I focus on issues related to primary non–take-up.

Whatever the cause, take-up of social welfare varies widely across programs and often falls short of 100 per cent.[20] In one review of a range of social welfare and housing programs in Organisation for Economic Co-operation and Development countries, researchers estimated that take-up rates tend to be only 40 per cent to 80 per cent.[21] The United States is no exception to this pattern.[22] For instance, in 2019, only 79 per cent of people who were eligible for the Earned Income Tax Credit claimed it, with the remaining 21 per cent forgoing an average benefit of US$2,461.[23]

Given such statistics, it is not surprising that a large body of literature has emerged to explain why people may not apply for these programs.[24] In the next section, I review some of this work using the help-seeking framework described earlier.

Factors Affecting the Decision to Seek Formal Help

STAGE 1: AWARENESS OF HELP

In the first stage of the framework, awareness of help, a person must establish whether resources might be available to them. In the context of formal help, one factor that may prevent a person from progressing through this stage is simply an unawareness of a program.[25] In one demonstration of how a lack of awareness can affect the decision to seek formal help, Bhargava and Manoli found that simply receiving a notice with information on the Earned Income Tax Credit increased take-up of the program, as did receiving additionally simplified information.[26]

Even if a person is aware of a program, they may still be uncertain about their own eligibility and thus the likely payoff of committing time and effort to apply. This uncertainty has been modeled theoretically, with researchers proposing that greater uncertainty of an application being successful suppresses application rates.[27] Other work has found that randomly informing some households of their likely eligibility for a program increased take-up relative to an uninformed control group,[28] providing evidence consistent with this idea.

STAGE 2: DESIRABILITY OF BEING HELPED

If a person determines that help might be available to them, they move to the second stage of the framework. In this stage, they must determine whether they would in theory want to be helped if they did not need to take any action to seek the help. What determines the desirability of being helped?

One critical factor will be the dollar amount of the benefit, which can take the form of either a one-time transfer or the sum of a stream of transfers over time. Perhaps unsurprisingly, there is robust evidence that the higher the program benefits, the more likely people are to apply for those benefits.[29]

Expectations about how quickly one might begin to receive benefits after applying may also affect the desirability of being helped. For example, a person who is facing immediate and acute financial need may be reluctant to apply for formal help if they believe that they will not be able to receive help sufficiently quickly.

In some cases, social welfare programs providing a stream of benefits require recipients to take certain actions or meet certain conditions to maintain those benefits.[30] For instance, to receive Supplemental Nutrition Assistance Program benefits, people must typically meet specific work requirements for as long as they are receiving the benefits.[31] Such conditions and requirements may affect the desirability of being helped for two reasons.[32] First, they increase the time and effort required to maintain the benefits. Second, they may be aversive purely for psychological reasons: people often dislike having their freedom restricted, even if they would have willingly chosen to take the action that is being required of them.[33]

Finally, a person may prefer to not receive formal help because they fear the shame or stigma associated with it.[34] That is, they may fear that receiving help would be a signal to themselves or others that they have failed, that they have negative attributes, or that they are part of a resented group.[35] Indeed, shame and stigma are and seemingly always have been central to the experience of poverty.[36] Influential theoretical work has placed these concepts at the center of the discussion on psychological costs of receiving formal help,[37] generating decades of work on the topic.[38] There is widespread enthusiasm for the idea and some evidence for its role in limiting take-up.[39] Nevertheless, not all research aiming to test the stigma hypothesis has found strong evidence for it, suggesting that other factors may be at least as important.[40]

STAGE 3: COSTS OF ACTION

If a person determines that they would in theory like to be helped but they have not yet taken action, they enter the third and final stage of the framework: evaluating the costs of taking action. One factor that may be particularly important in the decision to seek formal help is the amount of time or effort required to apply for it.[41] As mentioned earlier, seeking formal help can be a long and cumbersome process.[42] The negative effects of time and effort costs on take-up have been modeled theoretically and demonstrated empirically.[43] Assisting applicants with the enrollment process overcomes some of these costs and consequently increases take-up, particularly if the assistance is extensive and tailored to the individual.[44] There is also some evidence that simplifying the application process increases take-up.[45]

It seems plausible that a person's willingness to incur these effort costs will interact with their beliefs about the benefit amounts: the larger and more certain the perceived benefits, the more willing they will likely be to exert the effort.[46] However, those who will have the largest benefit amounts and will be the most likely to qualify for benefits (i.e., those who are in greatest need) may also have the highest time and effort costs of securing those benefits. Prior work has argued that relative to people with financial slack, people facing financial scarcity have less mental bandwidth and face greater demands on their time.[47] Thus, the people who need the benefits the most may also be least able to take action to access those benefits.

Although it may seem unrealistic that a person in need would be unwilling to travel locally or fill out an application in exchange for potentially substantial benefits, prior work has repeatedly documented that seemingly small inconveniences, or "hassle costs," can have massive effects on behavior[48] – even when a person actively intends on taking an action.[49] For instance, the hassle costs associated with needing to take several buses to a social welfare program office may be enough to discourage a person from applying for benefits.[50] It is typically theorized that the effect of hassle costs on behavior is driven by the fact that people place more weight on outcomes occurring in the present or near future than on those in the more distant future.[51] Because seeking formal help often entails paying an immediate effort cost in return for a future (and often uncertain) benefit, people may procrastinate on putting in that effort, potentially delaying take-up indefinitely.[52]

INFORMAL FINANCIAL HELP

What Is Informal Financial Help?

I next turn to informal help, or help that is provided by an individual acting in a personal capacity.[53] For the purposes of this review, I focus on helping interactions in which the individuals know each other personally, such as a person in need asking a friend or family member for a financial loan or gift.[54] When I use the term *informal help*, I am referring to this kind of interaction.

Compared with formal help requests, informal help requests will almost by definition be more visible to one's social circle. People may seek informal help through direct asks, through indirect asks (e.g., hints), or by soliciting the help of a third party who can serve as an intermediary.[55] Regardless of the method, informal help can generally be requested much more quickly than formal help.[56] If the request is accepted, the help can also typically be provided quickly. For instance, a helper may be able to give cash or send money through a financial technology application in a matter of minutes.

One important difference between formal and informal help relates to what happens after a request is submitted. In the case of formal help, requests are largely processed in a non-negotiable and codified way. With informal help, this will not necessarily be true. A help-seeker may be able to sway the potential helper in their decision of whether to help, how much to help, and what the terms of the help would be.[57] Moreover, some pieces of the arrangement may remain unclear or unspoken. For instance, many informal loans have open-ended repayment costs and timelines.[58] There may be no contracts at all, or perhaps only vague verbal or psychological contracts.[59] Such ambiguity can result in the two parties interpreting the same interaction in very different ways, thereby creating the potential for future disagreement or conflict.[60]

Informal Help Usage

Perhaps unsurprisingly, data on informal help usage are scarcer than data on formal help usage. However, the data that do exist reveal a few striking patterns.

First, most people feel that they have friends or family who could help them financially. For instance, the Consumer Financial Protection Bureau found that nearly three-quarters of American survey respondents believed that their friends or family would loan them money to help them make ends meet, with or without an expectation of repayment.[61]

Second, many people seem to take advantage of these opportunities for receiving informal help.[62] A global survey conducted by the World Bank asked respondents from whom they had borrowed money in the past 12 months.[63] The results revealed that 14 per cent of US respondents reported having borrowed from friends or family, compared with 23 per cent who borrowed from a bank or another type of formal financial institution (excluding credit cards), 17 per cent who borrowed from a store, and 1 per cent who borrowed from another private lender, such as a payday lender or pawn shop. The same survey revealed that informal loans seem to be even more prevalent on a global scale: across the 142 countries surveyed, 24 per cent of respondents reported having borrowed from friends and family over the same period.

In particular, friends and family seem to serve as a critical safety net for a significant proportion of people. A Federal Reserve Board survey of Americans found that among people who could not cover a $400 emergency expense using cash or its functional equivalent, 29 per cent said that they would borrow from friends and family to cover the gap (compared with 45 per cent who would put it on a credit card paid off over time and 5 per cent who would use a payday loan, deposit advance, or overdraft).[64] These results are consistent with findings from other studies conducted in the United States and abroad.[65]

Third, although informal loans and gifts are used by people of all income levels, they seem to be a particularly important source of financial support for people who are lower income, are more liquidity constrained, or have traditionally been excluded from more formal banking systems, such as racial minorities and immigrants.[66]

Finally, despite the simplicity, inexpensiveness, and speed of informal financial help,[67] as well as its apparent importance in the global economy, people often report disliking it and wanting to limit their reliance on friends and family.[68] This suggests that people face costs to asking for or receiving informal financial help. Indeed, as access to formal credit increases, people seem to shift to it.[69] The fact that the fraction of informal credit in total lending is larger in countries with less-developed formal banking sectors is also consistent with the proposition that if borrowers have a choice, they prefer to use formal credit markets.[70]

In the next section, I review the literature on some of these costs of seeking informal financial help. To organize the discussion, I again use the help-seeking framework described earlier.

Factors Affecting the Decision to Seek Informal Help

STAGE 1: AWARENESS OF HELP

Beginning with the first stage of the framework, awareness of help, the primary question a person in need must answer is whether another person would be willing and able to help. A potential helper's actual willingness to help will be affected by a wide range of variables, such as the helper's beliefs about why the person needs help and what kind of help it is.[71] When the person in need recognizes that those variables matter, their beliefs about the variables may in turn affect their estimates of the likelihood that a potential helper would agree to help.

Generally, the higher the perceived likelihood of a potential helper agreeing to help, the more likely the person in need should be to ask. Prior work measuring these beliefs has found that people consistently and often dramatically underestimate the likelihood that others would agree to help if asked.[72] This underestimation may prevent some people from ever progressing beyond the first stage.

STAGE 2: DESIRABILITY OF BEING HELPED

Recall that in the second stage, a person in need must determine whether they would in theory want to be helped if they could get the help without taking any action. As with formal help, one factor that will determine the desirability of receiving informal help is how much the person in need believes they could receive from a given potential helper, conditional on them agreeing to help at all. The more the potential helper can or is willing to provide, the more willing the person in need should be to ask. However, just as people tend to underestimate the probability that others will agree to help, there is also evidence that they underestimate how much others will help them, should they help at all.[73] That is, people in need underestimate others' helpfulness on both the extensive and the intensive margins.

A second factor falling into this stage that is also shared with the formal help-seeking factors is shame. Many cultures (including American culture) have a long history of attributing financial need to individuals' personal failings (e.g., laziness, immorality, incompetence) rather than to environmental circumstances or luck.[74] Many people in poverty internalize these attributions and consequently feel ashamed of their financial situation.[75] The fear of shame and judgment, in turn, can lead people to withdraw from social interactions and hide their struggles from others rather than seek help from them.[76]

Relatedly, a lack of privacy can also affect the desirability of receiving informal help. Receiving informal help often requires revealing personal and sensitive information to the potential helper – information the help-seeker might prefer to keep confidential.[77] This can be aversive not only because people may be ashamed of their financial need or fear judgment,[78] but also because they simply value privacy more generally.[79]

A fourth factor that can affect the desirability of being helped is that of indebtedness or reciprocity. A key feature of informal loans and gifts is that the recipient may be expected to return the favor in the future.[80] Although debt relationships can be seen as a sign of social inclusion and can strengthen social bonds,[81] people are often averse to feeling indebted to others.[82] The obligation to reciprocate can feel like a burden,[83] and debt relationships can generate or reinforce subordination.[84] In addition, being indebted to someone with whom one has a personal relationship (as is the case with informal loans) can produce problems that would not be present with formal loans. Whereas formal loans are secured through material collateral, informal loans are usually secured through social collateral.[85] This means that if the borrower defaults on the loan, they risk souring the relationship with their lender and potentially damaging their reputation.[86] An expectation that they will feel indebted, will need to reciprocate, or will face social sanctions if they default may prevent people in need from asking friends and family for help.

Fifth, a person may not want to be helped because of altruism or prosociality: the person in need may not want to take resources away from a helper lest it harm the helper. Although altruism has been studied extensively as a reason for giving,[87] it is surprisingly understudied as a reason for not requesting. Nevertheless, there is some circumstantial evidence,[88] and it seems intuitively plausible.

Finally, sometimes a person in need may want to save a potential helper's goodwill and willingness to help until it is most needed. To the extent that a person in need both recognizes that a potential helper's willingness or ability to help is exhaustible and believes that they may need more help in the future, they may prefer to not have help in lower-need situations to ensure they can get help in the higher-need situations. Like altruism, this topic has not received much attention in the literature.

STAGE 3: COSTS OF ACTION

If a person determines that they would want to be helped but has not yet taken action, they reach the final stage of the framework: evaluating the costs of taking action. Unlike with formal help, time and effort do not seem to be major factors preventing people from seeking informal help. However, there are many hedonic costs associated with having the conversation to ask for help that are independent of the costs of being helped (described in Stage 2) – that is, people often experience a "pain of asking."[89] Asking for help can be awkward and uncomfortable, and it requires navigation of complex social rules, norms, and cues.[90] It also exposes a person to the possibility of rejection, which can be hedonically painful and weaken a relationship.[91] Some work has argued that asking can be painful even if the help is ultimately given.[92]

Moreover, even though evidence demonstrates that people are uncomfortable asking for most types of help, there is reason to believe that people may be particularly uncomfortable asking for financial help. In addition to the standard unflattering assessments people may make about a person facing financial hardship (described earlier), people are often uncomfortable with monetizing formerly non-monetary interactions,[93] even when monetizing may be more efficient.[94]

DISCUSSION

Even in situations in which help would be of great material value, people often choose to not seek it. In this chapter, I have reviewed a range of factors that can affect whether a person seeks formal and informal financial help. I group these factors into three stages: awareness of the help, the desirability of being helped if the person could get the help without taking action, and the costs of taking action to seek the help.

Why is it important to understand why a person does or does not seek needed help? The case for formal help is fairly clear: knowing why people do and do not seek help from social welfare programs is essential for informing public policy. For instance, understanding the effect of time and effort costs on the decision to apply for a program is fundamental for predicting the extent to which a simplification of the program's application would increase take-up.

The case for informal help may be less obvious. Because formal and informal help are likely partial substitutes,[95] changes in informal helping interactions (whether through seeking or giving behavior) may affect decisions to seek formal help. Similarly, changes to formal help policies may affect decisions to seek informal help. Understanding when and how these processes occur can provide policy makers with more accurate estimates of the psychological and economic consequences of policies.

For example, suppose a policy maker is considering cutting a social welfare program that serves a displaced population with few community ties. Because these individuals may not have many sources of informal help, they may be particularly constrained in their ability to switch to it as access to formal help declines. These individuals may experience large economic losses as a result of the policy change. Alternatively, imagine that the program is instead serving a population with relatively strong community ties. These individuals may be able to switch to informal help more readily, thereby attenuating the magnitude of the economic losses. However, such a policy change may affect more than the recipients' economic well-being. First, as discussed in the "Factors Affecting the Decision to Seek Informal Help" section, people may experience a range of psychological costs from seeking informal help, such as shame and a loss of privacy. Thus, if the loss of the formal help program leads to an increase in informal help-seeking, there may also be a higher incidence of these psychological costs. Second, and much more important, the decrease in formal help provisions and possible subsequent increase in informal help-seeking would effectively shift the burden of helping away from the government and onto someone else: the help-seeker's friends and family. This, of course, can be a major strain on a community.

This last example highlights a critical point: formal help programs can affect not just the recipients of the formal help programs but also their broader communities. Careful consideration of these dynamics can provide policy makers with a more comprehensive and holistic view of how formal help policies affect communities' well-being. Conversely, ignoring the role of informal help when developing formal help policies can result in misguided estimates of the policies' effects.

A somewhat distinct question arising from this discussion is how to determine whether people should be seeking help more or less frequently in a given context. In this review, I have focused on people in need, describing the benefits and costs of seeking help, but of course (and as previewed in the last example), seeking help by definition also affects others, whether they are transferring resources or turning down requests. In some cases, seeking help can even affect third parties who are not directly involved in the interaction. To identify the optimal level of help-seeking, one must also consider its effects on these other parties.

In the context of formal help, the most obvious way in which help-seeking affects these other parties is through taxpayer funds: more help-seeking typically means that more help is provided and more taxes are spent. On the one hand, taxpayers and other observers may be concerned about fraudulent or incorrect claims,[96] and they may resent social welfare program recipients if they believe that benefits are excessive or undeserved.[97] On the other hand, spending on social welfare programs can generate wealth distributions that are closer to most people's ideals.[98] In addition, reducing poverty and inequality through such spending can confer a wide range of benefits to non-recipients, including increased economic output, decreased crime, and lowered governmental health expenditures.[99]

In the context of informal help, evidence suggests that some people dislike being asked for help and go out of their way to avoid the possibility of being asked.[100] Indeed, the literature on negative social capital documents the effects of excessive help-seeking in a community and its costs on potential helpers.[101] At the same time, there is also evidence that people often enjoy helping others,[102] suggesting that removing barriers to help-seeking may sometimes benefit both the recipient and the helper. Having a firmer understanding of when help-seeking will have positive versus negative effects on potential helpers and third parties can shed light on the optimal level of help-seeking in a given context and the extent to which it should be encouraged.

If one determines that help-seeking should be encouraged, the next question becomes how should it be encouraged? Specifically, which factors that prevent people from seeking help should be addressed? One way to answer this question is to target the factors that have the largest impact on behavior. If awareness of help is the largest bottleneck in the process, increase awareness. If the desirability of being helped is the largest bottleneck, increase the benefits, decrease the costs, or both. This approach implicitly assumes that the goal is to increase the overall amount of help-seeking.

However, increasing the overall amount of help-seeking might not be the most efficient or equitable approach if helping resources are limited and some people would benefit more from those resources than others. In such a case, an alternative strategy might be to concentrate on increasing help-seeking among people who would benefit most from the help – for instance, those who are in greatest need.[103] People who are in relatively greater need may, importantly, face different help-seeking barriers than people who are in lesser need. For instance, perhaps those who are neediest tend to be unaware of a program, whereas those who are less needy tend to be aware but not apply for other reasons. Addressing the barriers that disproportionately affect the neediest people (in this case, by increasing program awareness) should increase help-seeking among that group while keeping it relatively constant among those who are less needy.[104] Assuming that the increase in help-seeking also results in more receipt of help, such a strategy will work to concentrate the limited resources among those who are neediest.[105] This, in turn, may produce a more economically efficient and equitable outcome than a strategy that does not take need into account.[106] More research is needed to understand how the factors discussed in this chapter correlate with need and, thus, which ones might be the best candidates for targeting.

If the ultimate goal is to increase the extent to which people in need receive help (as opposed to simply seek it), a radically different approach may sometimes be preferable: rather than requiring people to actively seek help to receive it, people in need could simply be defaulted into receiving the help (resources permitting) and given an option to opt out.[107] For formal help, this might involve using existing tax or other administrative records to automatically enroll people known to be eligible for a particular program, whereas for informal help, it might involve helpers proactively offering help instead of waiting for an ask.[108] The effects of such an approach would be twofold. For anyone who is not seeking help because of factors in the awareness-of-help or costs-of-action stages, the default would automatically overcome those factors to connect those people to needed resources. At the same time, for anyone who is not seeking help because of factors in the desirability-of-being-helped stage, providing the option to opt out would allow those people to maintain their preference to not be helped.

NOTES

1 All Consumer Financial Protection Bureau statistics are calculated from the 2017 National Financial Well-Being Survey data.
2 See Ansara, D.L., & Hindin, M.J. (2010). Formal and informal help-seeking associated with women's and men's experiences of intimate partner violence in Canada. *Social Science & Medicine, 70*(7), 1011–18. https://doi.org/10.1016/j

.socscimed.2009.12.009; Broese van Groenou, M., Glaser, K., Tomassini, C., & Jacobs, T. (2006). Socio-economic status differences in older people's use of informal and formal help: A comparison of four European countries. *Ageing and Society*, *26*(5), 745–66. https://doi.org/10.1017/S0144686X06005241; Grinstein-Weiss, M., Fishman, G., & Eisikovits, Z. (2005). Gender and ethnic differences in formal and informal help seeking among Israeli adolescents. *Journal of Adolescence*, *28*(6), 765–79. https://doi.org/10.1016/j.adolescence.2005.01.002; and Neighbors, H.W., & Jackson, J.S. (1984). The use of informal and formal help: Four patterns of illness behavior in the black community. *American Journal of Community Psychology*, *12*(6), 629–44. https://doi.org/10.1007/BF00922616.

3 *Help* is often defined quite broadly as resources that alleviate suffering, improve quality of life, or facilitate attainment of a goal. See Fisher, J.D., Nadler, A., & Whitcher-Alagna, S. (1982). Recipient reactions to aid. *Psychological Bulletin*, *91*(1), 27–54; Gross, A.E., & McMullen, P.A. (1982). The help-seeking process. In V.J. Derlega & J. Grzelak (Eds.), *Cooperation and helping behavior* (pp. 305–26). Academic Press; and Lee, F. (1997). When the going gets tough, do the tough ask for help? Help seeking and power motivation in organizations. *Organizational Behavior and Human Decision Processes*, *72*(3), 336–63. In the context of financial help, such definitions could include charity funds, money received through panhandling, credit cards, and even predatory services that provide some benefit to the person in need, such as payday loans. As mentioned in the next section, however, the framework presented in this chapter is intended to apply to what the person in need perceives as help, regardless of how it has previously been categorized in the literature. For a broader discussion on definitions of help, see also McGuire, A.M. (1994). Helping behaviors in the natural environment: Dimensions and correlates of helping. *Personality and Social Psychology Bulletin*, *20*(1), 45–56; and Wispé, L.G. (1972). Positive forms of social behavior: An overview. *Journal of Social Issues*, *28*(3), 1–19.

4 In this chapter, I focus on psychological or behavioral economic factors that could affect the decision to seek help. However, I also review some factors from the standard economic model. For discussions of the standard economic model and more behavioral models of help-seeking, see Baicker, K., Congdon, W.J., & Mullainathan, S. (2012). Health insurance coverage and take-up: Lessons from behavioral economics. *Milbank Quarterly*, *90*(1), 107–34; Bhargava, S., & Manoli, D. (2015). Psychological frictions and the incomplete take-up of social benefits: Evidence from an IRS field experiment. *American Economic Review*, *105*(11), 3489–529. https://doi.org/10.1257/aer.20121493; and Moffitt, R. (1983). An economic model of welfare stigma. *American Economic Review*, *73*(5), 1023–35.

5 See Broadhurst, K. (2003). Engaging parents and carers with family support services: What can be learned from research on help-seeking? *Child & Family Social Work*, *8*(4), 341–50; Duckworth, A.L., & Gross, J.J. (2020). Behavior change. *Organizational Behavior and Human Decision Processes*, *161*(Suppl.), 39–49; Goldsmith, H., Jackson, D., & Hough, R. (1988). Process model of seeking mental health services: Proposed framework for organizing the research literature on help-seeking. In H. Goldsmith, E. Lin, R. Bell, & D. Jackson (Eds.), *Needs Assessment: Its Future* (pp. 49–64). National Institute of Mental Health; Heckman, J.J., & Smith, J.A. (2004). The determinants of participation in a social program: Evidence from a prototypical job training program. *Journal of Labor Economics*, *22*(2), 243–98; Liang, B., Goodman, L., Tummala-Narra, P., & Weintraub, S. (2005). A theoretical framework for understanding help-seeking processes among survivors of intimate partner violence. *American Journal of Community Psychology*, *36*(1–2), 71–84; Pavuluri,

M.N., Luk, S.L., & McGee, R.O.B. (1996). Help-seeking for behavior problems by parents of preschool children: A community study. *Journal of the American Academy of Child & Adolescent Psychiatry, 35*(2), 215–22; and Srebnik, D., Cauce, A.M., & Baydar, N. (1996). Help-seeking pathways for children and adolescents. *Journal of Emotional and Behavioral Disorders, 4*(4), 210–20.

6 Prior work has modeled problem recognition as a precondition to the decision to seek help. See Broadhurst (2003); Goldsmith et al. (1988); Liang, B., Goodman, L., Tummala-Narra, P., & Weintraub, S. (2005). A theoretical framework for understanding help-seeking processes among survivors of intimate partner violence. *American Journal of Community Psychology, 36*(1–2), 71–84; Pavuluri et al. (1996); and Srebnik et al. (1996).

7 Consider, for instance, the role of networks and social norms in the use of formal help (not pictured in Figure 8.1). Prior work has demonstrated that a person's decision to seek formal help depends on the extent to which those around them use it: the more that people in a given person's network use formal help, the more likely it is that the target person will use it. Such network effects can operate through a range of channels, with different channels corresponding to different stages of the help-seeking framework. For example, the more people in a network use a particular social welfare program, the more likely it is that a given person in the network will become aware of the program (Stage 1 of the framework), the less ashamed they may feel about receiving the benefits (Stage 2), and the easier it may be for them to navigate the application process (Stage 3). For general discussions on networks and social norms, see Brock, W.A., & Durlauf, S.N. (2001). Interactions-based models. In J.J. Heckman & E. Learnier (Eds)., *Handbook of Econometrics* (Vol. 5, pp. 3297–380). Elsevier; Elster, J. (1989). Social norms and economic theory. *Journal of Economic Perspectives, 3*(4), 99–117; and Manski, C. F. (2000). Economic analysis of social interactions. *Journal of Economic Perspectives, 14*(3), 115–36. For theory and evidence on how networks affect social welfare program take-up and usage, see Bertrand, M., Luttmer, E.F., & Mullainathan, S. (2000). Network effects and welfare cultures. *Quarterly Journal of Economics, 115*(3), 1019–55; Borjas, G.J., & Hilton, L. (1996). Immigration and the welfare state: Immigrant participation in means-tested entitlement programs. *Quarterly Journal of Economics, 111*(2), 575–604; Chetty, R., Friedman, J.N., & Saez, E. (2013). Using differences in knowledge across neighborhoods to uncover the impacts of the EITC on earnings. *American Economic Review, 103*(7), 2683–721; Furtado, D., Papps, K.L., & Theodoropoulos, N. (2021). Who goes on disability when times are tough? The role of work norms among immigrants. *European Economic Review, 143*, Article 103983; Kroft, K. (2008). Takeup, social multipliers and optimal social insurance. *Journal of Public Economics, 92*(3–4), 722–37; Lindbeck, A., Nyberg, S., & Weibull, J.W. (1999). Social norms and economic incentives in the welfare state. *Quarterly Journal of Economics, 114*(1), 1–35; and Rege, M., Telle, K., & Votruba, M. (2012). Social interaction effects in disability pension participation: Evidence from plant downsizing. *Scandinavian Journal of Economics, 114*(4), 1208–39.

8 See Duckworth and Gross (2020).

9 For discussions of information deficit models and the value of simply providing information, see, e.g., Pappalardo, J.K. (2012). Product literacy and the economics of consumer protection policy. *Journal of Consumer Affairs, 46*(2), 319–32; and Sturgis, P., & Allum, N. (2004). Science in society: Re-evaluating the deficit model of public attitudes. *Public Understanding of Science, 13*(1), 55–74.

10 Goldsmith et al. (1988); Liang et al. (2005); and Pavuluri et al. (1996).

11 For instance, suppose that people in need typically believe that being helped would in theory be desirable if they did not need to do anything to get it, but they find the

process of taking action to get the help aversive. In such a case, a policy maker who wants to encourage help-seeking could lower the barriers associated with taking action to secure the help (i.e., address Stage 3 factors). If instead the opposite were true, the policy maker might try to focus their resources on making the help itself more attractive (i.e., address Stage 2 factors). See Broadhurst (2003); Pavuluri et al. (1996); and Srebnik et al. (1996).

12 See Liang et al. (2005).

13 See Broadhurst (2003) and Liang et al. (2005).

14 See Austin, R. (2004). Of predatory lending and the democratization of credit: Preserving the social safety net of informality in small-loan transactions. *American University Law Review*, 53(6), 1217–57; Srebnik et al. (1996); and Pescosolido, B.A. (1992). Beyond rational choice: The social dynamics of how people seek help. *American Journal of Sociology*, 97(4), 1096–138. Unfortunately, relative to wealthier individuals, people living in financial hardship may in general have fewer options for addressing their struggles. See Jachimowicz, J.M., Frey, E., Matz, S., Jeronimus, B.F., & Galinsky, A. (2022). The sharp spikes of poverty: Financial scarcity is related to higher levels of distress intensity in daily life. *Social Psychological and Personality Science*, 13(8), 1187–98.

15 See De La Rosa, W., Sharma, E., Tully, S.M., Giannella, E., & Rino, G. (2021). Psychological ownership interventions increase interest in claiming government benefits. *Proceedings of the National Academy of Sciences*, 118(35), Article e2106357118. https://doi.org/10.1073/pnas.2106357118; and Small, D.A., Gelfand, M., Babcock, L., & Gettman, H. (2007). Who goes to the bargaining table? The influence of gender and framing on the initiation of negotiation. *Journal of Personality and Social Psychology*, 93(4), 600–13. https://doi.org/10.1037/0022-3514.93.4.600.

16 See Ansara and Hindin (2010); Broese van Groenou et al. (2006); Grinstein-Weiss et al.; and Neighbors and Jackson (1984).

17 U.S. Census Bureau. (2021). *About program income and public assistance*. Retrieved December 11, 2021, from https://www.census.gov/topics/income-poverty/public-assistance/about.html.

18 See Beckmann, A. (2006). *Access, participation, and take-up rates in defined contribution retirement plans among workers in private industry, 2006* (Compensation and Working Conditions). U.S. Bureau of Labor Statistics. https://www.bls.gov/opub/mlr/cwc/access-participation-and-take-up-rates-in-defined-contribution-retirement-plans-among-workers-in-private-industry-2006.pdf; Craig, P. (1991). Costs and benefits: A review of research on take-up of income-related benefits. *Journal of Social Policy*, 20(4), 537–65. https://doi.org/10.1017/S0047279400019796; Goedemé, T., & Janssens, J. (2020). *The concept and measurement of non-take-up: An overview, with a focus on the non-take-up of social benefits* (Deliverable 9.2, InGRID-2 Project 730998-H2020). InGRID-2; Hernanz, V., Malherbet, F., & Pellizzari, M. (2004). *Take-up of welfare benefits in OECD countries: A review of the evidence*. Organisation for Economic Co-Operation and Development. https://doi.org/10.1787/525815265414; van Oorschot, W. (1998). Failing selectivity: On the extent and causes of non-take-up of social security benefits. In H.J. Andreß (Ed.), *Empirical poverty research in a comparative perspective* (pp. 101–32). Routledge; and Witte, A.D., & Queralt, M. (2002). *Take-up rates and trade offs after the age of entitlement: Some thoughts and empirical evidence for child care subsidies* (Working Paper No. 8886). National Bureau of Economic Research. https://doi.org/10.3386/w8886.

19 See Hernanz et al. (2004) and van Oorschot (1998). For an example of how somewhat ambiguous eligibility criteria may lead to secondary non-take-up, see Parsons, D.O. (1991). Self-screening in targeted public transfer programs. *Journal of Political Economy*, 99(4), 859–76.

20 Currie, J. (2004). *The take-up of social benefits* (IZA Discussion Paper No. 1103). Institute of Labor Economics.

21 Hernanz et al. (2004).

22 U.S. Department of Health and Human Services. (2021). *Welfare indicators and risk factors: 20th Report to Congress.* https://www.aspe.hhs.gov/sites/default/files/2021-07 /welfare-indicators-and-risk-factors-20th-report.pdf?_ga=2.82104336.727716163 .1630444897-1041677647.1630444897.

23 Internal Revenue Service. (2022). *EITC participation rate by states tax years 2012 through 2019.* Retrieved April 3, 2023, from https://www.eitc.irs.gov/eitc-central /participation-rate/eitc-participation-rate-by-states; Internal Revenue Service. (2023). *Statistics for tax returns with the Earned Income Tax Credit (EITC).* Retrieved April 3, 2023, from https://www.eitc.irs.gov/eitc-central/statistics-for-tax-returns -with-eitc/statistics-for-tax-returns-with-the-earned-income.

24 See Craig (1991); Kerr, S. (1983). *Making ends meet: An investigation into the non-claiming of supplementary pensions.* Bedford Square Press of the National Council for Voluntary Organisations; and van Oorschot (1998).

25 See Aizer, A. (2007). Public health insurance, program take-up, and child health. *Review of Economics and Statistics, 89*(3), 400–15; Bertrand, M., Mullainathan, S., & Shafir, E. (2006). Behavioral economics and marketing in aid of decision making among the poor. *Journal of Public Policy & Marketing, 25*(1), 8–23. https://doi .org/10.1509/jppm.25.1.8; and Kissane, R. J. (2003). What's need got to do with it? Barriers to use of nonprofit social services. *Journal of Sociology & Social Welfare, 30*(2), 127–48.

26 Bhargava & Manoli (2015).

27 See Halpern, J., & Hausman, J.A. (1986). Choice under uncertainty: A model of applications for the social security disability insurance program. *Journal of Public Economics, 31*(2), 131–61. https://doi.org/10.1016/0047-2727(86)90015-0; and Kleven, H.J., & Kopczuk, W. (2011). Transfer program complexity and the take-up of social benefits. *American Economic Journal: Economic Policy, 3*(1), 54–90.

28 See Daponte, B.O., Sanders, S., & Taylor, L. (1999). Why do low income households not use food stamps? Evidence from an experiment. *Journal of Human Resources, 34*(3), 612–28. https://doi.org/10.2307/146382; Finkelstein, A., & Notowidigdo, M. J. (2019). Take-up and targeting: Experimental evidence from SNAP. *Quarterly Journal of Economics, 134*(3), 1505–56; and Goulet, J.L., Rosenheck, R., & Leslie, D. (1999). Effectiveness of a targeted mailing outreach program on SSI applications and awards. *Social Service Review, 73*(4), 579–87. https://doi.org/10.1086/514446.

29 Daponte et al. (1999); Krueger, A.B., & Meyer, B.D. (2002). Labor supply effects of social insurance. In A.J. Auerbach & M. Feldstein (Eds.), *Handbook of public economics* (Vol. 4, pp. 2327–92). Elsevier; McGarry, K. (1996). Factors determining participation of the elderly in Supplemental Security Income. *Journal of Human Resources, 31*(2), 331–58. https://doi.org/10.2307/146066; Riphahn, R.T. (2001). Rational poverty or poor rationality? The take-up of social assistance benefits. *Review of Income and Wealth, 47*(3), 379–98; and Warlick, J.L. (1982). Participation of the aged in SSI. *Journal of Human Resources, 17*(2), 236–60. https://doi.org/10.2307/145471.

30 For example, see Besley, T., & Coate, S. (1992a). Workfare versus welfare: Incentive arguments for work requirements in poverty-alleviation programs. *American Economic Review, 82*(1), 249–61.

31 Food and Nutrition Service. (2019). *SNAP work requirements.* Retrieved December 13, 2021, from https://www.fns.usda.gov/snap/work-requirements.

32 One could also view the actions required to maintain benefits as being equivalent to the actions required to (repeatedly) acquire benefits for the first time, in which

case this factor would fall into Stage 3. See also Fisher et al. (1982); Gross, A.E., Wallston, B.S., & Piliavin, I.M. (1979). Reactance, attribution, equity, and the help recipient. *Journal of Applied Social Psychology*, 9(4), 297–313. https://doi.org /10.1111/j.1559-1816.1979.tb00804.x; and Yaniv, G. (1997). Welfare fraud and welfare stigma. *Journal of Economic Psychology*, 18(4), 435–51. https://doi.org /10.1016/S0167-4870(97)00016-0.

33 See Brehm, J.W. (1966). *A theory of psychological reactance*. Academic Press; Brehm, J.W. (1989). Psychological reactance: Theory and applications. In T.K. Srull (Ed.), *Advances in consumer research* (Vol. 16, pp. 72–5). Association for Consumer Research; and Falk, A., & Kosfeld, M. (2006). The hidden costs of control. *American Economic Review*, 96(5), 1611–30. https://doi.org/10.1257/aer.96.5.1611. Also see the literature on conditional cash transfers versus unconditional cash transfers for a more general discussion of the benefits and costs of imposing conditions alongside financial resources: Baird, S., Ferreira, F.H.G., Özler, B., & Woolcock, M. (2014). Conditional, unconditional and everything in between: A systematic review of the effects of cash transfer programmes on schooling outcomes. *Journal of Development Effectiveness*, 6(1), 1–43. https://doi.org/10.1080/19439342.2014.890362; Khan, M.E., Hazra, A., Kant, A., & Ali, M. (2016). Conditional and unconditional cash transfers to improve use of contraception in low and middle income countries: A systematic review. *Studies in Family Planning*, 47(4), 371–83. https://doi.org/10.1111/sifp .12004; Knotz, C.M. (2018). A rising workfare state? Unemployment benefit conditionality in 21 OECD countries, 1980–2012. *Journal of International and Comparative Social Policy*, 34(2), 91–108. https://doi.org/10.1080/21699763.2018. 1472136; Robertson, L., Mushati, P., Eaton, J.W., Dumba, L., Mavise, G., Makoni, J., Schumacher, C., Crea, T., Monasch, R., Sherr, L., Garnett, G.P., Nyamukapa, C., & Gregson, S. (2013). Effects of unconditional and conditional cash transfers on child health and development in Zimbabwe: A cluster-randomised trial. *Lancet*, 381(9874), 1283–92. https://doi.org/10.1016/S0140-6736(12)62168-0; and Schubert, B., & Slater, R. (2006). Social cash transfers in low-income African countries: Conditional or unconditional? *Development Policy Review*, 24(5), 571–8. https://doi .org/10.1111/j.1467-7679.2006.00348.x.

34 Stigma could come into play in Stage 3 of the framework rather than Stage 2 if, for instance, the application process itself is highly visible to others, but – once approved – benefit receipt is private. See Friedrichsen, J., König, T., & Schmacker, R. (2018). Social image concerns and welfare take-up. *Journal of Public Economics*, 168, 174–192.

35 Goffman, E. (1963). *Embarrassment and social organization*. Wiley. https://doi.org /10.1037/11302-050.

36 See Chase, E., & Walker, R. (2013). The co-construction of shame in the context of poverty: Beyond a threat to the social bond. *Sociology*, 47(4), 739–754. https:// doi.org/10.1177/0038038512453796; Dawney, L., Kirwan, S., & Walker, R. (2020). The intimate spaces of debt: Love, freedom and entanglement in indebted lives. *Geoforum*, 110, 191–199. https://doi.org/10.1016/j.geoforum.2018.11.006; Piff, P.K., Wiwad, D., Robinson, A.R., Aknin, L.B., Mercier, B., & Shariff, A. (2020). Shifting attributions for poverty motivates opposition to inequality and enhances egalitarianism. *Nature Human Behaviour*, 4(5), 496–505; Ravallion, M. (2015). *The economics of poverty: History, measurement, and policy*. Oxford University Press; and Walker, R. (2014). *The shame of poverty*. Oxford University Press.

37 Moffitt (1983).

38 For examples, see Besley, T., & Coate, S. (1992b). Understanding welfare stigma: Taxpayer resentment and statistical discrimination. *Journal of Public Economics*,

48(2), 165–83. https://doi.org/10.1016/0047-2727(92)90025-B; Blumkin, T., Margalioth, Y., & Sadka, E. (2015). Welfare stigma re-examined. *Journal of Public Economic Theory, 17*(6), 874–86. https://doi.org/10.1111/jpet.12109; Blundell, R., Fry, V., & Walker, I. (1988). Modelling the take-up of means-tested benefits: The case of housing benefits in the United Kingdom. *Economic Journal, 98*(390), 58–74. https://doi.org/10.2307/2233304; Currie, J., & Grogger, J. (2001). Explaining recent declines in food stamp program participation [with comments]. *Brookings-Wharton Papers on Urban Affairs, 2001*, 203–44; Rogers-Dillon, R. (1995). The dynamics of welfare stigma. *Qualitative Sociology, 18*(4), 439–56. https://doi.org/10.1007/BF02404490; Walker (2014); and Yaniv (1997).

39 See Friedrichsen et al. (2018); Hall, C.C., Zhao, J., & Shafir, E. (2014). Self-affirmation among the poor: Cognitive and behavioral implications. *Psychological Science, 25*(2), 619–25. https://doi.org/10.1177/0956797613510949; Kissane (2003); and Riphahn (2001).

40 See Bhargava and Manoli (2015); Currie (2004); and Currie & Grogger (2001).

41 Currie (2004).

42 See Bertrand et al. (2006) and Kleven and Kopczuk (2011).

43 See Blundell et al. (1988); Kleven & Kopczuk (2011); Bitler, M. P., Currie, J., & Scholz, J.K. (2003). WIC eligibility and participation. *Journal of Human Resources, 38*, 1139–79. https://doi.org/10.2307/3558984; Currie & Grogger (2001); Kabbani, N.S., & Wilde, P.E. (2003). Short recertification periods in the U.S. food stamp program. *Journal of Human Resources, 38*, 1112–1138. https://doi.org/10.2307/3558983; and Kissane (2003).

44 See Aizer, A. (2003). Low take-up in Medicaid: Does outreach matter and for whom? *American Economic Review, 93*(2), 238–41; Aizer (2007); Finkelstein & Notowidigdo (2019); Flores, G., Abreau, M., Chaisson, C.E., Meyers, A., Sachdeva, R.C., Fernandez, H., Francisco, P., Diaz, B., Diaz, A.M., & Santos-Guerrero, I. (2005). A randomized, controlled trial of the effectiveness of community-based case management in insuring uninsured Latino children. *Pediatrics, 116*(6), 1433–41. https://doi.org/10.1542/peds.2005-0786; and Schanzenbach, D.W. (2009). *Experimental estimates of the barriers to food stamp enrollment* (Discussion Paper No. 1367–90). University of Wisconsin–Madison, Institute for Research on Poverty.

45 See Kronebusch, K., & Elbel, B. (2004). Enrolling children in public insurance: SCHIP, Medicaid, and state implementation. *Journal of Health Politics, Policy and Law, 29*(3), 451–89; Summer, L., & Thompson, J. (2008, September 30). *Best practices to improve take-up rates in health insurance programs.* Office of the Assistant Secretary for Planning and Evaluation. https://aspe.hhs.gov/sites/default/files/private/pdf/75636/report.pdf; and van Oorschot, W. (1998). Failing selectivity: On the extent and causes of non-take-up of social security benefits. In H. J. Andreß (Ed.), *Empirical poverty research in comparative perspective* (pp. 101–132). Routledge.

46 See Currie (2004) and Halpern & Hausman (1986).

47 See Mani, A., Mullainathan, S., Shafir, E., & Zhao, J. (2013). Poverty impedes cognitive function. *Science, 341*(6149), 976–80; Mullainathan, S., & Shafir, E. (2013). *Scarcity: Why having too little means so much.* Macmillan; and Giurge, L.M., Whillans, A.V., & West, C. (2020). Why time poverty matters for individuals, organisations and nations. *Nature Human Behaviour, 4*(10), 993–1003. https://doi.org/10.1038/s41562-020-0920-z.

48 See Gilovich, T.D., & Griffin, D.W. (2010). Judgment and decision making. In S.T. Fiske, D.T. Gilbert, & G. Lindzey (Eds.), *Handbook of social psychology* (pp. 542–88). Wiley; and Leventhal, H., Singer, R., & Jones, S. (1965). Effects of fear and specificity

of recommendation upon attitudes and behavior. *Journal of Personality and Social Psychology, 2*(1), 20–29. https://doi.org/10.1037/h0022089.

49 Sheeran, P., & Webb, T.L. (2016). The intention–behavior gap. *Social and Personality Psychology Compass, 10*(9), 503–18. https://doi.org/10.1111/spc3.12265.

50 See Bertrand, M., Mullainathan, S., & Shafir, E. (2004). A behavioral-economics view of poverty. *American Economic Review, 94*(2,), 419–423; and Bertrand et al. (2006).

51 See Duckworth & Gross (2020); Frederick, S., Loewenstein, G., & O'Donoghue, T. (2002). Time discounting and time preference: A critical review. *Journal of Economic Literature, 40*(2), 351–401; and O'Donoghue, T., & Rabin, M. (2000). The economics of immediate gratification. *Journal of Behavioral Decision Making, 13*(2), 233–50. https://doi.org/10.1002/(SICI)1099-0771(200004/06)13:2<233::AID-BDM325>3.0.CO;2-U.

52 See, for example, Bertrand et al. (2004), (2006); Bhargava, S., & Conell-Price, L. (2022). *Serenity now, save later? Evidence on retirement savings puzzles from a 401(k) field experiment* (Working Paper). Social Science Research Network. https://doi.org/10.2139/ssrn.4056407; Currie (2004); and Madrian, B.C., & Shea, D.F. (2001). The power of suggestion: Inertia in 401(k) participation and savings behavior. *Quarterly Journal of Economics, 116*(4), 1149–87. https://doi.org/10.1162/003355301753265543.

53 See Ansara & Hindin (2010); Broese van Groenou et al. (2006); Grinstein-Weiss et al. (2005); and Neighbors & Jackson (1984).

54 See Bar-Tal, D., Bar-Zohar, Y., Greenberg, M.S., & Hermon, M. (1977). Reciprocity behavior in the relationship between donor and recipient and between harm-doer and victim. *Sociometry, 40*(3), 293–8; and Deri, S., Stein, D.H., & Bohns, V.K. (2019). With a little help from my friends (and strangers): Closeness as a moderator of the underestimation-of-compliance effect. *Journal of Experimental Social Psychology, 82,* 6–15.

55 Garonzik-Wang, J.M., Berger, J.C., Ros, R.L., Kucirka, L.M., Deshpande, N.A., Boyarsky, B.J., Montgomery, R.A., Hall, E.C., James, N.T., & Segev, D.L. (2012). Live donor champion: Finding live kidney donors by separating the advocate from the patient. *Transplantation, 93*(11), 1147–50. https://doi.org/10.1097/TP.0b013e31824e75a5.

56 See Austin (2004); and Collins, D., Morduch, J., Rutherford, S., & Ruthven, O. (2009). *Portfolios of the poor: How the world's poor live on $2 a day.* Princeton University Press.

57 See Guérin, I., Morvant-Roux, S., & Servet, J.-M. (2011). Understanding the diversity and complexity of demand for microfinance services: Lessons from informal finance. In B. Armendáriz & M. Labie (Eds.), *The handbook of microfinance* (pp. 101–21). World Scientific Publishing. https://doi.org/10.1142/9789814295666_0005; Guérin, I., Roesch, M., Venkatasubramanian, G., & D'Espallier, B. (2012). Credit from whom and for what? The diversity of borrowing sources and uses in rural southern India. *Journal of International Development, 24*(S1), S122–37. https://doi.org/10.1002/jid.1785; and Morduch, J., & Schneider, R. (2017). *The financial diaries.* Princeton University Press.

58 See Adams, D.W. (1989). Taking a fresh look at informal finance. *Economics and Sociology, 1592,* 5–23. https://doi.org/10.4324/9780429034572-2; and Morduch & Schneider (2017).

59 Rousseau, D.M. (2001). Schema, promise and mutuality: The building blocks of the psychological contract. *Journal of Occupational and Organizational Psychology, 74*(4), 511–41. https://doi.org/10.1348/096317901167505.

60 Dezső, L., & Loewenstein, G. (2012). Lenders' blind trust and borrowers' blind spots: A descriptive investigation of personal loans. *Journal of Economic Psychology, 33*(5), 996–1011. https://doi.org/10.1016/j.joep.2012.06.002.

61 Calculated from the 2017 National Financial Well-Being Survey data.
62 See Dezső & Loewenstein (2012); Board of Governors of the Federal Reserve System. (2017). *Report on the economic well-being of U.S. households in 2016.* https://www.federalreserve.gov/publications/files/2016-report-economic-well-being-us-households-201705.pdf; McKean, L., Lessem, S., & Bax, E. (2005). *Money management by low-income households: Earning, spending, saving, and accessing financial services.* Center for Impact Research; and Morduch & Schneider (2017).
63 All World Bank statistics are calculated from the 2014 Global Financial Inclusion database.
64 Board of Governors of the Federal Reserve System. (2017).
65 See Desmond, M. (2016). *Evicted: Poverty and Profit in the American City.* Crown; McKean et al. (2005); Morduch & Schneider (2017); Arrowsmith, S., & Pignal, J. (2010). *Initial findings from the 2009 Canadian Financial Capability Survey "Working Paper."* Statistics Canada, Special Surveys Division; and World Bank. (2015). *Global Financial Inclusion (Global Findex) Database 2014.* https://doi.org/10.48529/9j25-hr41.
66 See, for example, Austin (2004); Bond, P., & Townsend, R. (1996). Formal and informal financing in a Chicago ethnic neighborhood. *Economic Perspectives, 20*(4), 3–28; Collins et al. (2009); Light, I., & Pham, M. (1998). Beyond creditworthy: Microcredit and informal credit in the United States. *Journal of Developmental Entrepreneurship, 3*(1), 35–51; Morduch & Schneider (2017).
67 See Bose, P. (1998). Formal–informal sector interaction in rural credit markets. *Journal of Development Economics, 56*(2), 265–280. https://doi.org/10.1016/S0304-3878(98)00066-2; Giné, X. (2011). Access to capital in rural Thailand: An estimated model of formal vs. informal credit. *Journal of Development Economics, 96*(1), 16–29. https://doi.org/10.1016/j.jdeveco.2010.07.001; Hoff, K., & Stiglitz, J.E. (1990). Introduction: Imperfect information and rural credit markets: Puzzles and policy perspectives. *World Bank Economic Review, 4*(3), 235–50; and Karaivanov, A., & Kessler, A. (2018). (Dis)advantages of informal loans – Theory and evidence. *European Economic Review, 102,* 100–28. https://doi.org/10.1016/j.euroecorev.2017.12.005.
68 See Collins et al. (2009); and Guérin et al. (2012).
69 Karaivanov & Kessler (2018).
70 See Karaivanov & Kessler (2018); and Lee, S., & Persson, P. (2016). Financing from family and friends. *Review of Financial Studies, 29*(9), 2341–86. https://doi.org/10.1093/rfs/hhw031.
71 See Applebaum, L.D. (2001). The influence of perceived deservingness on policy decisions regarding aid to the poor. *Political Psychology, 22*(3), 419–42; Tscharaktschiew, N., & Rudolph, U. (2016). The who and whom of help giving: An attributional model integrating the help giver and the help recipient. *European Journal of Social Psychology, 46*(1), 90–109; Weiner, B., Osborne, D., & Rudolph, U. (2011). An attributional analysis of reactions to poverty: The political ideology of the giver and the perceived morality of the receiver. *Personality and Social Psychology Review, 15*(2), 199–213; Hagerty, S.F., & Barasz, K. (2020). Inequality in socially permissible consumption. *Proceedings of the National Academy of Sciences, 117*(25), 14084–93; Schroeder, J., & Epley, N. (2020). Demeaning: Dehumanizing others by minimizing the importance of their psychological needs. *Journal of Personality and Social Psychology, 119*(4), 765–91; and Schroeder, J., Waytz, A., & Epley, N. (2017). Endorsing help for others that you oppose for yourself: Mind perception alters the perceived effectiveness of paternalism. *Journal of Experimental Psychology: General, 146*(8), 1106–25.

72 See Bohns, V. K. (2016). (Mis)understanding our influence over others: A review of the underestimation-of-compliance effect. *Current Directions in Psychological Science, 25*(2), 119–23. https://doi.org/10.1177/0963721415628011; Deri et al. (2019); Flynn, F.J., & Lake, V.K.B. (2008). If you need help, just ask: Underestimating compliance with direct requests for help. *Journal of Personality and Social Psychology, 95*(1), 128–43. https://doi.org/10.1037/0022-3514.95.1.128; and Newark, D.A., Flynn, F.J., & Bohns, V.K. (2014). Once bitten, twice shy: The effect of a past refusal on expectations of future compliance. *Social Psychological and Personality Science, 5*(2), 218–25. https://doi.org/10.1177/1948550613490967.

73 Newark, D.A., Bohns, V.K., & Flynn, F.J. (2017). A helping hand is hard at work: Help-seekers' underestimation of helpers' effort. *Organizational Behavior and Human Decision Processes, 139*, 18–29. https://doi.org/10.1016/j.obhdp.2017.01.001.

74 See, for example, Cozzarelli, C., Wilkinson, A.V., & Tagler, M.J. (2001). Attitudes toward the poor and attributions for poverty. *Journal of Social Issues, 57*(2), 207–27. https://doi.org/10.1111/0022-4537.00209; Robinson, J.W. (2009). American poverty cause beliefs and structured inequality legitimation. *Sociological Spectrum, 29*(4), 489–518. https://doi.org/10.1080/02732170902904681; and Smith, K.B., & Stone, L.H. (1989). Rags, riches, and bootstraps: Beliefs about the causes of wealth and poverty. *Sociological Quarterly, 30*(1), 93–107.

75 See Chase & Walker (2013); Dawney et al. (2020); and Walker, R. (2014). *The shame of poverty*. Oxford University Press.

76 See Chase & Walker (2013); Gladstone, J.J., Jachimowicz, J.M., Greenberg, A.E., & Galinsky, A.D. (2021). Financial shame spirals: How shame intensifies financial hardship. *Organizational Behavior and Human Decision Processes, 167*, 42–56. https://doi.org/10.1016/j.obhdp.2021.06.002; and Tessler, R.C., & Schwartz, S.H. (1972). Help seeking, self-esteem, and achievement motivation: An attributional analysis. *Journal of Personality and Social Psychology, 21*(3), 318–26.

77 Austin (2004); Collins et al. (2009); and Morduch & Schneider (2017).

78 Austin (2004); Collins et al. (2009); and Morduch & Schneider (2017).

79 See Acquisti, A., John, L.K., & Loewenstein, G. (2013). What is privacy worth? *Journal of Legal Studies, 42*(2), 249–74. https://doi.org/10.1086/671754; and Farrell, J. (2012). Can privacy be just another good? *Journal on Telecommunication and High Technology Law, 10*, 251–65.

80 See Adams (1989).

81 Guérin et al. (2011); Banerjee, A., Breza, E., Chandrasekhar, A.G., Duflo, E., Jackson, M.O., & Kinnan, C. (2021). *Changes in social network structure in response to exposure to formal credit markets* (Working Paper 28365). National Bureau of Economic Research. https://doi.org/10.2139/ssrn.3245656.

82 See Greenberg, M.S. (1980). A theory of indebtedness. In K.J. Gergen, M.S. Greenberg, & R.H. Willis (Eds.), *Social exchange: Advances in theory and research* (pp. 3–26). Springer US. https://doi.org/10.1007/978-1-4613-3087-5_1; and Greenberg, M.S., & Shapiro, S.P. (1971). Indebtedness: An adverse aspect of asking for and receiving help. *Sociometry, 34*(2), 290–301. https://doi.org/10.2307/2786418.

83 Collins et al. (2009); Guérin et al. (2012).

84 Guérin et al. (2011); Morduch & Schneider (2017).

85 See, for example, Adams (1989); Guérin et al. (2011), (2012); Karlan, D., Mobius, M., Rosenblat, T., & Szeidl, A. (2009). Trust and social collateral. *Quarterly Journal of Economics, 124*(3), 1307–61; and Light & Pham (1998).

86 See Dezső & Loewenstein (2012); Karaivanov & Kessler (2018); Karlan et al. (2009); and Lee & Persson (2016).

87 See, for example, Andreoni, J. (1990). Impure altruism and donations to public goods: A theory of warm-glow giving. *Economic Journal, 100*(401), 464–77. https:// doi.org/10.2307/2234133; Batson, C.D., Ahmad, N., Lishner, D.A., & Tsang, J.-A. (2002). Empathy and altruism. In C.R. Snyder & S.J. Lopez (Eds.), *Handbook of positive psychology* (pp. 485–98). Oxford University Press; Brown, A.L., Meer, J., & Williams, J.F. (2019). Why do people volunteer? An experimental analysis of preferences for time donations. *Management Science, 65*(4), 1455–68. https://doi .org/10.1287/mnsc.2017.2951; and Ottoni-Wilhelm, M., Vesterlund, L., & Xie, H. (2017). Why do people give? Testing pure and impure altruism. *American Economic Review, 107*(11), 3617–33. https://doi.org/10.1257/aer.20141222.

88 See Barnieh, L., McLaughlin, K., Manns, B.J., Klarenbach, S., Yilmaz, S., Hemmelgarn, B.R.; Alberta Kidney Disease Network. (2011). Barriers to living kidney donation identified by eligible candidates with end-stage renal disease. *Nephrology Dialysis Transplantation, 26*(2), 732–8. https://doi.org/10.1093/ndt/gfq388; Porter, D.J., & Preston, S.D. (n.d.). *Helping you by not helping me: Altruistic motivations for refusing help* (Working paper). Department of Psychology, University of Michigan; and Sieverdes, J.C., Nemeth, L.S., Magwood, G.S., Baliga, P.K., Chavin, K.D., Ruggiero, K.J., & Treiber, F.A. (2015). African American kidney transplant patients' perspectives on challenges in the living donation process. *Progress in Transplantation, 25*(2), 164–75. https://doi.org/10.7182/pit2015852.

89 See Bénabou, R., Jaroszewicz, A., & Loewenstein, G. (2022). *It hurts to ask* (Working paper 30486). National Bureau of Economic Research. https://doi.org/10.3386 /w30486; and Jaroszewicz, A., Loewenstein, G., & Bénabou, R. (2023). *The pain of asking and being asked for help* (Working paper). Harvard University, Carnegie Mellon University, and Princeton University.

90 For examples, see Babcock, L., & Laschever, S. (2009). *Women don't ask: Negotiation and the gender divide*. Princeton University Press; Barnieh et al. (2011); Bohns, V.K., & Flynn, F.J. (2010). "Why didn't you just ask?" Underestimating the discomfort of help-seeking. *Journal of Experimental Social Psychology, 46*(2), 402–9. https://doi .org/10.1016/j.jesp.2009.12.015; Collins, N.L., & Feeney, B.C. (2000). A safe haven: An attachment theory perspective on support seeking and caregiving in intimate relationships. *Journal of Personality and Social Psychology, 78*(6), 1053–73. https://doi .org/10.1037/0022-3514.78.6.1053; Downey, G., & Feldman, S.I. (1996). Implications of rejection sensitivity for intimate relationships. *Journal of Personality and Social Psychology, 70*(6), 1327–43; Grant, H. (2018). *Reinforcements: How to get people to help you*. Harvard Business Review Press; and van Rooy, R. (2003). Being polite is a handicap: Towards a game theoretical analysis of polite linguistic behavior. In J. Halpern (Chair) & M. Tennenholtz (Ed.), *Proceedings of the 9th Conference on Theoretical Aspects of Rationality and Knowledge* (pp. 45–58). Association for Computing Machinery.

91 See Baumeister, R.F., & Leary, M.R. (1995). The need to belong: Desire for interpersonal attachments as a fundamental human motivation. *Psychological Bulletin, 117*(3), 497–529; Beck, L.A., & Clark, M. S. (2009). Offering more support than we seek. *Journal of Experimental Social Psychology, 45*(1), 267–70; Downey & Feldman (1996); Eisenberger, N.I., Lieberman, M.D., & Williams, K.D. (2003). Does rejection hurt? An fMRI study of social exclusion. *Science, 302*(5643), 290–92; Kross, E., Berman, M.G., Mischel, W., Smith, E.E., & Wager, T.D. (2011). Social rejection shares somatosensory representations with physical pain. *Proceedings of the National Academy of Sciences, 108*(15), 6270–5; Leary, M.R. (1990). Responses to social exclusion: Social anxiety, jealousy, loneliness, depression, and low self-esteem. *Journal of Social and Clinical Psychology, 9*(2), 221–9; Leary, M. R. (2005).

Sociometer theory and the pursuit of relational value: Getting to the root of self-esteem. *European Review of Social Psychology, 16*(1), 75–111; MacDonald, G., & Leary, M.R. (2005). Why does social exclusion hurt? The relationship between social and physical pain. *Psychological Bulletin, 131*(2), 202–23; and Romero-Canyas, R., Downey, G., Berenson, K., Ayduk, O., & Kang, N. J. (2010). Rejection sensitivity and the rejection–hostility link in romantic relationships. *Journal of Personality, 78*(1), 119–48.

92 See Bénabou et al. (2022) and Jaroszewicz et al. (2023).

93 Ariely, D. (2008). *Predictably irrational.* HarperCollins. https://www.harpercollins.com/9780061629532/the-predictably-irrational/; Clark, M.S. (1984). Record keeping in two types of relationships. *Journal of Personality and Social Psychology, 47*(3), 549–57; and Clark, M.S., & Mills, J. (1979). Interpersonal attraction in exchange and communal relationships. *Journal of Personality and Social Psychology, 37*(1), 12–24. https://doi.org/10.1037/0022-3514.37.1.12.

94 See Camerer, C. (1988). Gifts as economic signals and social symbols. *American Journal of Sociology, 94*(Suppl.), S180–S214; and Ellingsen, T., & Johannesson, M. (2011). Conspicuous generosity. *Journal of Public Economics, 95*(9–10), 1131–43. https://doi.org/10.1016/j.jpubeco.2011.05.002.

95 See Jachimowicz et al. (2021); Karaivanov & Kessler (2018); and Lee & Persson (2016).

96 See Cappelen, A. W., Cappelen, C., & Tungodden, B. (2021). *Second-best fairness: The trade-off between false positives and false negatives* (Discussion Paper No. 18/2018), Norwegian School of Economics, Department of Economics; Feagin, J.R. (1972). Poverty: We still believe that God helps those who help themselves. *Psychology Today, 6*(6), 101–110; and Yaniv (1997).

97 See Besley & Coate (1992b); and Lepianka, D., Oorschot, W. V., & Gelissen, J. (2009). Popular explanations of poverty: A critical discussion of empirical research. *Journal of Social Policy, 38*(3), 421–438. https://doi.org/10.1017/S0047279409003092.

98 See Norton, M.I., & Ariely, D. (2011). Building a better America – One wealth quintile at a time. *Perspectives on Psychological Science, 6*(1), 9–12. https://doi.org/10.1177/1745691610393524; and Starmans, C., Sheskin, M., & Bloom, P. (2017). Why people prefer unequal societies. *Nature Human Behaviour, 1*(4), Article 0082. https://doi.org/10.1038/s41562-017-0082.

99 See Holzer, H.J., Whitmore Schanzenbach, D., Duncan, G.J., & Ludwig, J. (2008). The economic costs of childhood poverty in the United States. *Journal of Children and Poverty, 14*(1), 41–61. https://doi.org/10.1080/10796120701871280; McLaughlin, M., & Rank, M.R. (2018). Estimating the economic cost of childhood poverty in the United States. *Social Work Research, 42*(2), 73–83. https://doi.org/10.1093/swr/svy007; and Ravallion (2015).

100 See Andreoni, J., Rao, J.M., & Trachtman, H. (2017). Avoiding the ask: A field experiment on altruism, empathy, and charitable giving. *Journal of Political Economy, 125*(3), 625–53; Dana, J., Cain, D.M., & Dawes, R.M. (2006). What you don't know won't hurt me: Costly (but quiet) exit in dictator games. *Organizational Behavior and Human Decision Processes, 100*(2), 193–201. https://doi.org/10.1016/j.obhdp.2005.10.001; Dana, J., Weber, R. A., & Kuang, J.X. (2007). Exploiting moral wiggle room: Experiments demonstrating an illusory preference for fairness. *Economic Theory, 33*(1), 67–80. https://doi.org/10.1007/s00199-006-0153-z; and DellaVigna, S., List, J.A., & Malmendier, U. (2012). Testing for altruism and social pressure in charitable giving. *Quarterly Journal of Economics, 127*(1), 1–56. https://doi.org/10.1093/qje/qjr050.

101 See Portes, A. (1998). Social capital: Its origins and applications in modern sociology. *Annual Review of Sociology, 24*, 1–24; and Wherry, F.F., Seefeldt, K.S., & Alvarez, A.S.

(2019). To lend or not to lend to friends and kin: Awkwardness, obfuscation, and negative reciprocity. *Social Forces, 98*(2), 753–93. https://doi.org/10.1093/sf/soy127.

102 See Batson et al. (2002); Aknin, L.B., Barrington-Leigh, C.P., Dunn, E.W., Helliwell, J.F., Burns, J., Biswas-Diener, R., Kemeza, I., Nyende, P., Ashton-James, C.E., & Norton, M.I. (2013). Prosocial spending and well-being: Cross-cultural evidence for a psychological universal. *Journal of Personality and Social Psychology, 104*(4), 635–52. https://doi.org/10.1037/a0031578; Aknin, L.B., Dunn, E.W., Whillans, A.V., Grant, A.M., & Norton, M.I. (2013). Making a difference matters: Impact unlocks the emotional benefits of prosocial spending. *Journal of Economic Behavior & Organization, 88*, 90–95. https://doi.org/10.1016/j.jebo.2013.01.008; Andreoni, J., Harbaugh, W.T., & Vesterlund, L. (2010). Altruism in experiments. In S.N. Durlauf & L.E. Blume (Eds.), *Behavioural and experimental economics* (pp. 6–13). Palgrave Macmillan UK. https://doi.org/10.1057/9780230280786_2; Batson, C.D., & Powell, A.A. (2003). Altruism and prosocial behavior. In *Handbook of psychology: Personality and social psychology* (Vol. 5, pp. 463–84). Wiley. https://doi.org/10.1002/0471264385.wei0519; Dickert, S., Sagara, N., & Slovic, P. (2011). Affective motivations to help others: A two-stage model of donation decisions. *Journal of Behavioral Decision Making, 24*(4), 361–76. https://doi.org/10.1002/bdm.697; and Walster, E., Berscheid, E., & Walster, G.W. (1973). New directions in equity research. *Journal of Personality and Social Psychology, 25*(2), 151–76.

103 Those who are in greatest need will often, but not always, be the ones who benefit the most from help. See Ravallion (2015); and Sadoulet, E., De Janvry, A., & Davis, B. (2001). Cash transfer programs with income multipliers: PROCAMPO in Mexico. *World Development, 29*(6), 1043–56.

104 See Bhargava & Manoli (2015); Finkelstein & Notowidigdo (2019); Heckman & Smith (2004); and Mkandawire, T. (2005). *Targeting and universalism in poverty reduction* (Social Policy and Development Programme Paper No. 23). UN Institute for Social Development.

105 See Bhargava & Manoli (2015); Currie (2004); and Ravallion (2015).

106 See Currie (2004); Kanbur, R. (1987). Transfers, targeting and poverty. *Economic Policy, 2*(4), 111–36; Mkandawire (2005); and Ravallion (2015).

107 See Camerer, C., Issacharoff, S., Loewenstein, G., O'Donoghue, T., & Rabin, M. (2003). Regulation for conservatives: Behavioral economics and the case for "asymmetric paternalism." *University of Pennsylvania Law Review, 151*(3), 1211–54. https://doi.org/10.2307/3312889; and Thaler, R.H., & Sunstein, C.R. (2003). Libertarian paternalism. *American Economic Review, 93*(2), 175–9. https://doi.org/10.1257/000282803321947001.

108 Bénabou et al. (2022).

CHAPTER NINE

Cash to US Families at Scale: Behavioral Insights on Implementation from the Baby's First Years Study

Lisa A. Gennetian, Sarah Halpern-Meekin, Lauren Meyer, Nathan A. Fox, Katherine Magnuson, Kimberly G. Noble, and Hirokazu Yoshikawa

Cash transfers are used to alleviate poverty in countries around the globe.[1] As of 2019, 166 of 205 nations reviewed by UNICEF had some form of child benefit that is functionally equivalent to cash transfers to families. In the nine months after the start of the COVID-19 pandemic, 272 new cash transfer programs arose in 133 countries, with 124 of these programs consisting of one-time lump sum transfers.[2] Such cash transfers have the dual aim of alleviating the detrimental effects of economic deprivation on families with children, particularly in times of economic crisis, while supporting the productivity of the children's caregivers (i.e., their ability to work before the pandemic).[3]

The United States is an outlier among Organisation for Economic Co-operation and Development nations in the proportion of gross domestic product allocated to social benefits to families, ranking nearly last on cash benefits.[4] The United States has been particularly resistant to legislating a cash-based (unconditional) child benefit of this scope for a number of reasons,[5] favoring instead a patchwork of safety net programs that target families' material needs, such as food and housing, and policies that reward employment by supplementing earnings.[6] To meet the goal of reducing child poverty by half, a 2019 consensus report by the National Academies of Sciences, Engineering, and Medicine recommended a bundle of policies, including a child-based allowance available to all families up to an income limit, irrespective of earnings or prior tax filings, with a larger amount available to families with children aged younger than 5 years.[7] Nevertheless, it took a pandemic and the resulting impact on the economy and financial well-being of Americans for an expanded child tax credit to be legislated. In 2021, the United States embarked on its first large-scale social experiment of disbursing cash allowances to all except the highest-income families with children.[8]

By reducing poverty, cash allowances can have positive impacts on families with children.[9] However, their distribution and uptake depend on successful implementation, the ease of receiving the money, and whether the intended near-universal reach to all eligible families is achieved. Implementing cash transfers on a large scale and ensuring that the intended beneficiaries receive the income can be challenging. Cash distribution channels and formats vary worldwide from pickup points at post offices to transfers via digital platforms.[10] The US context is especially challenging because no existing system is available to efficiently and quickly deliver financial supports to families with children during times of crisis.[11] This is, in part, because existing financial benefit systems in the United States are typically designed with steps and requirements to determine eligibility, including proof of need based on income,[12] and systems in the United States that allocate funds to people have become increasingly focused on compliance rather than on preventing poverty or providing assistance.[13]

In this chapter, we describe an approach used to disburse cash to families with children in the United States as part of a multisite, randomized controlled study of poverty reduction called Baby's First Years (BFY).[14] The behavioral economic insights that informed the design and implementation of the study's cash transfer mechanism offer useful considerations regarding population inclusion and reach in large-scale programs.

US CONTEXT AND MECHANISMS FOR DELIVERING SOCIAL BENEFITS AND CASH SUPPORT TO FAMILIES WITH CHILDREN

President Johnson's War on Poverty (the Great Society programs) is a useful starting point to understand the history of means-tested safety net programs in the United States. The official poverty measure that drives much of the means testing of existing safety net programs stems from this era, when this measurement tool was created to assess the resources families had to purchase food.[15] This measure required making determinations about income, individuals' relationships with others in a household, and citizenship.[16] Doing so required proof and methods of documentation, giving rise to validation processes that have since shaped US government programs intended to provide economic support to individuals and families.[17]

The United States has several narrow mechanisms for delivering in-kind benefits supporting basic needs such as food, housing, and health care through federal agencies (e.g., the US Department of Agriculture, Department of Health and Human Services, and Department of Housing and Urban Development) and their state and local equivalents, in addition to two wide-reaching systems for delivering cash: Social Security and the tax system. The US Social Security system is charged with distributing a guaranteed monthly pension to retirees that is drawn from tax contributions from the working-age population. The tax system is responsible for the distribution of any cash refunds. Hence, the receipt of cash transfers through the tax system hinges on people filing taxes. Social Security and the Earned Income Tax Credit have had particularly large antipoverty effects for older adults and families with children, respectively.[18]

Starting in 2020, pandemic cash relief in the United States relied on the tax system for distribution. Expanded economic support to US families was also provided through existing food benefits via electronic benefits cards and earnings replacement (i.e., unemployment insurance paid directly into former earners' bank accounts).[19] The pandemic cash relief in the United States was largely effective in reaching individuals and families who were already connected to these systems, for example, those who had filed taxes in the past two years and who had already met the eligibility criteria for them. Many individuals received cash infusions as intended through the tax system, but those who were not already integrated into this system (e.g., a retired grandparent raising a grandchild) did not.[20] In addition to certain adjusted gross income limits, other requirements, such as the child living with the tax filer for more than half the year and being related to the tax filer through blood, marriage, legal adoption, or fostering, interfered with the scope of benefit receipt.[21]

BEHAVIORAL INSIGHTS AND CASH TO FAMILIES IN THE UNITED STATES

Receiving social benefits in the United States demands time and mental resources. Stigma, fear, and distrust also play a role in affecting families' pursuit and receipt of social benefits.[22] These concerns among individuals arise from social norms and stereotypes that can be fostered and diffused by broader political landscapes. For example, even when families are eligible, government rules such as the public charge rule, which considers benefit receipt as a factor in residency and citizenship, can have chilling effects even among citizens.[23] Moreover, the US benefit system has evolved toward a focus on compliance and fraud detection, with hurdles and barriers for benefit claimants referred to as ordeal mechanisms that are intended to screen in only the most deserving. However, these same ordeals also dissuade eligible people from receiving benefits. The framework of administrative burden reveals how these mechanisms result in a variety of learning, psychological, and compliance costs that disrupt and interfere with receipt and use of benefits.[24] Behavioral economics expands on this view by additionally considering how individuals construe the world and recognizing that individuals do not always behave in the ways that rational cost–benefit frameworks propose. Hence, context and psychological biases may make certain burdens especially consequential for families with children residing in poverty by increasing the demands on their attention and cognitive load.[25]

These contextual and psychological factors reflect ways in which economic support can be designed to either disrupt or facilitate receipt and use of benefits, particularly at population scale. They include choice designs that shape initial enrollment and resulting uptake and retention, general hassle factors, social influences and norms, and psychological biases that make individuals responsive to frames and anchors. Can deliberate design of these features matter? The evidence is still emerging. For example, a recent study of housing code compliance across three US metro areas found that personalized letters with a clear call to action regarding upcoming inspections, last-chance notifications of fines to correct violations, and postcards strategically timed during conventionally peak periods of fine violations were each found to increase compliance.[26] However, a host of personalized and related individualized outreach randomized interventions intended to reduce informational and educational barriers to filing for the Earned Income Tax Credit had no substantive impact on uptake,[27] suggesting that broader, systemic barriers may be more influential.

First, starting with the enrollment stage, the structure and presentation of choices can affect uptake and subsequent decisions that affect receipt of benefits. Defaults, or preset courses of action that take effect without relying on individuals to make active decisions,[28] may overcome procrastination and inertia resulting from the overwhelming nature of complex choices. Influential across many domains, defaults are found to be particularly effective in consumer domains (vs. other domains, such as environmental conservation efforts).[29] The ways in which the implication of not enrolling is presented can also matter: An active choice statement conveying specific consequences of not participating (e.g., "I wish to not receive the informational pamphlets about my children's development" compared with a more passive "I do not want to receive these materials") has also been shown to influence subsequent receipt.[30]

Second, "sludge" or "dark patterns" – unjustified frictions that impede users – can disrupt access to public benefits or services.[31] Whereas nudges aim to support beneficial choices, friction either discourages behavior that is in a person's best interest (sludge) or encourages behavior that is not (dark patterns).[32] Sludge often includes duplicative paperwork or waiting time, either in person or online, and compliance standards such as proof of eligibility and recertification requirements.[33] A recent Biden administration executive order aims to reduce these examples of sludge in programs critical to families by allowing options such as online purchasing of items covered by Supplemental Nutrition Program for Women, Infants, and Children benefits and by expanding presumptive and automatic enrollment across safety net programs.[34]

Third, family life and economic resources are often dynamic and uncertain. Instability in labor market income, for example, can wreak havoc on family life if income fluctuation causes households to reach earnings and income eligibility cliffs, resulting in a sudden loss of benefits. These negative income shocks can increase demands on cognitive load and escalate present bias, causing individuals to put more weight on the present relative to the future.[35] An increase in wages can result in a decrease or often complete loss of public benefits that are critical to family stability, particularly childcare and housing subsidies,[36] an effect that is magnified when families are enrolled in multiple programs. These types of uncertainty differ from the cognitive load demands due to structural features of social benefit receipt related to wait time, appointments, and forms. Uncertainty and confusion in understanding the tax system and tax credits make it difficult to rationally weigh the cost of an immediate loss in benefits against the future benefit of a tax refund.[37] Solutions such as benefits calculators, alignment of eligibility and rules across safety net programs, and tax refunds dispersed monthly instead of annually serve as examples that could reduce some types of uncertainty.[38]

Fourth, social influences and norms beyond the specific design of social benefits programs can affect perceptions. Many social programs presume help-seeking behavior rather than agency and autonomy as a starting point,[39] and this can increase perceptions of victimization among eligible recipients. Restrictions on what participants can redeem from their benefits, conditions on accessing benefits, and general quality of the physical environment and treatment by workers demean rather than empower participants and influence broader community narratives about the friendliness and generosity of public systems.[40] Uneven power dynamics can engender mistrust in the government that further prevents people in poverty and members of other marginalized populations from accessing public programs.[41]

Finally, all humans have psychological biases that cause them to implicitly respond to framing, cues, anchoring, and reference points and that affect behaviors such as earmarking of money for certain purposes.[42] On the one hand, these strategies can be useful to individuals as mental tools to assist with budgeting.[43] On the other hand, guilt and expectations of how to use funds can interfere with the success of mental tools such as earmarking.[44] Indeed, although such biases can be useful in reducing mental demands related to expending money and directed toward family objectives (e.g., the Dutch child benefit was found to particularly increase spending on children's items such as clothing),[45] such biases can also be exploited. A third of borrowers surveyed reported use of predatory credit such as payday loans, pawn loans, deposit advance loans, auto titles, and non-bank installment loans even though they had savings available.[46]

Each of these behaviorally informed aspects intersects with the design of cash support in the United States. Paying attention to these types of design details beyond or within existing US systems – whether from the perspective of families meant to receive benefits or from practitioners and policy makers charged with implementing benefits – is relatively nascent. Implications for large-scale reach and the extent of cost savings, if any, are also not well understood.

THE BABY'S FIRST YEARS STUDY

The BFY intervention is a monthly, predictable, unconditional cash gift disbursed to low-income parents with newborns, starting at the child's birth. This US study was designed to answer questions about infusions of income and children's well-being, specifically the causal impact of poverty reduction during the earliest years of children's development. From July 2018 to June 2019, 1,000 parents were recruited shortly after giving birth at one of 12 hospitals across four US metro areas (New Orleans, New York City, the Twin Cities in Minnesota, and the greater Omaha, Nebraska, area). After consenting to participate in a child development research study, the parents who had given birth were informed about the opportunity to participate in a cash gift lottery. Among consenting parents, 40 per cent were subsequently randomly assigned to receive an unconditional monthly gift of US$333 (US$3,996/year), and 60 per cent were randomly assigned to receive a US$20 unconditional monthly gift (US$220/year).[47] At the time of study consent, the parents were promised the cash gift for the first 40 months of their child's life. Because the pandemic disrupted capstone in-person data collection of children's developmental outcomes at the 36-month follow-up, funds were raised to extend the cash gift such that families will receive it until the child is 52 months old, with the capstone child development data to be collected when the child is aged 4 years, or at an approximately 48-month follow-up. The study team has since raised funds such that families will receive the monthly cash gift for a total of 76 months and data will be collected when children are aged 6 and 8 years.

One of the key tasks undertaken during the decade leading up to the study's launch was how to translate poverty reduction into a feasible income intervention. Examples from other nations, including the use of mobile money technologies (e.g., Kenya's Give Directly study), in-person distribution at sites such as post offices, and direct deposits in bank accounts, were not feasible for a US research trial, nor were they reasonable from the perspective of population scale at the time.[48] Mobile money and electronic benefit card equivalents did not have the current level of sophistication now applied through private organizations such as Propel (https://www.joinpropel.com/about-us) and Give Directly (https://www.givedirectly.org/). Fewer than half of individuals and families residing in poverty have an account in a bank or an equivalent financial institution insured by the Federal Deposit Insurance Company, thus making direct deposit less tractable. Directly handing out cash would require cumbersome tracking and monitoring, especially given the monthly disbursements. With these considerations in mind, we landed on a debit card mechanism. In summer 2014, we launched and successfully pilot tested the feasibility and implementation of cash disbursement through a debit card that was ultimately used for the cash gift in the large-scale study.[49]

BEHAVIORAL ECONOMICS AND THE BFY CASH GIFT

The BFY cash transfer is predictable and monthly, thus reducing the mentally taxing nature of income uncertainty and instability prevalent in low-income US households, whether it is a result of the characteristics of low-wage work, the eligibility and recertification requirements of public benefits, or other reasons.[50] Unlike existing US anti-poverty programs, the BFY cash transfer has low administrative burden, with little required documentation or certification of income eligibility. Once enrolled, parents continued to receive the cash gifts on an opt-out (vs. opt-in) basis; that is, the payments automatically continued unless a parent requested otherwise. The MasterCard debit card used to disburse the monthly cash allotment was labeled (i.e., cobranded) with a "4 My Baby" logo, primarily to differentiate it from other electronic benefit cards available at the four study sites, as shown in Figure 9.1. The debit card was handed to the parent at the time of consent to receive the cash transfer, approximately one to two days after the child's birth, and immediately activated. The cash disbursement is coupled with a text or email reminder on the day of each month corresponding to the child's birth date (e.g., a parent whose child was born on June 23 would receive the payments by midnight on the evening of the 22nd of each month). Many of these design features may elicit earmarking of the funds as "for the baby," in contrast to psychologically neutral expenditure decisions predicted by classical economic theory. However, parents in the BFY study received no restrictions or guidance on how to spend the money. The types of use of the money that could be interpreted as "for my baby" might, and likely do, vary widely, from purchasing specific items for the baby, such as diapers, to ensuring a home is clean or putting the funds toward rent or supporting the parent's education and job training. Table 9.1 summarizes the implementation and design

Table 9.1. Behavioral economic concepts in the design of the BFY cash gift

BFY cash gift feature	How it was operationalized and implemented	Behavioral economic insight
In-person or personalized introduction and card activation	Interviewers introduced and explained the card, showed the card, and were available to answer any questions.	Fresh start; timing influences motivation: trust (skepticism re. free money); co-occurring at nurturing and bonding moment with baby; joy Reduce enrollment inertia
Opt out	A cash gift is available on the card unless the participant calls to opt out.	Default effects; easy and low hassle: no recertification or reenrollment hassles
Automatic (repeated)	The cash gift is preprogrammed to automatically transfer to the debit card.	Spending habit formation
Monthly	Reduces mental demands of budget smoothing that quarterly or annual distribution would require; also aligns with normed expectations of other public benefit programs.	Scarcity and cognitive load
At time of childbirth and each month on date of child's birth date	Spending is associated with children and children's environments.	Psychology of preference formation
Monthly text or email reminder (optional)	For those who provided consent, text and email notifications for cash gift disbursements are sent, bringing attention to the money available for that month.	Scarcity and cognitive load
Predictable time period with no recertification or redetermination requirements (i.e., parents continue receiving the cash gift even if their circumstances change)	Low hassle, certainty, planning horizon; formal tracking of accumulated resources on card are available through BFY hotline, MasterCard login portal, or both Simplified receipt and use of money, in contrast with determination, eligibility, and recertification mechanisms that act as screening for many means-tested programs	Hassle factors as psychological barriers

(Continued)

Table 9.1. Continued

BFY cash gift feature	How it was operationalized and implemented	Behavioral economic insight
Unconditional; no limitations or restrictions on spending choices	Seamless availability of monthly cash	Affirmation and decision agency; scarcity and cognitive load
Debit card network is MasterCard, with MasterCard customer service line	An international financial tool that is mainstream	Social influences: normed to mainstream financial inclusion
No credit history required	Uncoupled from any credit-approval limitations; not tied to a formal banking structure (i.e., no bank account required but also not an avenue to build credit)	Hassle factors as psychological barriers: no friction related to eligibility determination
4MyBaby card branding with extra customer service	Cash gift transferred from a trusted, charitable organization source; uncoupled with history of experiences with social benefits programs; fresh start coupled with birth of baby Color of debit card is green, to differentiate it from other electronic public benefit cards	Social influences: uncoupled from stigma of other social benefits; reduced judgment of parenting
No alternative credit or debt functions	BFY cash gift money accumulates up to a large maximum; can be used at any point; not possible to overdraw on the card, thus preventing overdraft fees	Scarcity and limited attention

Note: BFY = Baby's First Years.

features of the BFY cash gift as informed by insights from behavioral economics previously described.

BFY CASH GIFT IMPLEMENTATION FINDINGS

As of August 2023, more than US$10 million has been disbursed to the BFY study families. Implementation of the cash gift has been highly successful. Every consenting parent walked out of the

Figure 9.1. The 4MyBaby card compared with other electronic public benefit cards available in each of the Baby's First Years study sites

Sources: Department of Children and Family Services. (n.d.). *Electronic benefits transfer (EBT)*. https://www.dcfs.louisiana.gov/page/electronic-benefits-transfer-ebt; Nebraska Department of Health and Human Services. (2022). *EBT (electronic benefits transfer)*. https://dhhs.ne.gov/Pages/EBT.aspx; Minnesota Department of Human Services. (2019). *How to use your Minnesota EBT card*. https://www.fmchs.com/images/documents/EBT.pdf; and New York State Office of Temporary and Disability Assistance. (2021). *Creating a personal identification number (PIN) for a P-EBT Food Benefit Card*. https://otda.ny.gov/SNAP-COVID-19/P-EBT-Card-PIN-Instructions.asp

hospital with an activated card with funds on it. As shown in Table 9.2, among the parents who consented to allow access to the data on their debit card transactions, very few cards exhibited no use in the first 12 months, and very few transactions failed because of insufficient funds or personal identification number (PIN) problems. Patterns of successful use do not statistically differ by observable characteristics of the parent, such as self-identified race or ethnicity, or by study site.

Parents can contact the MasterCard or 4MyBaby support line regarding questions and difficulties related to use of the debit card.

Table 9.2. Descriptive analyses of transactions from the 4MyBaby debit card over the first year of cash gift receipt

| | Over first 12 months after birth of child | | |
Characteristic of the transaction	Total sample	$20 monthly cash gift group	$333 monthly cash gift group
n	839	484	355
Use of 4MyBaby card, %			
Haven't used the card	2	3	0
Used the card every month	29	12	52
Other	69	85	48
Success of transactions			
Average no. of approved transactions	57.84	22.3	106.3
Average no. of failed transactions, insufficient funds	3.44	2.63	4.56
Average no. of failed transactions, personal identification number problems	2.95	2.26	3.90
Overview of expenditures, US$			
Amount of annual net approved transactions (total)	1,786.25	215.96	3,927.16
Average amount spent by participant per month	141.87	17.12	311.95
Total amount spent	1,511,792.38	105,319.94	1,406,472.38

Table 9.3 describes these varying types of customer support. The phone number for the MasterCard support line is printed on the back of the card, with an automated call service available 24/7 for most requests. The 4MyBaby card hotline number is printed on the front of the card with call and text service available, connected to a person during typical business hours. The 4MyBaby card hotline offers more comprehensive language translation, free replacement cards with follow-up communication to ensure that callers received them, and support for completing MasterCard's paperwork for fraudulent claims (including postage and envelopes as needed). The 4MyBaby hotline also supports parents' requests for proof-of-gift documentation that may be needed for receipt of government benefits. A summary of the total number and nature of 4MyBaby hotline calls is presented in Table 9.4. Contacts were made by call, text, or email; however, the vast majority of contact attempts happened via

Table 9.3. Support line features, by support entity

Support line feature	MasterCard support line	4MyBaby card hotline
24/7, 365 operation	Yes, for everything except card replacements	No, only available 10:00 a.m.–6:00 p.m. Eastern Time and not available on holidays
Support available via SMS text	Yes	Yes, for some services
Person-to-person support	No, service is automated	Yes
Spanish and English support available	Some; not all services or at all times	Yes
Free card replacement	No	Yes
Card replacement verification	No	Yes, follow-up communication when card is not activated within two weeks of send date
Instant card replacement	No, funds cannot be accessed until the replacement card is received and activated	Yes, card can be activated instantly and information provided to the participating parent for immediate use
Knowledge of back-end system customizations for the study	No	Yes
Support in completing MasterCard's paperwork for fraudulent claims (including postage and envelopes as needed)	No	Yes
Proof-of-gift documentation	No	Yes
Support liaising with benefit program administrators when cash gift is incorrectly factored into income eligibility	No	Yes
Information about upcoming Baby's First Years study activities	No	Yes
Communication of contact information changes to the study team	No	Yes

Table 9.4. Nature of BFY customer service calls from May 2018 to March 2022

Nature of calls	*n*
Uncategorized: no issue, call back or no contact, spam call, wrong number)	1,430
Replacement card request (lost, broken, stolen, expired, no details provided)	891
Activate new card or reset PIN request	802
Balance or transaction check	574
Card issues (e.g., frozen card, PIN not working, cannot check balance, funds not transferring to new card)	364
Other	151
Issue was resolved	141
Inquiries from non-participants	121
Age 1 visit	103
Contact information (update, verification, etc.)	96
General 4MyBaby card questions (how to use card, card issuer website, etc.)	92
Fraudulent activity claim	80
Incorrect or missing payment	65
Age 2 visit	48
Study incentive checks (any questions or issues)	47
Social benefits, clawback support, proof of gift letter request	42
BFY or 4MyBaby card withdrawal request	10
4MyBaby card gift extension	10
Age 3 visit	7
Total	5,074

Notes: BFY = Baby's First Years; PIN = personal identification number.

phone. Approximately 80 per cent of the parents in the BFY study had called at least once through March 2022, with an average total of 25 calls to the line per week.

The debit card mechanism is not foolproof.[51] We have garnered insights regarding the challenges of disbursing cash through a debit card as designed in the BFY study. First, algorithms that automate cash disbursement to recipients each month on the day of their child's birth date sometimes freeze or fail. These issues are rare: for the first two years of the children's lives, 99 per cent of payments were automatically disbursed on the correct day.[52] However, for families expecting the monthly cash infusion, this failure can be unnerving and put them at financial risk. Second, the debit card cannot carry more than US$10,000, and planned payments that would put a parent's account over that limit cannot be disbursed. In these cases, funds must be removed from the account for subsequent disbursements to be made. To date, only four participants have been affected by hitting the maximum allotment on the debit card. Third, as with all credit or debit cards, the 4MyBaby card expires after three years, well before the study's intention to stop disbursement of the cash gift. For many parents in the study, even when address information could be confirmed, mail was not a reliable mechanism for receiving the card or letters because of challenges with receiving mail, unreliable carrier service, or lack of a reliable mailing address (e.g., as a result of housing insecurity or homelessness), and multiple attempts to mail cards were needed. In the end, most parents' cards were replaced before the expiration date after they contacted one of the two hotlines. In other cases, replacement card requests were made after the expiration date.

DISCUSSION AND CONCLUSION

Feasible policy implementation strategies in the United States for getting benefits and financial support to people quickly, as might be needed in circumstances of financial or public health crises, on a large scale and with universal reach, are nascent. We draw on implementation lessons offered from the first randomized controlled trial of a monthly unconditional cash gift, the BFY study, launched in 2018, on approaches to disbursing cash to US families with young children as an exemplar of a strategy that is informed by behavioral economic insights, inclusive, and potentially achievable at scale.

The BFY study team considered how the setup of cash disbursement would affect cognitive load and attentional demands, inertia and choice anxiety, and mental tools that might support family objectives in allocation of the money gift. The cash gift was automatically available to the parent after the birth of the study's focal child, and it was guaranteed to be available monthly over the child's first three years of life (irrespective of shifting household financial or family structure). Cobranded with a 4MyBaby logo, the MasterCard debit card was differentiated from other types of electronic benefit cards and activated upon the parent's consent at hospital bedside, with money loaded each month on the day of the child's birth date, accompanied by a text reminder. The card allowed for ATM cash withdrawals with a small fee and in-person and online point-of-sale transactions where MasterCard was accepted.

Analyses of card transactions and of calls made to the study customer service team suggest successful implementation of the BFY study approach to disbursing cash, both in terms of ease of access and use and in terms of financial inclusion. The monthly cash gifts are typically drained by the end of the family's disbursement cycle, with a majority of the funds spent through point-of-sale transactions online and a variety of vendors. In semistructured interviews, parents reported few issues with using the BFY money. Although some needed additional support immediately after their enrollment – for example, to confirm whether it counted as taxable income – or occasional assistance with card logistics (such as resetting a PIN or reissuing a lost card), they understood how to use the debit card and did not struggle to find retailers and vendors who would accept it. That is, the administrative burdens they faced in terms of learning and redemption costs were low.[53]

The parents who participated in the BFY study represent diverse racial and ethnic backgrounds; many were not born in the United States, and they reside in communities with a history of exclusion and racism. Systemic discrimination shapes the financial tools to which people have access, with those from minoritized groups, women, and those with lower incomes less likely to be banked.[54] This has implications for the mechanisms through which unconditional cash transfers can occur. For example, preliminary data from the BFY study suggest that only two-thirds received the 2020–2021 pandemic-related stimulus payments. Any system predicated on recipients having bank accounts requires the additional step of working with potential recipients to create accounts. Although this may support the goal of working toward inclusion in the traditional financial services sector, some may be reluctant to engage with traditional banks, particularly in light of previous negative experiences; moreover, such steps impede goals of rapid disbursement of funds in cases of crisis.[55]

Several challenges prevail in the US context for equitable distribution of social benefits to and financial support of families with children. Administrative burdens related to eligibility, documentation, and related criteria for safety net programs impose direct and implicit costs on eligible families. With government systems oriented toward compliance and monitoring, demands such as proof of identification (e.g., a Social Security number) and child or household member residential and relationship requirements add complexity and contribute to stigma, fear, and related negative ripple effects as people interact with programs. The risks of doing something wrong feel elevated, and the consequences of doing so are stark, ranging from lost benefits to charges of fraud. Furthermore, as demonstrated through recent distribution of the 2021 expanded child tax credit, the tax system is not inclusive of non–tax filers (those who have very limited or no formal earnings); it is not designed to efficiently disburse funds to those who cannot receive direct deposits to bank accounts or do not have known addresses; and given the annual scope of much of the Internal Revenue Service's (IRS's) work and its chronic underfunding,[56] staff and technical capacity to manage predictable, frequent distribution of funds are limited. Working with other US systems such as Social Security is certainly one option for distribution. Reinvesting and expanding the role and capacity of the IRS is another. Yet another is to look to alternative cash distribution mechanisms. The implementation success of the BFY cash gift disbursement and debit card, coupled with strategies applied by a variety of recent guaranteed income pilots in the United States, can add further guidance on structural and behavioral elements to consider in efforts to achieve population reach and scale when providing economic support to families in the United States.[57]

NOTES

1 Bastagli, F., Steward, D., & Orton, I. (2020). *Universal child benefits*. UNICEF. https://www.unicef.org/media/72916/file/UCB-ODI-UNICEF-Report-2020.pdf.
2 Ibid.
3 See Artuc, E., Cull, R., Dasgupta, S., Fattal, R., Filmer, D., Gine, X., Jacoby, H., Jolliffe, D., Kee, H.L., Klapper, L., Kraay, A., Loayza, N., Mckenzie, D., Ozler, B., Rao, V., Rijkers, B., Schmukler, S.L., Toman, M., Wagstaff, A., & Woolcock, M. (2020). *Toward successful development policies: Insights from research in development economics* (Policy Research Working Paper No. 9133). World Bank. https://openknowledge.worldbank.org/handle/10986/33289; and Baird, S., Ferreira, F.H.G., Özler, B., & Woolcock, M. (2013). Relative effectiveness of conditional and unconditional cash transfers for schooling outcomes in developing countries: A systematic review. *Campbell Systematic Reviews*, 9(1).
4 In 2016, Canada introduced the Canada Child Benefit program, which provides benefits ranging from $5,000 to $6,400 per year to qualifying families, depending on the family's income and children's ages. The United Kingdom launched a child benefit in 1998, and it remains to this day. Denmark's Børne-og Ungeydelse is structured similarly, giving an unconditional cash transfer to children in households under a certain income threshold, and Australia's Family Tax Benefit gives the option of biweekly or annual lump sum payments to income-poor children aged younger than 20 years. See Bastagli et al. (2020); Collyer, S., Curran M.A., Garfinkel, I., Harris, D., Stabile, M., Waldfogel, J., & Wimer, C. (2020). *What a child allowance like Canada's would do for child poverty in America*. Century Foundation. https://tcf.org/content/report/what-a-child-allowance-like-canadas-would-do-for-child-poverty-in-america/?session=1. Also see Organisation for Economic Co-operation and Development. (2019). *Family cash benefits*. https://www.oecd.org/els/soc/PF1_3_Family_Cash_Benefits.pdf.
5 Individualism, racialization of poverty, and neoliberalism each broadly influence these critiques. Other concerns about the lack of conditions for cash receipt include increased inflation, government dependency, spending on substances such as alcohol and tobacco, and lack of investment, all of which have little evidence to prove their association with receipt of cash transfers (Handa, S., Daidone, S., Peterman, A., Davis, B., Pereira, A., Palermo, T., Yablonski, J. [2018]. Myth-busting? Confronting six common perceptions about unconditional cash transfers as a poverty reduction strategy in Africa. *World Bank Research Observer*, 33[2], 259–98).
6 See National Academies of Sciences, Engineering, and Medicine. (2019). *A roadmap to reducing child poverty*. National Academies Press. https://doi.org/10.17226/25246; and Aizer, A., Hoynes, H.W., & Lleras-Muney, A. (2022). *Children and the US social safety net: Balancing disincentives for adults and benefits for children* (Working Paper No. 29754). National Bureau of Economic Research.
7 See National Academies of Sciences, Engineering, and Medicine (2019); and Shaefer, H.L., Collyer, S., Duncan, G., Edin, K., Garfinkel, I., Harris, D., Smeeding, T.M., Waldfogel, J., Wimer, C., & Yoshikawa, H. (2018). A universal child allowance: A plan to reduce poverty and income instability among children in the United States. *RSF: The Russell Sage Foundation Journal of the Social Sciences*, 4(2), 22–42. https://doi.org/10.7758/rsf.2018.4.2.02.
8 Before 2021, the child tax credit was worth up to $2,000 per eligible child and available to many middle- to higher-earning families. The 2021 child credit tax expansion differs from the initial US child tax credit enacted in 1997 in two key

ways. First, although the initial version has been expanded over the years to offer slightly higher amounts and to reach more middle- and higher-income families, the 2021 expansion is unique in its universality, that is, everyone except for the very highest earners with a child is eligible for some nonzero amount irrespective of their earnings or tax filings (Marr, C., Cox, K., & Sherman, A. [2021]. *Build Back Better child tax credit changes would protect millions from poverty – permanently*. Center for Budget and Policy Priorities). Second, the amount and disbursement structure of the 2021 expansion differs substantively from its earlier versions, providing up to US$3,600 for each child aged younger than 6 years (and up to US$3,000 for each child aged 6–17 years); in comparison, the maximum available before this expansion was US$2,000. Moreover, these dollars were automatically disbursed on a monthly basis, whereas the credit had only previously been available as a lump sum. The maximum credit is available to taxpayers with a modified adjusted gross income (AGI) of US$75,000 or less for singles, US$112,500 or less for heads of household, and US$150,000 or less for married couples filing a joint return and qualified widows and widowers. Above these income thresholds, the extra amount above the original US$2,000 credit – either US$1,000 or US$1,600 per child – is reduced by US$50 for every US$1,000 in modified AGI (Internal Revenue Service. [2022a]. *IRS: Expanded credits for families highlight tax changes for 2021; many people who don't normally file should file this year*. Retrieved February 15, 2022, from https://www.irs.gov /newsroom/irs-expanded-credits-for-families-highlight-tax-changes-for-2021 -many-people-who-dont-normally-file-should-file-this-year).

9 See Gennetian, L.A., Aber, J.L., De Hoop, J., & Shafir, E. (2021). Behavioral insights and cash transfers to families with children. *Behavioral Science and Policy Journal, 7*(1), 71–92; and Collyer et al. (2020).

10 Gennetian et al. (2021).

11 Gennetian, L.A. (2020, March 20). *Challenges of equitable rapid response cash payments*. EconoFact. https://econofact.org/challenges-of-equitable-rapid-response-cash -payments

12 Herd, P., & Moynihan, D.P. (2018). *Administrative burden: Policymaking by other means*. Russell Sage Foundation.

13 Rettig, C.P. (2022). *Fiscal year 2022: Agency financial report*. Internal Revenue Service. https://www.irs.gov/pub/irs-pdf/p5456.pdf.

14 Noble, K., Magnuson, K., Gennetian, L.A., Duncan, G., Yoshikawa, H., Fox, N., & Halpern-Meekin, S. (2021). Baby's First Years: Design of a randomized controlled trial of poverty reduction in the United States. *Pediatrics, 148*(4), e2020049702. https://doi.org/10.1542/peds.2020-049702.

15 Fisher, G.M. (2008). Remembering Mollie Orshansky – The developer of the poverty thresholds. *Social Security Bulletin, 68*(3), 79.

16 Burt, M.R., Pindus, N., & Capizzano, J. (2000). *The social safety net at the beginning of federal welfare reform: Organization of and access to social services for low-income families* (Occasional Paper No. 34). Urban Institute. https://www.urban.org/sites/default /files/publication/43746/309309-occa34.pdf.

17 See Gordon, C. (2016). *Growing apart: A tattered safety net: Social policy and American inequality*. Retrieved February 20, 2022, from https://scalar.usc.edu/works/growing -apart-a-political-history-of-american-inequality/a-tattered-safety-net-social -policy; and Danziger, S. K. (2010). The decline of cash welfare and implications for social policy and poverty. *Annual Review of Sociology,36*(1), 523–45. https://doi .org/10.1146/annurev.soc.012809.102644.

18 Bitler, M., Hoynes, H.W., & Whitmore Schazenbach, D. (2020). *The social safety net in the wake of COVID-19* (Working Paper 27796). National Bureau of Economic Research. https://www.nber.org/papers/w27796.

19 Shahin, J., & Long, C. (2021). *State guidance on coronavirus P-EBT* (Guidance Document No. FNS-GD-2020-0109). U.S. Department of Agriculture. https://www.fns.usda.gov/snap/state-guidance-coronavirus-pandemic-ebt-pebt; Kovalski, M.A., & Sheiner, L. (2020, July 20). *How does unemployment insurance work? And how is it changing during the coronavirus pandemic?* Brookings. https://www.brookings.edu/blog/up-front/2020/07/20/how-does-unemployment-insurance-work-and-how-is-it-changing-during-the-coronavirus-pandemic/.

20 Karpman, M., Maag, E., Kenney, G.M., & Wissoker, D.A. (2021, November 4). *Who has received advance child tax credit payments, and how were the payments used?* Urban Institute. https://www.urban.org/research/publication/who-has-received-advance-child-tax-credit-payments-and-how-were-payments-used.

21 Internal Revenue Service. (2022b, July 14). *2021 Child Tax Credit and advance Child Tax Credit payments – Topic B: Eligibility for Advance Child Tax Credit payments and the 2021 Child Tax Credit* (Fact Sheet 2022-32). https://www.irs.gov/credits-deductions/2021-child-tax-credit-and-advance-child-tax-credit-payments-topic-b-eligibility-for-advance-child-tax-credit-payments-and-the-2021-child-tax-credit.

22 Levine, J. (2013). *Ain't no trust: How bosses, boyfriends, and bureaucrats fail low income mothers and why it matters.* University of California Press.

23 Haley, J., Kenney, G., Bernstein, H., & Gonzalez, D. (2020, June 18). *One in five adults reported chilling effects on public benefit receipt in 2019.* Urban Institute. https://www.urban.org/research/publication/one-five-adults-immigrant-families-children-reported-chilling-effects-public-benefit-receipt-2019.

24 See, for example, Chudnovsky, M., & Peters, R. (2020). The unequal distribution of administrative burden: A framework and an illustrative case study for understanding variation in people's experience of burdens. *Social & Policy Administration, 55*(4), 527–42; Moynihan, D., Herd, P., & Harvey, H. (2015). Administrative burden: Learning, psychological, and compliance costs in citizen-state interactions. *Journal of Public Administration Research and Theory, 25*(1), 43–69. https://doi.org/10.1093/jopart/muu009; and Herd & Moynihan (2018).

25 See, for example, Haushofer, J., & Fehr, E. (2014). On the psychology of poverty. *Science, 344*(6186), 862–67. https://doi.org/10.1126/science.1232491; Mullainathan, S., & Shafir, E. (2013). *Scarcity: Why having too little means so much.* Picador; and Gennetian, L.A., & Shafir, E. (2015). The persistence of poverty in the context of financial instability: A behavioral perspective. *Journal of Policy Analysis and Management, 34*(4), 904–36.

26 Linos, E., Quan, L.T., & Kirkman, E. (2020). Nudging early reduces administrative burden: Three field experiments to improve code enforcement. *Journal of Policy Analysis and Management, 39*(1), 243–65.

27 Linos, E., Prohofsky, A., Ramesh, A., Rothstein, J., & Unrath, M. (2022). Can nudges increase take-up of the EITC? Evidence from multiple field experiments. *American Economic Journal: Economic Policy, 14*(4), 432–52.

28 See Jachimowicz, J.M., Duncan, S., Weber, E.U., & Johnson, J.E. (2019). When and why defaults influence decisions: A meta-analysis of default effects. *Behavioural Public Policy, 3*(2), 159–86. https://doi.org/10.1017/bpp.2018.43; and Thaler, R.H., & Sunstein C. (2021). *Nudge: The Final Edition.* Penguin Books.

29 Jachimowicz et al. (2019).

30 Eriksson, K., & Simpson, B. (2012). What do Americans know about inequality? It depends on how you ask them. *Judgement and Decision Making, 7*(6), 741–5.
31 Sunstein, C. (2020). Sludge audits. *Behavioural Public Policy, 6*(4), 654–73. https://doi .org/10.1017/bpp.2019.32.
32 Thaler, R.H. (2018). Nudge, not sludge. *Science, 361*(6401), 431. https://doi:10.1126 /science.aau9241.
33 See, for example, Barrows, A. (2019, April 16). Work requirements are socially toxic sludge. *Behavioral Scientist.* https://behavioralscientist.org/work-requirements -are-socially-toxic-sludge/; Ku, L., Brantley, E., & Pillai, D. (2019). The effects of SNAP work requirements in reducing participation and benefits from 2013 to 2017. *American Journal of Public Health, 109*(10), 1446–51. https://doi.org/10.2105 /AJPH.2019.305232; and Heinrich, C.J., Camacho, S., Henderson, S.C., Hernández, M., & Joshi, E. (2022). Consequences of administrative burden for social safety nets that support the healthy development of children. *Journal of Policy Analysis and Management, 41*(1), 11–44. https://doi.org/10.1002/pam.22324.
34 Exec. Order No. 14058, 3 C.F.R. 704 (2022). https://www.govinfo.gov/content/pkg /CFR-2022-title3-vol1/pdf/CFR-2022-title3-vol1-eo14058.pdf.
35 See Gennetian & Shafir (2015); and Madrian, B.C. (2014). Applying insights from behavioral economics to policy design. *Annual Review of Economics, 6,* 663–88. https://doi.org/10.1146/annurev-economics-080213-041033.
36 Anderson, T., Coffey, A., Daly, H., Hahn, H., Maag, E., & Werner, K. (2022). *Balancing at the edge of a cliff: Experiences and calculations of benefit cliffs, plateaus, and trade-offs.* Urban Institute. https://www.urban.org/sites/default/files/publication/105321 /balancing-at-the-edge-of-the-cliff_0.pdf.
37 Ibid.
38 National Conference of State Legislatures. (2019). *Moving on up: Helping families climb the economic ladder by addressing benefit cliffs.* Retrieved March 31, 2023, from https:// www.ncsl.org/human-services/addressing-benefits-cliffs.
39 Gaines-Turner, T., Simmons, J.C., & Chilton, M. (2019). Recommendations from SNAP participants to improve wages and end stigma. *American Journal of Public Health, 109*(12), 1664–7. https://doi.org/10.2105/AJPH.2019.305362.
40 Chrisinger, B. (2017). Ethical imperatives against item restriction in the Supplemental Nutrition Assistance Program. *Preventative Medicine, 100,* 56–60. https://doi.org /10.1016/j.ypmed.2017.04.009.
41 Chilton, M., Rabinowich, J., Council, C., & Breaux, J. (2009). Witnesses to hunger: Participation through Photovoice to ensure the right to food. *Health and Human Rights, 11*(1), 73–85. https://doi.org/10.2307/40285219.
42 Chetty, R. (2015). Behavioral economics and public policy: A pragmatic perspective. *American Economic Review, 105*(5), 1–33. https://doi: 10.1257/aer.p20151108.
43 Sussman, A.B., & O'Brien, R.L. (2016). Knowing when to spend: Financial consequences of earmarking to encourage savings. *Journal of Marketing Research, 53*(5), 790–803. https://doi-org.proxy.lib.duke.edu/10.1509/jmr.14.0455.
44 Ibid.
45 Kooreman, P. (2000). The labeling effect of a child benefit system. *American Economic Review, 90*(3), 571–83.
46 Bianchi, N., & Levy, R. (2013). *Know your borrower: The four need cases of small-dollar credit consumers.* Center for Financial Services Innovation. https://s3.amazonaws .com/cfsi-innovation-files/wp-content/uploads/2017/01/26054909/Know-Your -Borrower-The-Four-Need-Cases-of-Small-Dollar-Credit-Consumers.pdf.
47 The cash gift treatment is equivalent to increasing the annual income of a family of three residing at the poverty line (US$21,330 in 2019) by approximately 19 per cent. The annual cash gift is similar in magnitude (in today's dollars) to income supplements

experienced by families in prior welfare-to-work experiments in the United States, which produced improvements of 0.15 to 0.20 standard deviations on the achievement of preschool and school-aged children (Duncan, G.J., Morris, P.A., & Rodrigues, C. [2011]. "Does money really matter? Estimating impacts of family income on young children's achievement with data from random-assignment experiments." *Developmental Psychology*, 47[5], 1263–79). The BFY gift amount is also comparable with the average US$3,200 lump sum income transfers to families with children that come through the Earned Income Tax Credit, shown to have similarly sized impacts on children's cognitive outcomes (Dahl, G.B., & Lochner, L. [2012]. The impact of family income on child achievement: Evidence from the Earned Income Tax Credit. *American Economic Review*, 102[5], 1927–56.) As feasible, agreements were secured with state and local officials to minimize risk of the cash gift interfering with eligibility for public benefits, including Temporary Assistance for Needy Families, Supplemental Nutrition Assistance Program, Medicaid, childcare subsidies, and Head Start. In two of the four sites, we secured state legislation to ensure this; other sites relied on administrative strategies in collaboration with the study investigators. The parents were informed of any risk to their income eligibility for other programs before consenting to receive the cash gift.

48 Gennetian et al. (2021).

49 Rojas, N.M., Yoshikawa, H., Gennetian, L.A., Rangel, M.L., Melvin, S., Noble, K., Duncan, G., & Magnuson, K. (2020). Exploring the experiences and dynamics of an unconditional cash transfer for low-income mothers: A mixed-methods study. *Journal of Children and Poverty*, 26(1), 64–84. https://doi.org/10.1080/10796126.2019.1704161.

50 See Hill, H., Morris, P., Gennetian, L.A., Wolf, S., & Tubbs, C. (2013). On the consequences of income instability for children's well-being. *Child Development Perspectives*, 7(2), 85–90; and Morduch, J., & Schneider, R. (2017). *The financial diaries: How American families cope in a world of uncertainty*. Princeton University Press.

51 Because the cash gift intervention is a component of a research study, several subgroups of otherwise eligible families were excluded, most importantly families who met the income criteria but who were not proficient in English or Spanish. Parents who were not going to go home with the baby; who, as determined by nurses or medical staff, should not be approached for medical or psychiatric reasons; whose infants were in the neonatal intensive care unit (NICU); or who did not expect to reside within 50 miles of the hospital were also excluded. Many of these features were mechanical and a function of the research study design criteria, although one could argue that cash support could be a mechanism toward reunification with a baby and an important support when a baby is in the NICU.

52 Of the 24,024 planned payments, 262 were not distributed automatically on the planned date.

53 See Barnes, C. Y. (2021). It takes a while to get used to: The costs of redeeming public benefits. *Journal of Public Administration Research and Theory*, 31(2), 295–310. https://doi.org/10.1093/jopart/muaa042; Moynihan, D., Herd, P., & Harvey, H. (2015). Administrative burden: Learning, psychological, and compliance costs in citizen-state interactions. *Journal of Public Administration Research and Theory*, 25(1), 43–69. https://doi.org/10.1093/jopart/muu009.

54 See Rao, S., & Malapit, H.J.L. (2015). Gender, household structure and financial participation in the United States. *Journal of Family and Economic Issues*, 36(4), 606–20. https://doi.org/10.1007/s10834-014-9426-z; and Rhine, S.L., & Greene, W.H. (2013). Factors that contribute to becoming unbanked. *Journal of Consumer Affairs*, 47(1), 27–45. https://doi.org/10.1111/j.1745-6606.2012.01244.x.

55 See Berry, C. (2006). *To bank or not to bank? A survey of low-income households* (BABC 04-3). Harvard University, Joint Center for Housing Studies. https://jchs.harvard.edu/sites/default/files/media/imp/babc_04-3.pdf; and Rao & Malapit (2015).

56 DeBot, B., & Marr, C. (2015, June 1). *Poor IRS service reflects Congress's deep funding cuts*. Center on Budget and Policy Priorities. https://www.cbpp.org/research/federal-tax/poor-irs-service-reflects-congresss-deep-funding-cuts.

57 Elmi, S. (2020). *Guaranteed income and cash infusions: A three-part series*. Aspen Institute.

CHAPTER TEN

Improving the Effectiveness of Cash Transfer Programs in Kenya

John Gachigi

BACKGROUND

Social protection has become increasingly important in the developing world and is a powerful tool to combat poverty and vulnerability to shocks across people's life cycle, including those resulting from natural disasters, pandemics, and manmade crises. Social protection coverage is also meant to foster inclusive growth through its impact on human capital and social cohesion. Such global recognition has led to social protection coverage emerging as a key measure of the achievement of several of the United Nations' 2030 Sustainable Development Goals (SDGs) and, in particular, Target 1.3 of SDG 1.

In the Kenyan context, *social protection* is defined as "a set of policies, programs, interventions and legislative measures aimed at cushioning all Kenyans against poverty, vulnerability, exclusion, risks, contingencies, and shocks throughout their life cycles, and promoting the realization of economic and social rights."[1] The government of Kenya (GoK) has implemented many poverty reduction programs over time. Yet, it recognizes that a substantial section of the population remains exposed to poverty owing to various vulnerabilities and that a majority of the poor, and particularly the ultra-poor, cannot cope with economic, social, and natural risks and shocks without additional support. This recognition has led to the initial implementation of several social protection interventions, one of which is a cash transfer program.

POLICY FRAMEWORK OF THE SOCIAL PROTECTION SECTOR

The overall policy environment for the social protection sector in Kenya is determined by the National Social Protection Policy of 2021, which provides overall strategic guidance and coordination for the sector. Social protection programming in Kenya is largely fashioned along the life cycle approach, tackling the various risks and vulnerabilities typically faced by children, youth, working-aged persons, aged persons, and persons living with disabilities across all age categories. This approach is complemented by programming that focuses on responding to covariate shocks. Both kinds of programs are guided by the concept of social protection floors, which are "nationally defined sets of basic social security guarantees that should ensure, as a minimum that, over the life cycle, all in need have access to essential health care and to basic income security which together secure effective access to goods and services defined as necessary at the national level."[2]

These social protection programs are led by cash-plus approaches that are aimed at adding value to the cash transfer stipends provided in the form of complementary interventions, such as economic inclusion to encourage an eventual exit, or "graduation," from poverty. At the same time, to ensure greater inclusivity, Kenya has increasingly used universal schemes as a way of overcoming the challenges of targeted programs.

The world is currently moving toward an inclusive life cycle approach with the aim of shifting from targeted programs to universal programs. The advantages of universal programs are reduction in errors of exclusion and therefore enhancement of the programs' political sustainability. Universal benefits also promote unity at the community level through inclusive involvement and hence enable governments to justify the rationale behind committing scarce resources to cash transfer programs. Proponents of universal programs argue that programs targeting the poor have trouble reaching the vulnerable and may instead increase, rather than decrease, inequalities. Hence, universal programs have the potential to overcome exclusion errors and therefore become effective in reaching poor people.[3]

The first universal scheme in Kenya was introduced in 2017, whereby all senior citizens aged 70 years or older were registered and enrolled in the cash transfer program regardless of their socio-economic status with the exception of public servant pensioners. The government has also initiated a pilot Universal Child Benefit program for Kenyan children who are aged zero to two years. The first cohort of enrolled beneficiaries was paid in December 2021 through mobile money.

INNOVATIONS FOR IMPROVED EFFECTIVENESS

To improve the effectiveness of the sector, the social protection system in Kenya has evolved in tandem with advancements in information and communication technologies (ICT). These changes have shaped key advances in the social protection sector, particularly those related to the design and delivery of social protection mechanisms, such as the development of new payment solutions using biometrics as an authentication factor and a refined grievance and case management system that has been decentralized to the grassroots level. Most recently, the COVID-19 pandemic, with its attendant restrictions and containment measures, has highlighted the need for and hastened the adoption of innovative ways of targeting people, especially digital targeting through advanced technological innovations.

INUA JAMII CASH TRANSFER PROGRAMS

The GoK has four cash transfer programs: the Cash Transfer for Orphans and Vulnerable Children (CT-OVC), the Older Persons Cash Transfer (OPCT), the Cash Transfer for Persons with Severe

Disability (PwSD-CT), and the Hunger Safety Net Programme (HSNP). These programs aim to address the needs of citizens across the life cycle. They are implemented under the brand name *Inua Jamii,* which means "uplifting the family," and target poor as well as vulnerable individuals and households. These programs provide basic consumption support through regular and predictable bimonthly stipends and are aimed at building recipients' capacity to live a life of dignity and to be able to exploit their human potential for their own socioeconomic development.

The specific objectives of the Inua Jamii cash transfer program include increasing food consumption and food security for beneficiary households; reducing morbidity and mortality of children aged younger than 5 years; increasing school enrollment, retention, and transition of children aged 4 to 18 years; reducing mortality of older persons and persons with severe disability; building the capacity of caregivers to care, retain, and protect beneficiaries within their households; increasing beneficiary households' capacity to cope with vulnerability; and increasing birth registration for orphans and vulnerable children and acquisition of death certificates for their deceased parents.[4]

The programs are implemented nationally in all 290 constituencies across Kenya's 47 counties and cover about 1,333,000 beneficiaries.[5] The total annual budget allocation for the cash transfer program is Ksh29.6 billion. Perhaps unique in the developing world, the funds transferred as part of Kenya's cash transfer are 100 per cent tax financed, making these programs fiscally sustainable.

The programs are based on categorical targeting, and targeted categories are identified on the basis of prevailing indicators of poverty and vulnerability. The programs provide benefits at either the individual or the household level; for the former, each individual in a household who meets a certain set of criteria receives the cash transfers, and for the latter, benefits are issued once to a household with at least one member who meets the relevant criteria.

CT-OVC was launched in 2004 as a pilot project to support orphans and vulnerable children facing poverty and dealing with the negative effects of the HIV/AIDS epidemic. The aim of the program was to support households that were living with or caring for orphans and vulnerable children, with the overall objective of supporting the poorest in society. The pilot project operated in three districts and supported 500 households. The program was later expanded, both geographically and numerically, to cover the whole country with a total of 353,000 current beneficiaries.[6]

The OPCT was introduced in 2007 with the objective of strengthening the capacities of older people and improving their lives and livelihoods. It targets extremely poor households that include persons aged 65 years or older who do not receive a regular pension. The program started as a pilot in three districts with only 300 beneficiaries and was further expanded in 2009 to 45 districts covering 33,000 beneficiaries. Currently, the program covers the whole country with a total of about 833,000 beneficiaries. In 2017, the government expanded the program through the introduction of a universal pension scheme program targeting senior citizens aged 70 years and older; this program provides an individual entitlement other than household benefits. The program is implemented in all regions of Kenya.[7]

The PwSD-CT is a national program launched in 2011 to support poor households with an adult or child with severe disability who requires 24-hour care and the support of a caregiver who is either a family member or a close relative. The program seeks to enhance caregivers' capacities through cash transfers and to improve the lives of persons with severe disabilities as well as to reduce the negative impact of disability on the household. The program started with 2,100 beneficiaries and was expanded nationally to 47,000 beneficiaries.[8]

The HSNP was started in 2008 and targets poor and vulnerable households in four arid counties of Kenya. The program aims to reduce extreme hunger and vulnerability by delivering regular and unconditional cash transfers to targeted households. Its main objective is to ensure effective, financially secure, and well-targeted use of safety net and cash transfer programs to support some of the most vulnerable and poorest citizens. The program currently covers about 100,000 households.[9]

In 2016, the GoK implemented a strategy to consolidate three of the four cash transfer programs under the Ministry of Labour and Social Protection; namely, the CT-OVC, OPCT, and PwSD-CT. The

Consolidated Cash Transfer (CCT) program is a flagship project under the social pillar of Kenya Vision 2030, which "aims to transform the country into a newly industrializing, middle-income country providing high quality of life to all its citizens in a clean and secure environment."[10] Kenya Vision 2030 is the long-term developmental blueprint for the country and is motivated by a collective aspiration for a better society by the year 2030. The aim of Kenya Vision 2030 is to create "a globally competitive and prosperous country with a high quality of life by 2030." It aims to transform Kenya into "a newly-industrializing, middle income country providing a high quality of life to all its citizens in a clean and secure environment."[11]

Previously, the cash transfer programs were managed in silos, which led to a duplication of many activities, double dipping, and an inefficient use of resources. To provide a framework for coordination, the Ministry of Labour and Social Protection established the Social Assistance Unit as part of the consolidation strategy. In 2020, the Social Assistance Unit was elevated to a fully-fledged Directorate of Social Assistance (DSA), and it will go a long way toward improving the effectiveness of the cash transfer program and efficient service delivery.

INNOVATIONS IN TARGETING OF POTENTIAL CASH TRANSFER BENEFICIARIES

Targeting is the process of identifying individuals and households eligible for the CCT program. The purpose of targeting is to make the best use of scarce resources by identifying those who most need the interventions and for whom the greatest poverty reduction impacts can be achieved. Before the CCT program, each program had its own targeting process, which was lengthy and manual. For the CCT program, a harmonized targeting approach was developed to enhance its efficiency and effectiveness.

This approach uses a standardized electronic harmonized targeting tool and a well-coordinated procedure for targeting and enrollment at least once every two years and recertification at least once every five years, subject to funds availability.[12] The harmonized targeting tool uses a proxy means-testing approach that derives its indicators and weights from a nationally representative household survey developed and piloted in three counties. The harmonized targeting approach will eventually replace all other methods of identifying beneficiaries of the National Safety Net Programme, making it a key element in increasing operational coordination and efficiency. The added advantage of this harmonized targeting tool is that it can be adapted and domesticated by other agencies dealing with health and food security through inclusion-specific indicators.

According to the 2020 operations manual for the CCT program, targeting is based on the following principles: ensuring that beneficiaries adhere to program eligibility criteria, households benefit from only one program (except for a household with a person aged older than 70 years living with an orphan or a person with severe disability), the program demonstrates transparency in its actions and processes, and the government and other program implementers treat community and other stakeholders with kindness and respect during the targeting process. There is also a need to ensure active participation of community members through established structures as well as to guarantee inclusivity of all citizens, irrespective of their social and cultural origins or standings.[13]

INNOVATIONS IN DELIVERY SYSTEMS

Payment is the process of disbursing funds to the beneficiaries through a secure, efficient, and reliable system. Providing regular, timely, and predictable payments to beneficiaries is a critical element of success for any cash transfer program. The CCT payments are made to beneficiary households every two months. The current transfer value is Ksh2,000 per month (Ksh4,000 per payment cycle), but the amount may vary as a result of the number of cycles being paid in lump sum or because of complementary programs targeting all or a section of CCT beneficiaries. The CCT delivers cash transfers through six banks, commonly known as contracted payment service providers (PSPs).

The key innovation that the GoK has undertaken in this area is the rollout of electronic payments. The evolution of cash transfer payments has gone through four phases. During the piloting stage, the government sent funds via Authority to Incur Expenditure to field officers, who would then collect money from the district treasuries by way of temporary imprests and travel to the field to go look for and pay the beneficiaries. Although the number of beneficiaries was small, the process was risky to the officers and very low in authenticity and accountability levels and therefore prone to abuse. In Phase Two, the payment was carried out through the Postal Corporation of Kenya (PCK). When the number of beneficiaries started increasing, the government contracted the PCK to be the channel for delivering funds to the beneficiaries. At the time, this looked like a better option, but the system largely remained manual. It had challenges in accountability and reconciliation. As a result, the government, in collaboration with development partners, opted for an electronic-based payment model that was secured with at least two-factor authentication to identify the beneficiaries.

Phase Three involved contracting two banks as PSPs. Biometrics of the beneficiaries and caregivers were taken, the payments were based on a 21-day cycle, the mode of payment was card based, and beneficiaries were mapped to a particular branch. In the course of payments, beneficiaries experienced biometrics failures, they still walked long distances, and cards were sometimes misrouted. Thus, it was still strenuous for the beneficiaries and the program to meet the objective of delivering and receiving the funds within a convenient distance. The transaction cost for this phase was 2 per cent of the amount disbursed. The fourth phase involved payment through multiple PSPs. The intention of this model was to give beneficiaries a chance to designate a PSP of their own choice from among the four contracted PSPs. This was intended to address the challenges of the long distances they were traveling to access funds through a paying agent, allow beneficiaries to operate a bank account from which they could easily withdraw wherever they were, have assets, be able to also deposit their own savings into the account, eliminate the need to withdraw all their funds within the payment window, allow them to take advantage of interoperability across the four banks, and provide an opportunity to change from one PSP to another if they are dissatisfied with service being offered.

This model has managed to address the major challenge of distance to the nearest paypoints, and uptake by beneficiaries has greatly improved. The requirement to provide proof of life every six months to ensure prompt action on deceased cases is also being alleviated, and the beneficiaries have been empowered to determine their PSP preference and hence access banking facilities at ease.

To ensure efficiency in delivery, payments are made electronically to a beneficiary's bank account of choice and with the use of two-factor authentication, which includes the national identification card and the biometric fingerprint of either the beneficiary or the caregiver. In exceptional cases in which the biometrics fail as a result of fingerprint challenges, or in circumstances in which beneficiaries are either bedridden or hospitalized, case-by-case exceptions are made for use of a personal identification number. This system ensures that all beneficiaries or caregivers receive their monthly stipends on time.

Steps have also been taken to leverage ICT in generating and updating the program payroll. The DSA, through the CCT information system, generates a payroll for all the enrolled beneficiary households on the basis of the specific program, entitlement amount, arrear amount, primary recipient and alternate recipient, and other specifics for PSPs. The entitlement and arrear amounts are automatically calculated, and the payroll list is automatically generated for each PSP and accessed by the PSP through a web service known as the application programming interface.[14] To ensure the security and reliability of the system, a PSP logs into the CCT information system with their user account and downloads their approved payroll list. To access the payroll list, the PSP must download the password-encrypted file and run the verify checksum to access the token password for the specific file. Only the defined PSP user can access the token password and file, and PSPs are unable to view the payroll lists of other PSPs. The downloaded file also includes a checksum process to ensure that the file's data integrity is maintained. Through these measures, the GoK is striving to ensure that payments are predictable, timely, and automated.

The CCT information system has several modules and submodules for effective functionality. These modules are illustrated in Figure 10.1.

Figure 10.1. CCT information system

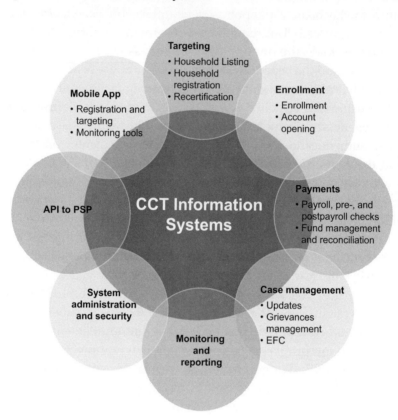

Notes: CCT = Consolidated Cash Transfer; API = application programming interface; PSP = payment service provider; EFC = error, fraud, and corruption.

These modules and submodules are interrelated, and they support one another for effective delivery of the cash transfer. The system is robust and secure, and it supports other agencies through integration, linkages, and data-sharing protocols.

INNOVATIONS IN GRIEVANCE AND CASE MANAGEMENT

The CCT program provides several avenues through which beneficiaries and the community can lodge grievances or cases either directly or indirectly. These are available through the grievance and case management system. The mechanism is open to the community and is designed to be easily accessible and simple to use. This system has been set up deliberately in this manner to ensure that beneficiaries and the community are made aware of the differences in the various complaint channels accessible to them. This knowledge enables them to decide on the most suitable channel to use for a grievance. The access channels include talking to a Beneficiary Welfare Committee member; visiting the subcounty officers, visiting the ministry headquarters, sending letters or emails to ministry headquarters, or calling through the toll-free telephone number. The toll-free line provides a route for people to raise concerns that are independent of direct local program administration. Standard grievance and case management forms are normally used to manually record issues received at the subcounty level. The respective forms are then scanned and updated into the grievance and case management module by the subcounty officers, along with other supporting documents.[15]

Four broad categories of grievance are normally of major concern to the beneficiaries, implementers, and other stakeholders: grievances, service requests, updates, and complaints. Grievances mainly arise when an individual or group is dissatisfied or discriminated against and excluded from participating in the cash transfer programs through wrong, unlawful, or unfair practices in CCT process. The grievances could be in areas such as targeting, enrollment, payments, and case management. For effective service delivery, grievances are treated with the utmost urgency because of the sensitivity and passions that they engender, especially for marginalized groups. Grievances are escalated and managed centrally at DSA headquarters. The general details of the grievance are recorded through a standard grievance and complaints management form and are subsequently captured in the grievance and case management module by the receiving party, with care taken to ensure sufficient information is gathered to initiate an investigation.[16]

Complaints may be raised by program beneficiaries, by members of the community in areas in which the program operates, or by members of the general public regarding any aspect of program implementation. The most commonly raised types of complaint may include payment-related complaints and complaints about the quality of service offered; card and account issues; misuse of funds by a caregiver; or error, fraud, or corruption. A standard update form is used to manually record all grievances and complaints, and the results are entered into the CCT Information System. The subcounty officers, with the support of Beneficiary Welfare Committees, are responsible for receiving, recording, and reporting complaints at the community level. Complaints are normally resolved at the subcounty level and, where necessary, escalated to ministry headquarters.[17]

INNOVATIONS IN COMPLEMENTARY PROGRAMS FOR AN EFFECTIVE CASH-PLUS AGENDA

To add value to the cash transfer programs, the government has introduced complementary interventions that are meant to combine social protection programs, such as cash transfers, with one or more types of complementary support such as additional inputs, services, and linkages to other sectors. These complementary interventions improve the cross-sectoral achievement of results, hence strengthening the return on investment of national efforts.

Complementary supports can be components that are integral elements of the social protection intervention, such as additional benefits or in-kind transfers and information about behavior change communication such as financial literacy to encourage savings and investment in income-generating activities. Other components are external to the intervention but offer explicit linkages to services provided by other sectors, such as the direct provision of access to services or facilitating linkages to services. In addition, there are other benefits or in-kind transfers, such as asset transfer in graduation programs as well as fortified foods, if food is not available.

Complementary programs support social protection programs through three pillars: skills training; access to health care, nutrition, and education, which involves nutrition counseling, school feeding, free primary and secondary day schools, and bursaries to secondary schools; and socioeconomic inclusion for beneficiaries through interventions such as life and business skills training, livelihood asset transfers, coaching and mentoring, financial literacy training and access to credit, and economic empowerment for various vulnerable groups.

Implementing complementary programs involves the identification of the main social protection programs that need complementing, establishing a strong monitoring and evaluation system that seeks to find the right mix and right level of intervention, being ready and willing to constantly adapt program parameters to optimize outcomes, and creating a strong central leadership to make ministries and programs work together. There is also the need to strengthen intersectoral links between national programs to maximize their impact and at the same time improve results even when there is no impact gap.

However, implementing complementary programs incurs challenges and obstacles such as institutional or professional arrogance, whereby some organizations feel they are better off than others. Other challenges include competing interests between organizations that cause conflict; inadequate policies and legal frameworks regarding complementarity interventions; and inadequate, and in some instances the absence of, data-sharing protocols that hinder intergradation of data systems and sharing of vital data.

A KEY INNOVATION: BENEFICIARY OUTREACH STRATEGY FOR EMPOWERING BENEFICIARIES

Beneficiary outreach is the process through which program information is communicated to its beneficiaries. The Inua Jamii Beneficiary Outreach Strategy is aimed at facilitating and empowering beneficiaries with information and knowledge to actively engage with a cash transfer program and understand its eligibility criteria; make informed choices and conveniently access their payments; understand their rights and responsibilities; and at the same time communicate effectively in the case of complaints and grievances.

The Beneficiary Outreach Strategy will thus enable the Inua Jamii program to become more responsive and accountable to the needs of the local communities by providing access to comprehensive program information and by effectively communicating with vulnerable, marginalized, and ultrapoor beneficiaries. It also provides a platform for beneficiaries to provide feedback to the program.

The primary objective of the outreach strategy is to improve beneficiary awareness of the key features of the Inua Jamii program, such as targeting, enrollment, payments, grievances, and case management. The second objective is to enable beneficiaries to effectively engage and communicate with the program by providing sufficient knowledge and understanding of beneficiary rights, responsibilities, and entitlements.[18]

The first challenge to communicating with the majority of beneficiaries is their reliance on limited sources of information, mainly from area chiefs and local elders. Radio and mobile phones are secondary sources of information. A second challenge is low awareness of beneficiary rights and responsibilities, which is compounded by caregivers' poor responsibility regarding how and where to spend cash. Often, caregivers do not report beneficiary deaths because they are afraid of losing the cash transfer benefits.[19]

The effectiveness of the cash transfer program can be improved by urgently addressing the challenges affecting the smooth implementation of the outreach strategy. First is the need to stay flexible, responsive, and adaptable in the choice of method, tools, and messages. Second, and equally as important, is understanding the unique characteristics and information use habits of beneficiary groups to create relevant communication. Third is to use the local knowledge of elders, chiefs, and county and subcounty staff to reach out to specific groups of beneficiaries. Fourth, is reaching out to beneficiaries through multiple modes of communication, which is paramount to raise awareness of and build recall of eligibility criteria, payment processes, available modes of lodging a complaint, and related information on the program. Fifth is the need for program staff from headquarters to the county and subcounty levels to connect and communicate regularly with all stakeholders to maximize internal efficiency and, where possible, provide quarterly updates.

INNOVATING BY USING BEHAVIORAL SCIENCE
TO IMPROVE PROGRAM IMPACT

Since 2018, the World Bank, ideas42, and the GoK have been working together to develop behavioral interventions that can help cash transfer recipients make productive investments. A package of behavioral interventions was developed to address key barriers faced by transfer recipients that hindered them from doing so, and the interventions were then refined through feedback from program participants. The package of interventions included posters that were developed to address social norms by expanding recipients' perceptions of how they could spend their payments; goal-setting and plan-making activities to help participants set realistic goals, identify how much they would save from each transfer, and finally calculate how many cash payments it would take to reach their goal; and a partitioning pouch that participants could use immediately upon cash receipt to separate the cash they planned to save from the cash they planned to spend immediately on consumption needs. These designs were supplemented by text message reminders sent at important times, such as when recipients could collect their cash, to ensure their goals and plans were top-of-mind.

To assess the impact of the behavioral designs, they were tested in a randomized controlled trial with 900 cash transfer recipients in March 2019.[20] The behavioral interventions led to significant increases of 9 per cent in the incidence of having a productive goal and 41 per cent in the amount saved from the transfer when compared with receiving the cash only. Restrictions resulting from the COVID-19 pandemic enacted in March 2020 affected the roll-out of a large-scale cluster randomized controlled trial to test the effectiveness of the nudge designs. However, a pilot of a qualitative phone survey to assess whether recipients found the behavioral designs useful during COVID-19 lockdowns, conducted in June 2020, provided evidence that recipients who received the behavioral designs were still able to use them, and although many recipients' goals and plans were disrupted as a result of the lockdowns and associated challenges, they were often able to adjust their investment goals and savings plans accordingly.[21]

COVID-19 RESPONSE THROUGH CASH TRANSFER

Like any other country, Kenya has been hard hit by the effects and repercussions of the COVID-19 pandemic since its outbreak in early 2020. At the onset of the pandemic in March 2020, it was estimated that 3.5 million households were in dire need of urgent social assistance in Kenya. However, the Inua Jamii National Safety Net Programme was not in a position to adequately meet the needs of the population affected by COVID-19. In responding to the pandemic, the GoK therefore allocated an additional Ksh10 billion to act as a cushion for members of society newly vulnerable because of the adverse effects of COVID-19.[22]

However, a policy brief report by Magongo and colleagues released in April 2020 indicated that the smooth implementation of cash transfer interventions was adversely affected by COVID-19 worldwide.[23] Particularly affected were programs that paid beneficiaries using cash and hence required physical contact, which were impeded by the COVID-19 protocols and other precautions taken by the government to reduce beneficiary exposure. However, implementing agencies had to devise innovative methods, which included the introduction of mobile money payment platforms as a safe alternative to digital cash transfers through banks and agents. This has enabled agencies to effectively reach the most vulnerable populations and at the same time protect them from infection.[24] The government has also embraced the mobile money payment platform, whereby beneficiaries are paid through their mobile phone. The advantage of mobile money payment is that it is real time, is easily accessible, and can be used to buy goods and services directly.

EMERGENCY RELIEF CASH TRANSFER INTERVENTIONS

The drought currently ravaging several parts of the country was declared a national disaster by Kenya's president on September 8, 2021. The drought has rendered about 2.5 million people food insecure and in need of urgent relief assistance. The Cabinet has approved a policy shift from provision of food to cash transfer and to automate the entire relief process from targeting through registration and payment.

Provision of cash transfers instead of famine relief has been hailed by development partners as one of the best policy shift innovations for reducing hunger and building resilience among drought-stricken citizens. Experience has shown that cash transfers have proven to be the most effective way to reach vulnerable persons in times of emergency because they provide for immediate needs, thus reducing vulnerabilities.

Previously, the logistics for the distribution of famine relief were very cumbersome, expensive, and time consuming. Famine relief was also subject to theft, leakages (the deliberate disappearances of relief food while in storage, during delivery or at distribution points), and long delays because it was controlled by cartels and bureaucrats. With the new cash transfers, money is delivered through mobile money platforms, which are quicker, spontaneous, real-time, and transparent because phone numbers are subject to validation by many agencies involved in the entire process.

Provision of cash transfers through a digital payment platform and especially mobile money transfers will have an immediate impact on vulnerable citizens, thus improving their livelihood. The money provided will, at the same time, have a multiplier effect because it will spur the local economy through the injection of additional cash for circulation.

IMPACTS OF CASH TRANSFER GRANTS

Studies on the impact of cash transfer programs have shown that the proportion of beneficiaries reporting positive impacts from the program on their household's welfare is very high for all the socioeconomic indicators measured. A study conducted through the Programme Implementation and Beneficiary Satisfaction Survey in 2018 produced evidence that the programs have contributed to diversification of the household diet; a significant improvement in children's school attendance; improved health of household members because they are now able to access health services; increased self-esteem of household members because they are now accepted by other society members and invited to participate in socioeconomic and cultural activities; and increased involvement in productive activities through asset ownership and engagement in income-generating enterprises. These findings are critical for welfare enhancement and poverty eradication in the country, and any effort that is perceived to have had an impact on the households cannot go unnoticed and is therefore very significant.[25]

The *Baseline Survey Report of Kenya's Inua Jamii 70 Years and Above Cash Transfer Programme* has shown that the primary objective of the cash transfer program is to improve the economic status and well-being of older people at an individual level. Receipt of monthly stipends has directly affected income at an individual level, leading to changes in recipients' patterns of expenditure, savings, and investment. The money supports older people to meet their basic needs, particularly for expenses that primarily benefit the older person as an individual rather than the household. The stipends help senior citizens to meet their health expenses, especially given the high levels of ill health and disability experienced by older people and considering the high levels of out-of-pocket health expenditures in Kenya. There is strong evidence to show that the ability of cash transfer interventions to contribute to family and community life are likely to lead to positive impacts on the dignity and empowerment of the beneficiaries.[26]

NOTES

1 Kenya, Ministry of Gender, Children, and Social Development. (2021). *Kenya Social Protection Policy, 2021*. https://www.socialprotection.go.ke/

2 Para. 1 of International Labour Organization. (2012). *Social protection floor*. Retrieved December 15, 2021, from https://www.ilo.org/secsoc/areas-of-work/policy-development-and-applied-research/social-protection-floor/lang--en/index.htm.

3 Kesteren, V., Dekker, M., Miroro, O., Gassmann, F., & Timár, E. (2018). *The business case for social protection in Africa* (Synthesis Report Series). INCLUDE. https://includeplatform.net/wp-content/uploads/2019/07/Synthesis-SP_final.pdf.

4 Kenya, Ministry of Labour and Social Protection, State Department of Social Protection, National Social Protection Secretariat. (2020a). *Kenya social protection sector annual report 2018/19*. https://www.socialprotection.go.ke/wp-content/uploads/2020/09/Kenya-Social-Protection-Sector-Annual-Report-2020-1.pdf.

5 Social Assistance Unit. (2020). *Consolidated cash transfer programme management information system report.*
6 National Social Protection Secretariat. (2018a). *Kenya's single registry for social protection.*
7 Ibid.
8 Ibid.
9 Ibid.
10 Kenya, Ministry of Labour and Social Protection, State Department for Social Protection. (2017). *Kenya social protection sector review 2017.* https://vision2030 .go.ke/.
11 Kenya, Ministry of Planning and National Development and Vision 2030. (2007). *Kenya Vision 2030: A globally competitive and prosperous Kenya.*
12 Director of Social Assistance. (2020). *Operations manual for Consolidated Cash Transfer Programme (revised) 2020.*
13 Ibid.
14 Banerjee, A., Duflo, E., Goldberg, N., Karlan, D., Osei, R., Parienté, J., Shapiro, J., Thuysbaert, B., & Udry, C. (2015). A multifaceted program causes lasting progress for the very poor: Evidence from six countries. *Science, 348*(6236), 1260799. https:// doi.org/10.1126/science.1260799.
15 Director of Social Assistance (2020).
16 Ibid.
17 Ibid.
18 Kenya, Ministry of Labour and Social Protection, Social Assistance Unit. (2018). *Beneficiary outreach strategy and action plan.*
19 Ibid.
20 ideas42. (2019). *Cash and change: Using behavioral insights to improve financial health in three cash transfer programs.* https://www.ideas42.org/wp-content/uploads/2019/09 /I42-1160_CashTransfers_paper_final-4.pdf.
21 Kezengwa, S., & MacLeod, K. (2021). *Utilizing pre-COVID behavioral designs during a pandemic: Experiences of Kenya's national cash transfer beneficiaries.* ideas42. https:// www.ideas42.org/blog/utilizing-pre-covid-behavioral-designs-during-a-pandemic -experiences-of-kenyas-national-cash-transfer-beneficiaries/.
22 UN Development Programme. (2020, April). *Articulating the pathways of the socio-economic impact of the coronavirus (COVID-19) pandemic on the Kenyan economy* (Policy Brief No. 4). Retrieved from https://data.unhcr.org/en/documents /download/78194.
23 Magongo, B., Lam, J. delBusto, I., Chibwana, C., Remetse, L., Li, S., & Coppel, E. (2020a). *South Africa social sector responses to COVID-19 policy brief.* https://www .researchgate.net/publication/340647086_South_Africa_social_sector_responses_to _COVID-19_Policy_Brief.
24 Magongo, B., Lam, J., del Busto, I., Chibwana, C., Remetse, L., Li, S., & Coppel, E. (2020b, April 14). *South Africa's social development sector response to COVID-19* (Policy brief). National Development Agency & IDinsight. Retrieved from https://www .researchgate.net/publication/340647086.
25 Ministry of Labour & East African Community. (2018). *Programme Implementation and Beneficiary Satisfaction Survey (PIBS) for the Kenya National Safety Net Programme.*
26 Kenya, Ministry of Labour and Social Protection, State Department for Social Protection, National Social Protection Secretariat. (2020b, July). *Baseline survey report of Kenya's Inua Jamii 70 years and above cash transfer programme.* https://socialprotection .org/discover/publications/baseline-survey-report-kenya%E2%80%99s-inua-jamii -70-years-and-above-cash-transfer.

PART THREE

Conclusions

CHAPTER ELEVEN

Cash Transfer Programs: Looking Back, Looking Forward

Saugato Datta, Jiaying Zhao, and Dilip Soman

LOOKING BACK: AN INTEGRATIVE SUMMARY

The first ten chapters in this book explored the many ways in which behavioral science can be applied to improve cash transfer programs. The five chapters in Part 1 provided a birds-eye view of welfare programs more generally. Chapter 1 provided a review of 87 cash transfer programs in the Global North and Global South and found that most distributed money via monthly payments, with very few providing lump sum payments. Programs in the Global North were smaller in scale in terms of both reach (the number of cash recipients) and size (the relative increase in income). Most programs tracked outcomes for only one or two years, and very few tracked them beyond five years. That said, cash transfers had positive impacts in the domains of health, assets, spending, and employment. Chapter 2 explored how behavioral science can inform the design and delivery of cash transfer programs and identified several behavioral barriers (cognitive scarcity, poverty identity, stagnation mindset, and present bias) that can impede their success. Recommendations to innovate, adapt, and scale cash transfer programs were offered, and several behavioral interventions (self-affirmation, goal setting, and plan making) that might help cash recipients achieve optimal outcomes were discussed. Chapter 3 offered practical lessons on how cash transfer programs could reach those populations who are hardest to reach by using targeting mechanisms, dedicated data management systems, and appropriate partnerships and stakeholder engagement. Chapter 4 highlighted the need to understand and consider the context of people's lives and environment when designing cash transfer programs. Small design features (timing of the cash transfer, reliability of payment schedule) and key design features (conditionality) are crucial in shaping trust, well-being, and self-empowerment of cash recipients and ensuring the success of these programs. Chapter 5 reviewed the landscape of basic income programs in Canada (a special case of cash transfer programs in which everyone in a given society receives a minimum income to meet basic needs) and described the positive impacts of basic income on recipients' health and well-being, with little negative impact on employment.

The five chapters in Part 2 took a deeper dive into the ways in which behavioral science could inform the design and delivery of programs. Chapter 6 proposed a new framework and examined the impact of five design features of cash transfer programs (scope, additional services, conditionality, payment mode, payment method) on the four-stage delivery chain of the programs (access, enroll, provide, manage). Existing literature and interviews with 16 academics and practitioners suggest that (1) a broader scope of cash transfers increases inclusivity and benefits to the recipients, (2) additional services can promote recipient engagement and outcomes, (3) conditionality can have a negative impact on access and recipient outcomes, and (4) recurring and lump sum payments can help promote better outcomes. Chapter 6 also called for researchers in this area to draw inspiration from developments in and research from the private sector in designing programs. Chapter 7 called for the need to design programs that provide both cash transfers and time transfers and discussed how cash transfer programs can serve to maximize time-saving benefits for recipients. The chapter offered a new model of cash transfer programs that facilitate time-saving benefits through more efficient targeting, disbursement, and evaluation. Chapter 8 outlined a range of factors that can affect whether a person seeks formal and informal financial help at three stages: from awareness of the help to the desirability of being helped and to the costs of taking action to seek help. Chapter 9 illustrated some of the ideas from earlier chapters through a case study; it described the Baby's First Years program and provided a behavioral framework to improve the program. Specifically, automatic and reliable cash payments through a debit card, personalized introduction to the card, monthly reminders, absence of conditionality, no credit history requirement, and 4MyBaby branding collectively helped recipients make better decisions by alleviating cognitive load and attentional demands, inertia, and choice anxiety and mentally earmarking the money for their babies. Chapter 10 presented another case study and described how the government of Kenya uses behavioral science to improve the effectiveness of its cash transfer programs, including universal schemes for all senior citizens and children.

AT A GLANCE: A CHECKLIST FOR POLICY MAKERS AND PRACTITIONERS

Although there were many actionable insights across the ten chapters, we recognize that it might be hard for practitioners to access them in a readily usable way. Therefore, drawing on all of the chapters, we have created a checklist of behaviorally informed prescriptions for policy makers and practitioners to use in designing, implementing, and evaluating future cash transfer programs to improve impact, inclusivity, and equality.

Guidelines for Recipient Targeting

- Target specific individuals who would benefit the most from the cash transfer program and its specific objectives, rather than households more generally. For example, target women for programs designed to improve maternal health or girls' education or target the family member who makes agriculture-related decisions for a program designed to improve agricultural productivity.

- Use targeting mechanisms that are appropriate for the socioeconomic circumstances that the target population or segment is currently experiencing.
- Use local knowledge of elders, chiefs, village, county, and subcounty staff to reach out to specific groups of recipients.
- Establish meaningful partnerships with on-the-ground stakeholders to reach the hardest to reach. Sometimes, the best partnerships might not be the most obvious (e.g., partnering with a mobile network or the distributor of a popular product).
- Consider targeting methods that can reduce or eliminate unnecessary barriers and costs for both cash recipients and program implementers.
- Remove barriers that have the largest impact on recipients. This involves an understanding of both procedural and psychological barriers.
- Consider setting up a default of automatically providing cash transfers to eligible recipients instead of requiring them to apply.

Prescriptions for Cash Delivery

- Digital delivery of payments is usually preferred over other forms (e.g., checks). It not only improves the speed and security of delivery, but it also reduces sludge by eliminating gatekeepers (e.g., bank officers who might want bribes) and reducing any psychological burdens (by making the act of receiving the payment invisible to others).
- Consider minimizing the conditionality of the cash transfer. Critically examine each condition to see whether the benefits, if any, are worth the downsides.
- Ensure the reliability of payments when digital payments are not possible.
- Consider a smaller number of larger payments over more numerous smaller ones, especially in cases in which the objectives of the cash transfer program might be supported by the purchase of high-ticket items.
- In cases in which there is significant seasonality in expense patterns or in incomes, align payment timing with periods of greatest need (e.g., disburse payment when cash is most needed).

- Ensure that payments are timely and that respective authorities are held accountable.
- Consider cash-plus services that would enhance the positive outcomes of cash transfers. These include time-saving services and other forms of support.
- Provide people with direct time transfers in addition to cash transfers.
- Build trust with recipients through in-person connections and interactions.

Guidelines for Governments, Stakeholders, and Service Providers

- Programs in the Global North need more support from governments, especially the removal of benefit cliffs with large lump sum payments. Actively seek such support from governments.
- Scaling is a challenge. Political buy-in is often needed to scale cash transfers from a pilot to a broader population.
- Work closely with key stakeholders from the beginning, and make them part of the entire behavioral design and scaling process. Avoid the temptation to design everything before communicating with these stakeholders.
- Be mindful of service providers' resource and bandwidth constraints.
- Look for ways to efficiently embed cash transfers into existing services and remove any unnecessary or redundant design features when creating new programs.
- Examine the interaction between federal and local programs to identify gaps (which need to be accounted for in program design) and overlaps (which call for reducing redundancies).
- Rethink how the various levels of government can work together to ensure coordinated delivery of cash transfers.
- Provide technical support and capacity building (e.g., digitization of program platforms) that are key to the successful delivery of programs.
- Use dedicated data management systems to store, analyze, and cross-check information on recipients, but pay special attention to data protection and privacy issues.

LOOKING FORWARD: A RESEARCH AGENDA FOR CASH TRANSFER STUDIES

Although we have identified many ways in which behavioral science can inform the design and delivery of cash transfer programs, our work has also raised new questions and new avenues for future research. Although each chapter has identified opportunities for future research, we compile some of the more common ones in the form of research questions. We hope that readers of this book are inspired to seek out answers to these questions.

1 What are the pros and cons of providing a single lump sum payment versus a series of ongoing payments? Under what conditions is the former better than the latter? What additional supports might be necessary to make the lump sum payment approach the preferred option?

2 Could programs adopt a self-selection approach in which recipients choose how to receive the cash transfer (e.g., mixing regular and lump sum payments, variable payment amounts)? What are the costs and benefits of the self-selection approach?

3 What are the optimal program designs that lead to more sustained reduction in poverty over time and lower fiscal burdens over the long run? How does the optimality change as a function of desired program outcomes and contextual factors more generally?

4 What are the long-term effects of cash transfers? Could longer-term outcomes be tracked beyond five years to examine the long-run effects of cash transfers and of program design features on outcomes?

5 What other approaches and methodologies (besides randomized controlled trials) could be used to evaluate the behavioral interventions (e.g., rigorous localized user testing, administrative data, A–B testing)?

6 What are the appropriate approaches to conduct a cost–benefit analysis of behavioral interventions (e.g., use a cost-effectiveness multiplier) in the domain of cash transfer programs?

7 How do design features (e.g., timing) of cash transfer programs help recipients achieve program outcomes? What are the relative effect sizes of each design feature?

8 How can the psychology of time be better integrated into the design of cash transfer programs? In particular, under what conditions is it better to provide time-saving services, and under what conditions is it better to provide cash?

9 How can machine learning algorithms best be used to predict creditworthiness of recipients for better targeting in cash transfer programs? More generally, how can machine learning better complement behavioral approaches?

10 What additional performance metrics (e.g., recipient satisfaction) covering various stages of engagement with a program (from enrollment to delivery) can be measured to evaluate the program's effectiveness?

11 What are the general equilibrium effects of cash transfer programs (e.g., what are the trade-offs between larger payments to a smaller set of recipients vs. smaller payments to a larger set of recipients)?

12 What additional design features of programs can benefit from a behavioral lens? In particular, how can the design of program-related communication and other materials (e.g., forms, scripts for service providers) benefit from an understanding of behavioral science?

Although there are numerous research questions that we still do not have good answers to, a look back at where the field was a few years ago will highlight how much progress has been made. Our point in this volume is simple – understanding the behaviors (and the frictions to desired behaviors) of cash transfer recipients as well as program staff is not only important but paramount, and it can potentially make or break otherwise sound programs. As such, we encourage proponents, policy makers, designers, and implementation staff to adopt a behavioral lens to continually improve programs and outcomes.

Contributors

Saugato Datta is a managing director at ideas42, where he oversees work on the application of behavioral science in low- and middle-income countries in partnership with government agencies, multilateral organizations, and non-governmental organizations. His current work spans organizational behavior, education, labor markets, agriculture, and social protection. He has also worked on global health and around resource conservation. Datta has a PhD in economics from the Massachusetts Institute of Technology and undergraduate and master's degrees from Cambridge University and the University of Delhi. In his spare time, he likes to listen to music, cook, eat, and contemplate an alternative career path involving interior decoration.

Oceana Ding studied cognitive science, psychology, and neuroscience at the University of Toronto. She is a user experience researcher currently working in financial technology. She partners with product, development, and design teams to evaluate user needs and apply data-driven insights to create user-centric experiences. In her spare time, she enjoys hiking, reading, and photography.

Ryan Dwyer is a PhD candidate in social psychology at the University of British Columbia and a Vanier Scholar. His research focuses on the psychology of money, technology, and happiness, with an emphasis on using randomized controlled trials to study the impact of direct cash transfers on vulnerable populations.

Evelyn L. Forget is a professor of economics and community health sciences at the University of Manitoba in Winnipeg. Her research examines the health and social implications of poverty and inequality, and she is often called upon by governments, First Nations, and international organizations to advise on poverty, inequality, and health and social outcomes. Her most recent books are *Basic Income for Canadians: From the COVID-19 Emergency to Financial Security for All* and (with Hannah Owczar) *Radical Trust: Basic Income for Complicated Lives*. She is a Fellow of the Royal Society of Canada and an Officer of the Order of Canada.

Nathan A. Fox is a Distinguished University Professor in the Department of Human Development and Quantitative Methodology at the University of Maryland. He conducts research on the effects of early experience on brain and behavioral development in infants and children.

John Gachigi is the director, State Department for Social Protection, in Kenya, where he is responsible for the implementation of the Consolidated Cash Transfer Programme (Inua Jamii). His role involves coordination of targeting, enrollment, payment, grievances, and case management. He is a doctoral student in development studies and has a background in sociology, community development, and social protection. He is a social protection specialist and also a master trainer using the TRANSFORM experiential learning methodology, and his special interest is promoting transformative leadership geared to creating positive changes. In his spare time, Gachigi enjoys farming, listening to music, and watching current affairs.

Lisa A. Gennetian is Pritzker Professor of Early Learning Policy Studies in the Sanford School of Public Policy at Duke University. She is an applied economist who brings insights from behavioral economics and child development to her research, which focuses on child poverty, cash transfers, financial security and stability, and children's development, with a lens toward causal mechanisms.

Sarah Halpern-Meekin is an associate professor in the School of Human Ecology and the La Follette School of Public Affairs at the University of Wisconsin–Madison. She is a sociologist whose research focuses on family, adolescence, social policy and the welfare state, class and inequality, and qualitative methods. Her research also focuses on the role of instability in family relationships and finances and on the ways public policy may affect these experiences.

Faraz Haqqi is a senior associate at ideas42 with experience in applying behavioral science to health, livelihoods, and governance issues in Sub-Saharan Africa and South and Southeast Asia. He holds an MPA from Cornell University and a BA from the University of Maryland at College Park.

Waleed Hussain is an analyst with the Ernst & Young Economics Advisory practice in Toronto. He works closely with a variety of public- and private-sector clients by combining economics and statistics to solve complex and multifaceted problems. Outside of work, Hussain balances his time between paddling in Lake Ontario and, in the colder months, reading about democratic theory and voting behavior.

Kyle Jacques is a monitoring and evaluation specialist with the UN Peacebuilding Fund in Khartoum, Sudan, where he assesses the impacts of multiple UN-supported peacebuilding programs. Previously, Jacques worked with the Peacebuilding Fund at the UN Headquarters in New York, as well as with the Danish Refugee Council as a research analyst in South Sudan. He holds a master's degree in global affairs from the University of Toronto and a bachelor's degree in political science from McGill University. In his spare time, Jacques likes drumming, cooking, and returning to Canada as often as possible to be with his family and friends.

Ania Jaroszewicz is a postdoctoral fellow at Harvard University, where she conducts behavioral economics research on poverty and informal helping interactions. She holds a PhD in behavioral decision research from Carnegie Mellon University. In her spare time, Jaroszewicz tries to be outdoors as much as possible.

Mukta Joshi is a projects director at ideas42. A development economist by training, Joshi has extensive experience in applied research across multiple disciplines (development finance and private-sector development) and geographies (North America, South Asia, Middle East, and North Africa). Before joining ideas42, Joshi worked at the World Bank and International Finance Corporation in Washington, DC. Joshi holds a PhD in development economics from Ohio State University and a master's in economics from Mumbai University India.

Catherine MacLeod is a senior associate at ideas42 and is currently working on international livelihoods programs. She focuses on bringing behavioral innovations to cash transfer and labor market programs, primarily in the Middle East/North Africa region and Sub-Saharan Africa. She holds an MSc in economics from the University of Amsterdam with a specialization in development economics and a BA in economics from Stony Brook University.

Marin MacLeod is the executive director of the Reach Alliance. She was a member of the Reach team that investigated the world's first iris-scanning cash assistance program for refugees in Jordan. Before joining the Reach Alliance, MacLeod led Grand Challenges Canada's approach to impact measurement across their maternal, newborn, and child health innovation portfolio. MacLeod has experience with program design, delivery, and evaluation, having worked across a range of public health issues in several countries. She holds a BA (Hons) from Queen's University as a Loran Scholar and a Master in Public Health degree from the University of Toronto.

Katherine Magnuson is a Vilas Achievement Professor of Social Work and the director of the Institute for Research on Poverty at the University of Wisconsin–Madison. Her research examines how disparities in socioeconomic status affect children's development and how these effects may be altered by policies and programs, especially early childhood education programs.

Lauren Meyer is the Baby's First Years national project director. She operationalizes multifaceted and complex projects aimed at supporting families and communities in raising healthy and strong children who can become the people they aspire to be.

Sherry Ning is a behavioral strategy consultant at ZS Associates, where she applies behavioral insights in navigating complex business challenges. She has a degree in psychology from the University of Toronto and has previously been a researcher at Behavioural Economics in Action at Rotman. Often curious about a million things at once, her published works cover topics ranging from neuroeconomics to the search for meaning in life. For leisure, Ning enjoys classical music, sci-fi thrillers, creative writing, and fencing.

Kimberly G. Noble is a professor of neuroscience and education at Teachers College, Columbia University. As a neuroscientist and board-certified pediatrician, her research focuses on how socioeconomic inequality relates to children's cognitive and brain development.

Sydney Piggott was a member of the Reach research team that investigated Ethiopia's Productive Safety Net Programme. She has degrees in international development and global affairs from McGill University and the University of Toronto. Piggott is a senior not-for-profit leader, researcher, and advocate for gender equity and social justice on a global scale who has led programs and community engagement in social impact organizations including Elevate, YWCA Canada, and the Equal Futures Network. When she is not working, Piggott is a volunteer in her community and passionate about supporting the innovative work of young changemakers.

Dilip Soman is a Canada Research Chair in behavioral science and economics at the Rotman School of Management, University of Toronto, and the project director of the Behaviourally Informed Organizations initiative. He has degrees in behavioral science, management, and engineering and is interested in the applications of behavioral science to welfare and policy. He is the author of *The Last Mile* (2015), coeditor of *The Behaviorally Informed Organization* (2021), and coeditor of *Behavioral Science in the Wild* (2022), all with the

University of Toronto Press. His non-academic interests include procrastination, cricket, travel, and taking weekends seriously.

Kaitlyn Stewart recently graduated from the University of British Columbia. She holds a Bachelor of Arts with a major in psychology and a minor in interpersonal development. She currently works as a research assistant for various labs in the faculties of psychology and education, where she pursues her research interests in poverty and addictions. Outside of academia, Stewart volunteers in the downtown east side of Vancouver assisting with harm reduction and overdose prevention. In her spare time, she enjoys making pottery, cycling, and skiing Vancouver's local mountains.

Daniella Turetski is a PhD student in behavioral marketing at the Rotman School of Management, University of Toronto, and a researcher at Behavioural Economics in Action at Rotman. Turetski's current research focuses on the ethics of choice architecture interventions, cash transfer program design, and complex emotions, such as regret and guilt. She received her Bachelor of Commerce from the University of Toronto, where she specialized in management, economics, and psychology. Outside of her academic pursuits, Turetski loves to bake and coordinates marketing strategies for a local professional theater company.

Renos Vakis leads the Mind, Behavior, and Development Unit at the World Bank, integrating behavioral science in the design of antipoverty policies. He has written extensively on issues related to poverty dynamics and mobility, aspirations, mental well-being, and social protection and has led numerous randomized trials on a range of antipoverty interventions in various settings. Vakis has also taught applied economics at Johns Hopkins University's School of Advanced International Studies. He holds a PhD from the University of California, Berkeley.

Colin West is a postdoctoral researcher in behavioral economics at the University of Toronto, Rotman School of Management. He conducts applied research on economic decision making and psychological well-being in the workplace. West completed his PhD at the University of California, Los Angeles, Anderson School of Management, and holds a bachelor's degree from Harvard. He has also worked as a consultant applying behavioral economics insights and methods at technology companies and non-governmental organizations.

Ashley Whillans is an assistant professor in the Negotiation, Organizations & Markets Unit at the Harvard Business School, where she teaches the Motivation and Incentives course to MBA students. Her research focuses on how decisions about time and money shape happiness. In both 2015 and 2018, she was named a Rising Star of Behavioral Science by the Behavioral Science and Policy Association. Whillans earned her BA, MA, and PhD in social psychology from the University of British Columbia. Her dissertation research on time and happiness won the 2018 Canadian Association for Graduate Studies Distinguished Dissertation Award for being the single best PhD thesis in Canada across the fine arts, humanities, and social sciences. In her spare time, she enjoys writing about research for popular press outlets such as *Harvard Business Review* and *The Wall Street Journal*.

Kevin Yin is an economist and postgraduate associate at Yale University. He holds a BA in economics and philosophy from the University of Toronto and an MA in development economics from Yale University. His research interests lie at the intersection of international economics and macrofinance, particularly understanding the nature of sovereign debt defaults and financial crises in emerging markets to find policies to mitigate them. Yin's current work involves modeling the trade of electricity across the global power grid and studying firm life cycles. Outside of research, Yin enjoys traveling and producing hip-hop and R&B music.

Hirokazu Yoshikawa is the Courtney Sale Ross University Professor of Globalization and Education and codirector of the Global TIES for Children center at New York University. As a community and developmental psychologist, his research focuses on children's development and the impact of public policies and programs, with particular attention to immigrants and immigration, early child-hood, and poverty reduction in the United States and in low-and middle-income countries.

Jiaying Zhao is the Canada Research Chair and associate professor in the Department of Psychology and the Institute for Resources, Environment and Sustainability at the University of British Columbia. Zhao uses psychological principles to design behavioral solutions to address financial and environmental sustainability challenges and received her PhD in cognitive psychology from Princeton University. Outside of work, Zhao is an avid culinary explorer (aka "foodie"), always on the lookout for the next succulent dish.

Xiao (Mimosa) Zhao is the director of analytics at a boutique consulting firm (The Evidence Network Inc.). She is most energized while exploring uncharted territory, managing research teams for success, and activating insights through both qualitative and quantitative analyses. Zhao holds degrees in design and engineering (BEng, Beijing Institute of Fashion Technology), English language and literature (BA, BIFT), and innovation management (MSc, University of Ottawa). She is currently pursuing her MBA at the Rotman School of Management, University of Toronto. Outside of her work and academic conquests, Zhao is an enthusiastic fan of both the NBA and Formula 1 racing.